How Trump Won

HOW TRUMP WON

The Inside Story of a Revolution

JOEL B. POLLAK
Breitbart News Senior Editor-at-Large
LARRY SCHWEIKART
#1 *New York Times* Bestselling Author

REGNERY
PUBLISHING
A Division of Salem Media Group

Regnery® is a registered trademark of Salem Communications Holding Corporation

Cataloging-in-Publication data on file with the Library of Congress
Paperback ISBN 978-1-62157-395-1
E-book ISBN 978-1-62157-538-2

Published in the United States by
Regnery Publishing
A Division of Salem Media Group
300 New Jersey Ave NW
Washington, DC 20001
www.Regnery.com

Manufactured in the United States of America

10 9 8 7 6 5 4 3 2 1

Books are available in quantity for promotional or premium use. For information on discounts and terms, please visit our website: www.Regnery.com.

Distributed to the trade by
Perseus Distribution
www.perseusdistribution.com

To *my mother-in-law, Rhoda Kadalie, a pioneering
black feminist, anti-apartheid struggle veteran, human rights activist,
and writer, who predicted proudly from the very beginning that
Donald Trump would win*
—Joel Pollak

To *the Deplorables*
—Larry Schweikart

CONTENTS

Introduction

When my co-author Larry Schweikart calls Trump's victory "the most astounding election in American history," he knows whereof he speaks.

Larry is a professional historian with decades of college teaching, ground-breaking historical research, and numerous popular history bestsellers to his credit. He has written extensively on the American presidency, particularly in the nineteenth century, and so he brings a long historical perspective to the astonishing events of 2016 that culminated in the election of Donald J. Trump as president of the United States.

He was also personally involved in Trump's paradigm-busting campaign, as a member of a group of volunteer analysts who were feeding data and analysis in key states to the Trump organization up through Election Night. Larry and his fellow "Renegade Deplorables" knew weeks ahead of Election Day that Trump was on a course to win Florida, Pennsylvania, and key states in the Midwest and become the forty-fifth president of the United States. On election night, they were able to reassure my former Breitbart News boss Stephen K. Bannon—by then the CEO of the Trump campaign organization—that when early voting totals seemed to be tipping the election to Hillary Clinton, these were merely the Democrat-heavy "early" votes being posted, and that the bulk of the "red" Election Day ballots had yet to arrive. The story of where they found their hard numbers, and how they were able to analyze the data, is behind-the-scenes election news that I, as a reporter, have been fascinated to learn.

When I was reporting from the Trump rallies all across the United States in the last two weeks of the campaign, I found myself thinking how Trump's "movement" was both like and unlike the resurgent conservatism that so many of us had imagined would emerge from the Tea Party—and really, that conservatives had been hoping and working for in vain ever since the Reagan era. Larry's analysis sheds some light on that question. He points out that Donald Trump is an updated version of an older kind of American conservatism, one that Reagan took for granted but one that we, in our post-nationalist generation, have begun to rediscover. He also has some interesting things to say about whether Trump's victory may have inaugurated a third American "party system," finally ousting the establishment that has been shutting down debate of critical political issues—and shutting the American people out of self-government—for decades. Maybe that's what the tens of thousands of Trump supporters I observed, and the dozens I interviewed, in the campaign's final push were sensing. Many of the Trump fans I spoke to conceded that their candidate wasn't perfect. They knew all about the numerous "scandals" that the media had pushed, one after another, in the ever-renewed hope that the campaign would finally "implode." But Trump was offering a historic opportunity for the people to take their government—and their own destiny—out of the control of a corrupt elite and into their own hands. And they took it—joyfully.

—Joel Pollak

■　■　■

Reporting for Breitbart News from the Donald Trump press plane in the last weeks of the 2016 election, my fellow author, veteran reporter Joel Pollak, had a unique ringside seat on history.

Not only was he one of the few able to observe the spectacular finale of the Trump campaign as an eyewitness, but from the "inside," as a member of the traveling press corps, he was confirming many of the things we "Deplorable" analysts were seeing from afar. As editor at one of the only media outlets—and that includes conservative media—that was not hostile to Trump, Joel may have been the *only* person on the press plane who was genuinely interested in what Trump was doing. It might be said that Joel was trying to get Trump, while his media cohorts were only interested in "getting" Trump. While the rest of the press corps, smugly oblivious to Trump's appeal and obsessed with "gotcha" moments, squandered their access to the candidate and his supporters on increasingly feeble attempts to trip up the candidate (or failing that, at least to make his supporters look really stupid), Joel used his opportunities to delve into the *sui generis* phenomenon that was the Trump campaign. He reported on the outsider Republican candidate's unprecedented approach to media and spectacle, his fresh message, and the reasons that it had such a broad appeal. As a matter of fact, Joel was so out of sync with the rest of the press corps that at one point he was nearly banished from the press plane. But he managed to soothe ruffled feelings among the other reporters, and stay on board.

Joel had covered the campaign from the West Coast, from all angles, since the beginning: Hillary Clinton events, Bernie Sanders rallies, and the early Republican primaries. But he joined the press plane at a truly critical point for Trump's candidacy. And the eyewitness story he tells—from Trump's debate performance in Las Vegas after the *Access Hollywood* tape release, when the candidate seemed almost to be conceding the election, to the final frenetic days of the campaign, with visits to seven different states in one day—could not be more fascinating.

His on-the-ground reporting, talking day in and day out over the very last leg of Trump's groundbreaking campaign to Trump voters—men and women; white, Hispanic, and black; straight and gay—who would be responsible for the electoral upset of the century, perfectly complements my historical perspective and my inside line to the campaign and to the data that ensured Trump's victory.

We start the story of Trump's historic campaign for the White House with a "cold open," as the filmmakers call it: Joel's campaign diary begins in Las Vegas with the Trump team just before the third presidential debate, as the last crucial weeks of the general election campaign were about to get under way. From there, we take a step back for a look at the bigger picture in my first chapter, as I delve into how Donald Trump won the most astounding victory in the history of the U.S. presidency. Then it's back to the frenetic closing weeks of the campaign, as Joel reports the excitement from the press plane.

Throughout the book, I offer both historical perspective and the perspective of someone with an inside line to the Trump organization. I look at the whole course of Trump's run for the presidency, from back in the summer of 2015, when a few analysts (who eventually became the "Renegade Deplorables") first saw that one candidate for the GOP nomination was different—that Donald Trump, by showing that he (unlike any other Republican) would fight, was offering hope to voters who had nearly given up believing their votes could ever dislodge the ensconced establishment from its death grip on power.

Meanwhile, also throughout the book, the installments of Joel's campaign diary give us all the chance to relive the wild ride of a lifetime that was the Trump campaign. Only this time it's even more fun—because everybody knows who wins!

—Larry Schweikart

On the Campaign Trail:
Las Vegas

Joel Pollak

October 19, 2016

The air shimmers in the high desert heat above the asphalt esplanade of the Las Vegas Strip.

In the distance stands the golden massif of the Trump International Hotel, commanding the very center of the boulevard—an optical illusion created by the fact that the road curves to the right as it heads toward downtown, while the tower is set just far enough from the prime property of the Strip to dominate the skyline, regardless.

Above it all, in ornate gold, the name: "TRUMP."

In the lobby, behind a phalanx of hotel security and Secret Service agents, a small gaggle of campaign employees gathers, whispering quietly among the curious hotel guests. Once in a while a senior staff member emerges from the bank of elevators at the far end of the lobby.

The rest pace nervously, smartphones in hand, as they exchange messages with colleagues high on a floor above, where the man himself is hunkered down with a close circle of advisors, preparing.

A few familiar faces mill about, a supporting cast.

There is Patricia Smith, the bereaved Benghazi mother, whose son Sean was killed while his country's leaders slept, and who had poured out her grief on the stage of the Republican National Convention in Cleveland. There are Diamond and Silk, two robust black women, volunteer emissaries for the ticket whose pro-Trump videos had made them an internet phenomenon. Even President Barack Obama's estranged Kenyan half-brother, Malik, poses for pictures with fans.

Kellyanne Conway, the pollster and campaign manager who is widely credited with creating the campaign's short-lived era of good fortune in late summer, makes a brief turn across the marble floor, poses for photographs, returns upstairs.

The small crowd becomes even more sparse as groups of staffers leave for the short but congested drive to the other side of the Strip, the venue for the third and final presidential debate of the brutal and bruising 2016 presidential election cycle.

Outside, at a sudden signal, traffic stops—everywhere, for miles.

A motorcade—local police, highway patrol, and Secret Service—rolls out of the Trump International Hotel and down the back streets to the University of Nevada, Las Vegas. For a few minutes more, at least, the real estate tycoon—who had struggled to secure his place among the hostile Vegas oligarchs—can bring Sin City to a standstill. The outsider can bring his rivals to attention.

But after November 8? Once the election is over, it seems they'll be able to ignore him again.

■ ■ ■

Donald Trump surprised many observers when he entered the presidential race, descending into the fray on an escalator in the Trump Tower in New York in June 2015. And he was continuing to surprise the political world. He had already upended Republican Party politics in his attempt to seize the forty-fifth presidency from the ambitious clutches of Hillary Clinton, who had been denied the prize eight years before.

The story about why Trump had come so far was a highly contested one.

The tale favored by Democrats and much of the media was that Trump appealed to the nascent bigotry in right-wing politics and was exploiting the grievances of Americans who felt they had not shared in the country's prosperity.

Hillary Clinton herself gave expression to that twofold explanation. As she would say, infamously: "You could put half of Trump's supporters into what I call the basket of deplorables." In that basket were the "racist, sexist, homophobic, xenophobic, Islamophobic"—"irredeemable," she said.

The rest of Trump's support, she said, were "people who feel that government has let them down, nobody cares about them, nobody worries about what happens to their lives and their futures, and they are just desperate for change."[1]

Trump had exploited both the deplorables and the marginalized, Clinton said, by using websites that had previously been on the fringe to amplify his message, appealing to old-fashioned bigotry and new economic resentment to earn millions of votes.

That wasn't so different from the standard left-wing narrative about virtually any Republican candidate. Then-Senator Barack Obama said much the same of the so-called "bitter clingers" in 2008—those who "cling to guns or religion or antipathy to people who aren't like them or anti-immigrant sentiment or anti-trade sentiment as a way to explain their frustrations."[2]

Yet Trump was a different kind of Republican candidate—starting with the fact that he had overcome sixteen other candidates and the resistance of the entire Republican establishment. But few understood how, or why.

Many of Trump's conservative critics—the #NeverTrump faction—chalked Trump's success up to the support he enjoyed among popular alternative media outlets such as talk radio, the Drudge Report, and my own Breitbart News. These, it was said, had enabled his rise, along with the mainstream media, which had been overly friendly and accommodating to Trump during the primaries—partly to drive up their own ratings, partly to undermine the Republicans' chance of winning the general election on the assumption that Trump would be a weak candidate.

But Trump's critics, whether of the Left or the Right, didn't generally waste much time or energy asking how his differences from your garden-variety Republican candidate were contributing to his remarkable success in the primaries. They were busy worrying about whether those differences amounted to authoritarian tendencies and racist "dog whistles." Trump had offensive views about Mexicans, Muslims, and others, it was said, and he was willing to tolerate violence at his political rallies, even encouraging retaliation against protesters. He threatened the media with new libel laws that would muzzle freedom of the press. And he practiced a centralized decision-making style at odds with the constitutional role of the president. Trump's success only showed that America was flirting with fascism, the argument went.

Accordingly, to his opponents, both left and right, it was important not only that Trump lose the election, but that his supporters be crushed by his defeat—so crushed that they would never again entertain any idea of another candidate like him.

Democrats had good hopes that this populist outsider would lose so badly—perhaps even losing control of the House of Representatives— that he might bring the long-delayed ambitions of the political Left, including so-called "comprehensive" immigration reform, to fruition. A thorough drubbing of Trump would be a definitive rejection of his "xeno-phobic" position on immigration.

And the Republicans who opposed Trump also looked forward to a settling of scores. Establishment types anticipated a Trump loss as an opportunity to purge the Republican Party of its pesky Tea Party base. Some conservatives looked forward to Trump's defeat as a chance to rid the GOP of the insufficiently conservative insurgents who were bringing it to defeat by choosing a candidate who was a mere reality-show Hol-lywood celebrity, a lifetime liberal who was hijacking their party and their cause with a vain cult of personality.

■ ■ ■

But to Trump supporters, the candidate was the antidote to the twenty-five-year consensus in Washington about free trade, open borders, and transactional politics.

At my own Breitbart News, one of the few media outlets (even on the Right) friendly to Trump, some described the candidate as a "populist-nationalist." The New York billionaire was giving voice to a broad working-class constituency—across the political spectrum—that felt the sting of competition from foreign trade and immigrant labor.

Trump had exhibited few clear political convictions in many decades of life in the spotlight. He had enjoyed cozy relationships with members of the political elite on both sides of the aisle, donating to both, and even praising Hillary Clinton and Barack Obama.

But when he did speak out on politics, he was remarkably consistent in his skepticism of trade deals and his conviction that America's leaders—whether Republican or Democrat—were failing to project the country's strength abroad.

Trump defied easy political categorization; he flip-flopped on some of the most important issues in contemporary political debate; he even seemed, at times, to forget, or to misstate, his own positions. But at the core of it all was an unapologetic patriotism that Americans had become unaccustomed to seeing in their politicians.

Trump's slogan, "Make America Great Again," was derided by seasoned political observers.

And it was easily the best and most effective slogan of any candidate in the field.

A decade earlier, conservative reformers had noted that their party's rhetoric of limited government had failed to connect to the concerns of suburban and working families. They proposed a new kind of conservatism—what some called a "national greatness" conservatism.[3]

Now Trump was giving it to them—only without the policy details, and with populist rhetoric about immigration and terrorism that resonated with millions of Americans but repulsed the party's cosmopolitan elite.

Some of Trump's supporters heralded his campaign as a long-awaited pushback against what they called "globalism." That was something different from the "globalization" leftists had railed against in the late 1990s. The anti-globalization movement had protested the integration of economic markets under the supervision of aloof international financial governing institutions. Some Trump fans complaining about "globalism" were concerned about that—but more were specifically concerned about the surrender of national sovereignty and culture that seemed to come in tandem with the new global economy.

Among the Trump fans who relished that confrontation were members of a movement called the "alt-right" (shorthand for "alternative right")—a heterogeneous group whose common theme was that its members shared political views on the right of the spectrum that were deemed beyond the normal boundaries of political discourse.

Some, for example, were monarchists convinced American democracy had been a failure. Others in the alt-right did have opinions that were not so benignly eccentric—a minority were racists and even neo-Nazis. Others, who were not racists, were frustrated that political correctness had ruled out the kind of frank discussions about race and culture that the Left pretended it wanted to have (when what it really wanted was to intimidate its opponents).

But all of them were misreading the man I saw on the campaign trail. Though he would later adopt terms such as "globalist" into his speeches, Trump was less ideological than some of his fans, or his foes, imagined.

Essentially, Trump was a nationalist, as well as an ambitious, accomplished, and competitive man who saw the poor job the country's politicians were doing and thought that it was possible to do better.

And, as far as campaigning for the nomination, he was right about that.

Trump, always a master of marketing, saw the Republican Party as an asset with a devalued brand, ripe for a takeover. There was huge demand for effective political leadership, as well as for strong political opposition.

Theoretically, the Grand Old Party should have provided those things. But it had become a target of ridicule over the preceding two decades, and its leaders had no idea how to respond.

Trump seized the opportunity—and was, perhaps, surprised by his own success.

It is actually possible to pinpoint the moment when Trump took control of the 2016 race. On July 10, 2015, Trump was three-and-a-half weeks into his campaign, and stuck in sixth place, with just 6.5 percent support among Republican primary voters in the RealClearPolitics average. Former Florida governor Jeb Bush was in first place, with 16.3 percent.

But that day, Trump met with the families of Americans who had been killed by illegal aliens. The families had reached out to other politicians, to no avail: few were interested in their bereavement. Trump was the first to take an active public interest in their grievance against the federal government.

One of the participants, Sabine Durden—herself an immigrant, and the mother of a biracial child who was killed by an illegal alien—later spoke exclusively to Breitbart News' Michelle Moons:

> [Trump] listened to each one of our stories and was visibly shaken and touched. We got hugged and he promised to continue to fight for us and our kids. We then went to a separate room where the press was staged. He addressed them and then gave each of us time to share our story. The press tried to pin him down on his previous comments. He stood his ground. I had a Coke bottle that read HERO on it and I told him that he should have it. He is my hero because he was the only one who got attention to this truly important issue.[4]

By July 19, just nine days later, Trump had surged to first place, and barely looked back. The number of people who have lost relatives to murder by illegal aliens is very small—hardly enough to form a constituency in one state, let alone the whole country. But they stood for all of the

Americans who had been ignored by government for so many years. And finally, someone was listening. Trump was on his way to victory.

Along the way, Trump not only upset the Republican establishment, but also grappled with a cohort of conservative opinion-makers, equally set against the party leadership but determined to reshape the GOP in their own more ideological mold.

Trump seemed to have little use for ideological arguments: to him, ideological rigidity was one more way the country's leaders had tied themselves up in knots, preventing government from doing what it was for—building infrastructure, defending the country, helping the weakest.

And so Trump threatened not only the political control of the Republican insiders but also the intellectual primacy of professional conservatives. He rose to the top of the Republican Party—the party of Ronald Reagan—without their help, and despite their resistance.

The other danger that both the Republican political establishment and the conservative ideological establishment saw was that if (or when) Trump failed, he would bring the whole edifice of Republicanism and conservatism down with him, perhaps never to be rebuilt.

That sense of imminent existential threat fueled many of the internal battles about Trump among the party's leading voices, whose debates took on a personal, almost fratricidal tone. (At times, Trump's own combative style of argument only added fuel to the fire.) Each side reached for whatever weapons came to hand. Trump's supporters on the Right were content to laugh with the media at the shortcomings of his rivals; Trump's conservative opponents eagerly joined the Left in labeling him and his supporters bigots.

When the election was all over, and—win or lose—it was time to begin anew with new challenges, would the feuding camps of Republicans and conservatives stumble as soon as they had to try to walk together again?

Losing in 2016 might be more costly for Republicans than it had been before. That year represented the best, and very possibly the last, opportunity for the new American conservative opposition movement that had begun in the waning days of 2008 and risen in earnest in the first months of Obama's tenure in office to succeed.

The financial crash of 2008 shook Americans' confidence in capitalism; the subsequent bailout of the banks shook their confidence in government and gave rise to a new backlash. That backlash became the Tea Party, which arose in opposition to Obama's economic stimulus, a near-trillion-dollar boondoggle that did little to create jobs but much to inflate the national debt. When the administration introduced Obamacare a few months later, shrouded in false promises, and pushed it through Congress over the unanimous objection of Republicans, the Tea Party became a potent political force that soon swept Democrats out of the House of Representatives.

The Tea Party grudgingly supported Mitt Romney's presidential run despite his moderate past, once it became clear that no other candidate could keep him from the GOP nomination. But when he lost to Obama, Tea Party activists felt a sense of disappointment and betrayal. In 2014, conservatives delivered the Senate to Republicans, only to watch in frustration as Congress failed to stop the president's agenda, whether on immigration or climate change or the Iran nuclear deal.

Trump presented himself as the answer to weak leadership in Washington—both by Obama on the global stage, and by Republicans on Capitol Hill. His main strength was that he emphasized strength; he won by winning.

Yet losing would leave no other solution, no real way forward. Trump was a tower—perhaps a tower of Babel, for which the climb heavenward was the main unifying purpose.

If it fell, its workers would scatter; incomprehensible to each other, they would never return again.

My place on the press plane in the last days of the 2016 presidential campaign was a ringside seat at the knock-down, drag-out, no-holds barred fight for the future of the Tea Party, the Conservative Movement, the GOP—and the Republic.

CHAPTER ONE

The Most Astounding Election in American History

Larry Schweikart

Joel's campaign diary will be an indispensable primary source for any objective and unbiased political history of the 2016 campaign. When such a history is finally written—if, indeed, any will ever be—they will declare this the most astounding election in American history. Its outcome, with businessman and former reality TV show star Donald J. Trump slashing through a crowded and talented field of Republican contenders to win the nomination, then battling a Democrat opponent in Hillary Clinton who, by all accounts, was a favorite not just to win the general election but to do so in a blowout, was the political equivalent of the American hockey team defeating the Soviets in the 1980 Olympics.

Trump, a man with virtually no political experience, with almost no support from party insiders, and with little large-scale funding besides his personal fortune, emerged seemingly out of nowhere to roundly defeat the largest stable of credible candidates the Republican

Party has ever fielded in the modern era and seized the nomination…easily. Then, astonishing supporters and detractors alike, he was elected president of the United States without the traditional armies of consultants and pollsters, or the seemingly necessary "ground game" that was required to merely win a primary, not to mention a general election. His Democratic Party opponent had not just the active support of a sitting president touted for his high public approval numbers but also the endorsements of every wing of the Democrat coalition, which in sheer voter registrations outnumbered the Republicans. And Trump had to beat not only Clinton but three other smaller-party candidates as well. All of this came despite the fact that his own party wasn't solidly behind him—with powerful Republican office-holders offering tepid and wavering support, at best, and #NeverTrump intellectuals churning out daily articles for venerable conservative magazines. On top of all of those apparently fatal disadvantages, Trump faced entirely monolithic and extraordinarily nasty opposition from almost every outlet of the so-called "news" media.

Jerome Hudson of Breitbart News has catalogued the number of times the "experts" insisted Trump had no chance. Just a few of their predictions:

- Ross Douthat of the *New York Times*: "Donald Trump will not be the Republican nominee"
- *Washington Post* editor James Downie: "Let's dispense with the notion that Trump has a real shot at winning in November"
- CNN contributor Hilary Rosen: Trump had lost the election "from the first day he announced"
- The Huffington Post: "Donald Trump will not…win the general election.…"
- The *Los Angeles Times*: "Hillary Clinton will beat Donald Trump" by seven percent with "perhaps a double digit landslide" (If you're going to be wrong, go big!)
- Fox contributor Karl Rove, who has recently repeatedly been wrong, on MSNBC: "Trump can't win [the] general

election" because conservatives will stay home (Surprise, Karl: conservatives—plus disenfranchised whites and union members—won the election for Trump)

- RealClearPolitics elections analyst Sean Trende on November 4, hedging his bet somewhat: "There's probably a 90% chance Trump loses"
- Bloomberg columnist Jonathan Bernstein: "Seriously, Trump Won't Win"
- The *New York Daily News*: promised a "yuge" November loss for Trump
- The *Nation*, reassuring its lefty readers: "Relax, Donald Trump can't win"
- *Forbes* specifically claimed, "Trump won't win Wisconsin"
- Frank Luntz, who tried to delete his Twitter predictions after Clinton's bid turned south, on Election Night: "Hillary Clinton will be the next President of the United States" (Oops)[1]

Yet Trump won.

Only two national pollsters, both of them viewed as "outliers," had Trump ahead on Election Day, November 8.

Yet Trump won.

Not a single major television network could even remotely be considered "friendly" to The Donald.

Yet Trump won.

How?

Now the story of how Trump won the most astounding election victory in our nation's history can be told. To explain exactly what Donald J. Trump did to be elected the forty-fifth president, I'll be drawing on the perspective of a group of outsiders. In addition to myself (a professional historian), we were a pollster, an aerospace engineer in the defense industry, an obstetrician, an investment banker, and one analyst who still wishes to remain entirely anonymous. We were not full-time politicos, but we managed to beat the professional politicos with our own analysis, predictions, and spot-on advice to the Trump campaign.

These amateurs saw Trump's strength early, and some of us predicted his success far earlier than anyone else. On Election Day, we came together to provide real-time data to the Trump campaign that even Team Trump didn't have. Using data from all of us, the pollster in our group of "Renegade Deplorables" was able to call states for Trump with certainty up to an hour before the major networks broke the news.

More important, though, is also the story of *why* Trump won—the "forgotten" Americans he spoke to, and the ideas that he talked about to appeal to them. In achieving what everyone said he couldn't, Trump realigned the Republican Party, making it "inclusive" for the first time in years and attracting the white working class for the first time since 1984. Trump won by taking states no one thought he had a chance of taking, and by stealing Clinton's own taken-for-granted voters out from under her nose. His election is a revolution in American politics that has realigned the political party system in dramatic fashion—possibly establishing a third "Party System" in American history (although the Republican Establishment has, so far, sidled up to Trump in a move that might prevent such a realignment).

Donald Trump's rise to be the nominee of the Republican Party in 2016—let alone the victor in the presidential race and, on January 20, 2017, president of the United States—was absolutely unforeseen just eighteen months earlier. It was so unlikely that only a handful of observers, including Ann Coulter, Bill Mitchell, and myself, had thought it even possible.[2] What had we seen that virtually *all* of the pollsters (save People's Pundit Daily and the USC/*Los Angeles Times* poll), *all* of the political pundits except Rush Limbaugh and Sean Hannity, and *all* of the talking heads on the news missed?

Reading Clinton–and Obama–Wrong

For one thing, those of us who saw Trump as a formidable candidate early on knew that for eight years, a majority of Americans had been deeply dissatisfied with the Obama administration. This was despite not only his handy reelection in 2012 but also polls purporting to show that Obama continued to be very popular, with a high approval rating. (Below, I delve into the 2016 election-cycle polling, whose utter and total failure means that Obama's approval rating must be suspect.) We saw that the Republican candidate had an opportunity to run against the weak, unpopular, and corruption-tainted Hillary Clinton. In short, we saw that a Republican had a solid shot at winning the White House. But we (and Donald Trump) were not alone in seeing that opportunity. Many contenders saw 2016 as the perfect moment to run for the presidency, producing the largest field of legitimate Republican candidates certainly in post–Civil War history and probably in all of American history. At various points one after another of them—Jeb Bush, Marco Rubio, and Scott Walker—was thought to be a "sure thing" to win the nomination. Waiting in the wings was the insurrectionary Reaganite conservative Texas Senator Ted Cruz.

They all failed. Walker, unable to sell his Wisconsin reform message to the broader Republican base, was one of the first to drop out. Bush, damaged by the "low energy" label Trump gave him, which he never shook, was soon gone, despite a mind-boggling expenditure of campaign money on ads. Rubio survived long enough to win Puerto Rico and Minnesota, but failed even to be competitive in his home state of Florida. As the "sure things" fell by the wayside, the unlikely duo of Cruz and Ohio Governor John Kasich stayed in the race, trying to derail Trump. Yet despite winning a few states, they dropped so far behind Trump that at the last minute the two of them, without hope of winning the nomination outright for themselves, were forced into an unholy alliance aimed merely at denying Trump the 1,237 delegates necessary to cement his victory on the first ballot at the convention.

That, too, failed.

At the end of the process, some sixteen months after the race for the nomination had begun, a man with no political experience at all, who had never held elected office, and who had never served in the military, had won the Republican nomination—convincingly. Trump won a record 13 million votes in the GOP primaries. He racked up 1,400 delegates at a time when Nate Silver and the other so-called experts at Silver's *FiveThirtyEight* blog were insisting he would have a hard time getting to 1,237.[3] He spurred excitement on the Republican side as no one in recent memory had, causing GOP primary vote totals to grow by 10 million from 2008.

Yet the Republican Party—especially the Old Guard, the likes of the Bushes, Mitt Romney, and John McCain—refused to fully embrace him. When it came to Donald Trump, the Republican Party establishment acted the part of a reluctant groom at a shotgun wedding.

The rejection of Trump by that establishment was a stunning display of disbelief and pride, for Trump's dominance was mind-boggling at times. In the primaries, he won every county in Florida— where he was opposed by *two* Florida natives—except for Miami, and every county in Virginia. He won every county save for a single New York district in a five-state sweep of the Northeast. Beaten in Ohio by the sitting governor, Trump was the *only* other candidate to win any county in that state. (In the general election, Trump would go on to carry Ohio by a whopping nine points, or four times the margin by which George W. Bush carried the state in 2004—without an ounce of statewide support from Governor John Kasich.) He took the entirety of the state in the California primary, with 75 percent of the vote. Never viewed as the "evangelical" candidate—that was Cruz's strong suit—Trump led in almost every state, and especially the Southern states of the "Bible Belt," among self-described evangelicals. Though his appeal was supposed to be limited to the "uneducated," Trump won the "college educated" and "some college" categories in almost every state.

A Very Predictable Primary Blowout

In April 2016, pundits were in near universal agreement that Trump could not reach the "magic number" of 1,237 delegates at the convention. Just one month later, they glumly admitted he couldn't be stopped. To many, the result seemed impossible, incredible, stunning.

To some of us, it was obvious.

I am on record as early as August *2015* predicting that Trump would win both the nomination and the election.[4] Actually, I think I made the prediction earlier. By March 2016 I had concluded that Trump would compile at least 1,300 delegates in the Republican primaries—while the "experts" such as Silver were still insisting he would have a very tough path to merely reach 1,237.[5]

In November 2015, I predicted Trump would win the general election with a relatively easy Electoral College victory—which I then defined as between 300 and 320 electoral votes—but a narrower popular vote margin. In 2016, I refined that prediction to say Trump would win seventy or so electoral votes from formerly blue states, but by margins of under 2 percent. And just two days out, I wrote that "300–320 [Electoral Votes] are entirely within reach," when most pundits were still saying Hillary would win by more than that much.[6]

Trump would in fact take Pennsylvania by 1.2 percent, Michigan by .3 percent, Wisconsin by 1.3 percent, and Florida by 1.3 percent. In "blue" states he lost, the margins were also razor thin in some cases: New Hampshire (under .5 percent), Minnesota (1.5 percent), and Virginia (4.9 percent, but only 200,000 votes). There were a few "blue blowouts," such as North Carolina, where Trump doubled Romney's 2012 margin, and Iowa, where Trump won by over nine percentage points. But by and large, this was a "big" victory won in tiny margins in a number of states. In short, for the sixteen months leading up to the 2016 election, I was pretty much correct, often even underestimating Trump's strength.

Donald Trump–Conservative, Nationalist, or Both?

A large portion of the so-called #NeverTrump opposition, led by *National Review* magazine, claimed (and I underscore "claimed") that they opposed Trump because he wasn't a real conservative. To the extent this was justified at all, they were going by some of Trump's previous positions on social issues (which he had recanted some time back), his military isolationism, and his rejection of pure "free trade" theories—with his criticism of trade deals including the North American Free Trade Agreement (NAFTA) and the Trans-Pacific Partnership (TPP) and his proposal to build a wall to stop illegal immigration from Mexico.

But in fact, much of modern "conservatism" is *not* traditional American conservatism as practiced by George Washington, John Adams, and Alexander Hamilton (Federalists), James Madison (a member of the original Republican Party), or Abraham Lincoln, Theodore Roosevelt, Warren Harding, and Calvin Coolidge (GOP members). The historical fact is that Ronald Reagan significantly *departed* from many traditionally conservative positions, claiming that overseas intervention was necessary to prevent our strategic position from eroding in the unprecedented circumstances of the Cold War. Reagan also agreed to the Simpson–Mazzoli immigration bill on the specious grounds that the Democrats would honor their promises. Until Reagan, virtually all of the conservative leaders of the Federalist, Madisonian, Whig, and Republican Parties would have *agreed* with Trump's major public policy stands.

With the exceptions of James Polk and Woodrow Wilson, most Democrat presidents would have agreed with Trump, as well.

As talk show host Rush Limbaugh has explained many times, Trump is not ideological. He does not see things in an ideologically "conservative" framework. He is a pragmatist, a problem solver who measures success not by adherence to a particular political ideology but by whether or not people are prosperous, employed, and safe. Pollster Richard Baris of People's Pundit Daily Polling—one of the very few pollsters to properly gauge Trump's popularity—has noted that Trump's appeal was "attitudinal," and that it crossed racial and ethnic lines, especially with African American men, who did not like political correctness and were always "open to Trump."[7]

What gave rise to Donald Trump? The answer seems obvious: the failure of conservatism to achieve anything in the past eight years. Despite two overwhelming election victories at the House and Senate levels, the Republicans steadfastly refused to use either of the *only* two weapons in their arsenal to stop Barack Obama—impeachment or a "government shutdown." Obviously either would have been a major battle, and quite possibly the GOP would have lost both. But when the representatives that they had elected did not even try to exercise their constitutional powers (of the purse, in the House; to call the president to account for unconstitutional actions, in the Senate), a large number of conservative voters came to see conservatism itself as hollow and toothless.

Jim McIngvale, the owner of Gallery Furniture, originally a Cruz supporter but later friendly to Trump, recalls attending a visit by Trump to a local Republican gathering in Texas. At that meeting, McIngvale asked the billionaire about his views on "American Exceptionalism." Trump did not answer with a traditional ideological response, such as one you might find in the "Pillars of Exceptionalism" that we outlined in *A Patriot's History of the Modern World*.[8] He did not respond with a theoretical defense of American freedom. Instead, Trump asked his own question: "How can you call us exceptional when we don't win? These other countries are eating our lunch. We need to make America great again." In other words, a philosophical conservatism that had failed its people was meaningless. Definitions of "exceptional" that did not reflect America's current condition were flawed. Only a practical conservatism that would result in a great and prosperous America was worth having. Before we can talk about exceptionalism, the United States must actually *be* exceptional—something that has not been true for the past twenty years, in Trump's view.

The New Conservatism Is the Old Conservatism

Trump-era conservatism entails the same program as the Washington-Lincoln-TR conservatism: negotiate deals based on strength that work to the betterment of the U.S., not one-sided deals that result in Boeing giving China all its patents (a threat to national security), to give one example. Washington and Hamilton believed in protective tariffs to ensure the domestic manufacture (and thus the reliable supply, in any foreign conflict) of guns and uniforms for the military. Today, that means a U.S. manufacturing infrastructure to supply computers, optics, and other necessities of modern warfare. Oh, and by the way, true free trade occurs when you can—by force or intimidation if necessary, as has happened before in American history (remember Commodore Perry and the Opening of Japan in 1853)—open foreign markets to American products.

To Washington and Lincoln, it was necessary for American security that the nation operate from shared values stemming from a love of America and its laws. Every illegal alien violates the latter by coming here illegally (or overstaying his visa). Many violate the former by elevating their own national language above English or seeing themselves as first "Mexicans" or "Muslims" and only tangentially as Americans. According to Trump, the assimilation process has to be restarted. That was exactly the policy under William McKinley, Teddy Roosevelt, and every president up to Lyndon Baines Johnson. For a fifty-year period in the twentieth century, we had virtually *no* immigration.

The new nationalist conservatism is feared by the political elites, who are globalist in their sympathies, as are *many* corporate leaders who benefit from the "cheap labor express." Yet the American people are conservative nationalists. They want a strong America, not one subservient to the UN, or international treaties, or the international bankers who wrecked the world economy. They yearn for Americans to set our own course, independent of the failures of China, Russia, and the European states unable to protect their own borders, to escape from sclerotic regional structures such as the European Union, or to exert their own national spirit. Trump represented a promise to return to traditional conservatism, nationalist conservatism.

Finally, traditionalists from Washington to Lincoln to Calvin Coolidge (perhaps excluding TR) believed in a relatively isolationist foreign policy. Harding negotiated the Washington Treaty to limit shipbuilding with the U.S. in the *lead*, so that we wouldn't need a big navy. Trump has indicated that the U.S. has been too eager to deploy troops around the world—something with which both Washington and Lincoln would have agreed.

Trump's traditional American nationalist conservatism explains his appeal to Democrats and independents as well as to the "conservative" and "very conservative" Republicans that pollsters found supported him. Trump is a departure from Reagan conservatism, but Reagan was a departure from Washington-Lincoln-Harding-Coolidge conservatism. Reaganism was needed in the 1980s, but times have changed and the world (and its threats) are much different today. Trump's 2016 campaign revealed a completely different attitude to the problems facing America from the previous eight years of do-nothing conservatism, which was itself the husk of an unusual variation on traditional American conservatism that was right for a particular moment in the Cold War.

Trump was signaling, as he put it in his announcement that he would run for office, his intention to Make America Great Again. And from the outset, his supporters took him seriously.

Very seriously.

This book is the story of how Donald J. Trump gained the presidency. Along the way, it offers up a hearty dose of behind-the-scenes activity in the key states of Ohio and Florida by a renegade bunch of part-time political junkies who came to be known as the "Deplorables"— a term Hillary Clinton gave to Trump's supporters when she called his voters a "basket of deplorables."

The only one of us who could claim full-time professional status as a political pundit was Richard Baris, the pollster whose operation was not taken seriously by the "real" pollsters. Baris had worked with a number of political campaigns, but in 2013 he created People's Pundit Daily (PPD). In his first polling in 2014, Baris found that there was a low response rate, and he discerned then that the "major" pollsters had not yet adjusted. So Baris developed a "large net" approach, then "let the data talk to me," as he puts it, rather than trying to force the polling results into a pre-established model.[9] In the 2016 election, PPD was the most accurate of all the polls.

Then there was "Deplorable Don," Donald Culp, an aerospace engineer at Wright Patterson Air Force Base in Ohio. Culp worked in artificial intelligence but was deeply interested in politics and had advised the local Republican Party on its voter outreach (which was successful in 2016). Culp would develop key internal voter assessment models that would prove uncannily accurate.

Another member of the Band of Deplorables was "Deplorable Greg," Greg Den Haese, an obstetrician-gynecologist from the Tampa, Florida, area whose hobby was politics, and who knew south Florida like the back of his hand.

Working independently, another south Floridian, an anonymous data miner named "Deplorable Drew," was funneling data to Team Trump that, as we later saw, almost exactly confirmed what Greg was compiling.

An anonymous analyst named Deplorable Dave from Dayton had deep inside knowledge of Ohio politics and specific battleground counties.

Finally, my years of writing about many American elections as a professional political historian had made me familiar with the political realities of Ohio, Arizona, and Florida. Members of the website FreeRepublic—particularly "SpeedyinTexas," "Ravi," and others—contributed data from time to time.

We were a part of another unusual and unique element of the Trump campaign, which eschewed traditional consultants and pollsters. Trump had access to knowledgeable volunteers eager to help in any way they could. Our band of Deplorable brothers, beginning long before Election Day, fed streams of information, voter registration changes, absentee ballot numbers, real-time early-voting observational data, polling, and other insights directly to the top of Team Trump. On Election Day itself, we confirmed trends in red counties in Florida that we knew would hand the state to The Donald, and we had—despite great concerns from Team Trump itself—already determined that Trump would win Ohio in a blowout. Our group of misfits and renegades "called" Florida an hour before the networks, Pennsylvania hours before, and Michigan days before. Our only miss of the night, Wisconsin, was a pleasant surprise. Our Deplorable Renegades knew probably before anyone else—except Hillary's campaign (see chapter nine for that fascinating story)—that Trump had won.

But before we go behind the scenes into the virtual bunker of the Renegade Deplorables, let's visit the excitement of the 2016 campaign trail, where veteran reporter Joel Pollak, senior editor-at-large of Breitbart News, was on the ground with tens of thousands of the voters who would soon give Donald Trump's presidential campaign the most astounding victory in American history—though Pollak didn't know it.

CHAPTER TWO

On the Campaign Trail:
Washington to North Carolina to New York

Joel Pollak

October 25, 2016

I board the red-eye flight in Los Angeles to Baltimore. I have booked two tickets, actually—the other is to Raleigh-Durham, North Carolina—because I have no real idea, until the last hours, where exactly Donald Trump and his campaign are going to be.

I have been offline for the preceding two days, in observance of the Jewish holidays of Shemini Atzeret and Simchat Torah. And for every one of those forty-eight-plus hours, I have been stewing quietly, eager for news.

I have broken some news of my own, actually, even while offline. My piece for Breitbart News that came out just before the last debate was an exposé, working with conservative filmmaker James O'Keefe and his Project Veritas, which revealed that Hillary Clinton's campaign has been inciting violence at Trump rallies and other Republican events for the previous year.[1] And my latest follow-up story links Clinton herself directly to the tactics of her henchmen behind a veil of "dark money" super PACs.[2] But I have to wait to see it online, and follow the reaction.

Every four years, Jewish holiday season coincides with the final stretch of the campaign. And every four years, it seems, while liberal Jewish voters are free to enjoy their holidays more or less secure in the knowledge that their candidates will win, conservatives are left to think glumly about the future and pray for miracles.

Midway between Rosh Hashanah, the Jewish New Year, and Yom Kippur, the Day of Atonement, the infamous *Access Hollywood* tape landed—hard.

The tape, made in 2005, recorded a conversation between Trump and TV host Billy Bush (a member of *that* Bush family) in which Trump boasted about the ability to grope women and get away with it because of his celebrity status. "Grab them by the pussy," he said, and Bush laughed.

The men did not realize their microphones were live; they were not on camera, but on a bus. The release of the video prompted Republicans to panic, and the mainstream media to rejoice.

As of October 25, just two weeks before the election, it seems that Trump has never really recovered from that shock. It seems odd that of all the things that could end Trump's prospects, it would be something so completely beyond the control of the campaign itself. Not one of the myriad campaign gaffes or stumbles, every one of which the media was sure would make the Trump campaign "implode," but an eleven-year-old video that someone had clearly looked very hard to find, and tried very hard to keep under wraps. It was also, clearly, a joke—not the kind of thing that Trump would have remembered or could have known to anticipate.

Not so, perhaps, the accusations that have followed—a slew of women suddenly breaking their silence, in some cases many decades old, to claim that Trump had tried to impose himself on them.

As sexual assault claims go, these are minor compared to Bill Clinton's long résumé: even according to the allegations, Trump seemed to have relented when women told him to stop. And their timing is suspect:

Why wait until October, and not bring these accusations up earlier, during the GOP primary?

The answer is not hard to guess. This was a coordinated hit, an "October surprise." And the claim has been given additional weight (pun intended) by the way the media has handled the apparently pre-packaged story of Trump's twenty-year-old feud with Alicia Machado, a former Miss Universe. Hillary Clinton had brought up Machado and her fight with Trump about her weight—he had just bought the pageant when the new champion ballooned—at the first presidential debate, and several interviews with Machado, clearly months in the making, were subsequently released.

Trump may have known that he would face questions about his past. Indeed, everyone already knows about his philandering, which had emerged as a point of criticism in the primary.

But this is different. The *Access Hollywood* video seems to have caught even Trump by surprise. And it has been delivered with the same media message we have all heard countless times throughout the primaries and the campaign for the general election, but never with such credibility as this: "The presidential race is over," as NBC News' Chuck Todd says.[3]

In late October, that certainly seems true—thanks to polls that plunged, after the media has done their part.

■ ■ ■

But Clinton has been suffering some embarrassing revelations of her own.

There are the daily releases from WikiLeaks, for example, the rogue organization founded by fugitive Julian Assange. WikiLeaks helped trigger the Arab Spring and other global upheavals by reporting the contents of U.S. diplomatic cables, thanks in part to American soldier Bradley (now Chelsea) Manning. Now Assange has access to Clinton campaign chair John Podesta's emails.

The result is a slew of embarrassing revelations about the Clinton operation—its apparent coordination with super PACs; its real feelings about Catholics; its internal admissions that the Clinton Foundation is rife with conflicts of interest; its panic as it has tried to anticipate the next Clinton gaffe or scandal.

The media have largely ignored the WikiLeaks revelations, however—each of which might have been enough to derail any other campaign, certainly a Republican one.

O'Keefe's videos have had an impact, too, showing that it was Clinton—not Trump—who had sown seeds of violent division in the country. The Democratic operatives who carried out what they referred to as "bird-dogging" used a system of text messages—a "Pony Express," one called it—to connect the Clinton campaign to its super PAC constellation, flouting laws that prevent campaigns and super PACs from coordinating their political activities. And they created a "double-blind" system so that the candidate herself would be insulated from most of their nefarious field operations.

Their goal had been to create a sense of "anarchy" around Trump—which they did, fooling even conservative Republicans who tended to blame Trump for the violence of which his rallies were actually the targets, rather than blaming the leftists who had deliberately fomented it.

Even the mainstream media have covered O'Keefe's video revelations about Chicago consultant (and convicted felon) Robert Creamer, who was at the heart of this scheme by the Democrats.

Still, most Democrats live in a bubble. More than one liberal friend on social media is aggrieved by the chant, "Lock her up," which Trump crowds have taken to repeating ever since the Republican National Convention. To the Left, that seems like the essence of mob justice; it smacks of totalitarian regimes.

I try, in vain, to explain to liberal friends and opponents that the slogan is an expression of the quite rational belief that Clinton has committed apparent crimes—mishandling classified materials, obstruction of justice, lying under oath—that would have seen any ordinary citizen prosecuted, and that her position shouldn't protect her from the same consequences.

But they will not hear it. It is not enough for them to support Clinton for political or ideological reasons, despite her flaws. Those flaws—including solid evidence of corruption and criminality—have to be wished away.

■ ■ ■

Hillary Clinton represents the ultimate decline of one of America's great political parties.

Much has been said and written about the advent of Trump as a sign of Republican malaise—and much of that is true. But as hard-core leftist CNN commentator Van Jones observed in May 2016, at least the Republicans played by the rules and allowed Trump to win a fair contest.[4] In the Democratic Party, the primary was rigged, legally and otherwise, in Clinton's favor.

The Democrats' "superdelegate" system is an undemocratic mechanism through which the party insiders can act in concert to prevent an insurgent candidacy—such as that of "democratic socialist" Senator Bernie Sanders of Vermont—from taking the nomination.

That much Sanders knew when he joined the fray. What he did not count on was Democratic National Committee (DNC) officials colluding with Clinton—supplying her in advance with debate questions, and the like—to defeat him.

The 2016 election seems to mark the final transition of the Democratic Party from a party of the working class to a party of gentry liberals.

On policy after policy, Clinton has targeted the sensibilities of her donors in New York, D.C., and San Francisco—and ignored the deeply felt anxieties of the people whose support she had courted in 2008. While, for example, in that election she wooed Appalachia in a last-ditch effort against Obama, in this election cycle she has called for coal mines to be put out of business.

But above all, 2016 is the election when Democrats have refused to reject, replace, or in any effective way stand up to a candidate with demonstrable ethical problems, who has a tendency to lie about nearly everything, and who likely ought to have been prosecuted by the Justice Department.

There were some decent Democratic alternatives—not all of whom actually ran for the 2016 nomination—but Democrats fell in lockstep behind Clinton, most with no degree of enthusiasm.

The slow erosion of the Democratic Party has been twenty years in the making, dating back to the Bill Clinton impeachment scandal of the late 1990s. President Clinton had revived the party by embracing the center—partly for the sake of expediency, but also after several years leading the "New Democrat" movement, which embraced market principles over traditional union-backed, statist approaches to achieving Democrats' core aims of economic equality.

Bill Clinton struggled to cultivate successors in the wake of the impeachment scandal, however. And while his wife, Hillary, is seen as a fellow moderate, in truth her political roots were as left-wing as Obama's—perhaps even more so.

Still, many of her political gestures throughout her career have been cynical, and a vote to authorize the Iraq War cost her dearly in the 2008 Democratic primary. Other Democrats who had made the mistake of adopting a hawkish stance were hounded out of the party by the Left.

Obama emerged from a wing of the party that had always considered Bill Clinton's pragmatism to be a disaster, and believed that under the right circumstances—such as a financial crisis, for instance—the country would turn toward left-wing policies as the only acceptable answer.

Obama's moment came in 2008, when he harnessed the anti-war movement to defeat Clinton and cast his other radical policies as the sensible alternative to a litany of Republican failures.

In his election and reelection, Obama showed Democrats that they could run as purist liberal-leftists and still win—provided that they were able to maximize the turnout of minority voters, and that they were willing to play by the hard Chicago rules necessary to bully Republicans into submission.

What was lost was not just the desire to do what most Americans recognized was in the national interest, but even the desire to be *seen* as doing it. In the process, the Democratic Party lost touch with a broad swath of the American public.

And so Democrats, as represented by Hillary Clinton, have become a thin coalition of the educated upper class and the dependent underclass, sustained by Wall Street donations, a power-hungry tech industry, and the culture patrol that is Hollywood and the mainstream media.

Saturday Night Live has portrayed a Trump voter as a drunk filled with resentment toward minorities.[5] Bill Clinton calls the typical Trump voter "your standard redneck."[6] Such is the Democrats' contempt for millions of Americans.

Worse, the party is completely out of ideas. Most of Clinton's policies and promises either pledge to extend what Obama has already done or are simply repetitions of his campaign promises from 2008 and 2012.

Clinton promises, for example, to grant women equal pay for equal work—something they already have had as a matter of law for decades, and which Obama strengthened in 2009 by extending the statute of limitations for women to file discrimination lawsuits.

What gives the Clinton campaign the momentum it enjoys—in spite of empty halls, canned questions, and public fatigue—is outrage at Donald Trump, especially his comments about women, Muslims, and illegal aliens from Mexico.

Democrats have used those comments to drive voter registration among all three of those groups, and to present their party as the vehicle for the aspirations of these three groups, in a coalition largely bound by tired identity politics.

Clinton has no achievements of which to speak—or, at least, to speak honestly. She claims credit for a program in the 1990s called SCHIP, which extended health insurance subsidies to children.

But the idea had not been hers alone, and it followed her disastrous stewardship of health care reform in 1993, which went down to ignominious defeat. Her tenure as secretary of State featured lots of globe-trotting—and little else to report.

The Bernie Sanders campaign represented a kind of *cri de coeur* from the party's activist base, pleading for a more authentic campaign than Clinton offered—one grounded in leftism and its utopias, one where the party would not be seen to have abandoned the antiwar standard it raised in 2008 over the Obama campaign, one where the candidate would be genuinely a stranger to Wall Street and to K Street, not beholden to large donors and interest groups.

Sanders offered his fans that hope for several months, but it was hard to take his campaign seriously after he breezily dismissed concerns about the unfolding Clinton email scandal at the first opportunity, at the Democratic presidential debate in Las Vegas in October 2015. He was "sick and tired of hearing about your damn e-mails," Sanders told Clinton. She seemed both surprised and relieved, for Bernie had effectively given the game away entirely.[7] That was the only issue on which Sanders could possibly have hoped to win the nomination—by pointing out Clinton's corruption and dishonesty.

Somehow, the man who railed against Wall Street was incapable of seeing self-dealing, cronyism, and greed when it originated in D.C. instead. By refusing to give credence to attacks on her emails—largely because they were a Republican preoccupation—Sanders made it easier for the party to unite around Clinton. And so they have rallied around their nominee without examining her record with any degree of objectivity.

Not for the first time, the Clintons have stretched the law for their own benefit—and escaped. The lesson for them, once again, is that they can get away with living by a different set of rules. And the potential for malfeasance once they are in the White House is practically infinite.

The rule of law is now at stake. It appears to be a risk Democratic stalwarts are willing to accept.

October 26, 2016

Hundreds of journalists crowd the presidential ballroom of the Trump International Hotel in Washington, D.C. They jostle each other to reach the front of the media section; they crane their necks and hold cameras high over their heads to catch the action in front; they live-stream from their cell phones and chatter with each other nonchalantly, trying to look less excited than they are.

This is the hotel's grand opening, and Trump has been roundly excoriated by the press for attending it in the last weeks of the presidential campaign. His taking a break from the presidential campaign to promote his business is the umpteenth incident that's said to demonstrate his fundamental unseriousness about the presidency and underline the fact that he's unqualified for the office he seeks. In any case, in the wake of the *Access Hollywood* tape, it seems increasingly unlikely that, qualified or unqualified, he'll ever have the chance to occupy that office.

But for a campaign that seems to have no chance of winning, Trump is commanding a lot of attention.

Trump appears at the front, looking strong but tired. His daughter, Ivanka, is wearing a stunning white dress and bright red lipstick; his sons appear at his sides, dapper and proud.

In her introduction, Ivanka is fully in executive mode—not a potential First Daughter, but a manager and entrepreneur. She does, however, address her father's critics, whom she says have tried to "discredit" his business success. This hotel, she says—winner of a competitive bid by the federal government—is the retort.

Then Trump speaks. He is defiant, strident, but also exhausted, his voice gravelly with fatigue.

He touts the hotel's success—"under budget, ahead of schedule"—as a model for what he hopes to do in government. He slams Obamacare, whose massive premium hikes are in today's headlines; he congratulates his ally Newt Gingrich, seated in the audience, on going toe-to-toe with Megyn Kelly of Fox News in a debate that went viral the night before.

But, win or lose, he says, "The United States is great. Its people are great.... The future lies with the dreamers, not the cynics and the critics."

It sounds almost like a valediction—not quite a concession speech, but parting words, phrases by which he hopes to be remembered. As if this event—this success, not the accusations of a dozen women, not the bitter recriminations of the columnists on the elite opinion pages—is what will stand for him, if the campaign fails.

The whole event then shifts from the ballroom to the lobby, a huge rectangular atrium with steel beams arcing through the center and crystal chandeliers suspended near the sumptuous bar.

The media rush through the doors in a scrum to find the best positions for photographs and interviews; the invited guests take a more leisurely route. They file into rows of chairs set near a raised stage. Above, on a catwalk, the hotel's large kitchen and custodial staff watch patiently.

There is an eerie, icy silence for several minutes, as if there is something less than festive about the occasion. The only noise is the occasional piercing shout from the protesters on the street outside—union picketers who have been there all morning, demanding that Trump allow workers at this hotel and his Las Vegas property to organize. (There is a smattering of Trump supporters outside, too, and of curious onlookers hoping to see the man himself, or perhaps just a glimpse of his infamous hair.)

And then Trump himself arrives, flanked by his family. He speaks into the microphone; he praises the sound in the room. He is handed the scissors; they are the biggest and most beautiful he has ever seen, he says. He praises the workers and the employees, again.

And then, after a moment of confusion when the red ribbon seems to have gone missing, the Trump family poses with their blades at the ready. A snip, a cheer—and the pealing of bells resounds from the hotel's tower.

At that, the gathering disbands. The journalists mill about, unsure whether they have seen something worth reporting or if they have been used as props in Trump's show—as they have been, so often, in this campaign. (Two infamous episodes spring to mind. In September, Trump staged a press conference where the media expected him to answer questions about President Obama's birth certificate, and instead paraded a slew of supportive retired military leaders before the cameras for half an hour before announcing that he accepted Obama's American birth. The following month, before the second presidential debate, the Trump campaign told the press he would answer questions about his past sexual conduct, only to produce several of Bill Clinton's accusers instead.)

The guests mill about the hotel atrium for a few minutes—and then there is a flutter of bags snapping closed, heels on marble, and wheels on concrete. Out into the brilliant sunshine we march, waiting for the traveling press bus to whisk us to the airplane, for the plane to bring us to the next event, and for the next event to tell us: What is the man thinking?

How will he face defeat?

■　■　■

In Charlotte, North Carolina, we file off the press plane and dutifully wait for the Secret Service to search our belongings before piling into rickety buses and heading downtown.

There, in the intimate setting of a former Baptist church—at seven hundred packed seats, one of the smallest venues Trump has addressed in the campaign thus far—he is to unveil what his campaign calls a speech on "urban policy," and what he calls a "New Deal" for African Americans.

The crowd is predominantly white, and genteel, though there are several groups of black supporters, primarily near the front. Everyone is well dressed, in their Sunday best; this is an elite group of supporters that has been pulled together for a last-minute invitation-only event.

The likely reason: poll numbers showing Trump drawing unusually large levels of support from blacks in Pennsylvania, nearly three out of ten. If he can drive that proportion up, perhaps he can win the Keystone State. Really.

After words of introduction, and an invocation, Trump fails to appear. His speechwriter, Steven Miller—a cerebral Jewish Republican from far-left Santa Monica, who had previously worked for Alabama Senator Jeff Sessions on the Senate Budget Committee—peers out occasionally from behind the curtains.

It transpires that Trump has been meeting backstage with a group of local African American "faith and community leaders." The insights he can garner from that meeting, not to mention the photo-op, are probably worth the hour-long delay.

Finally, Trump emerges. The crowd applauds happily at first, as if relieved—then lustily, chanting his name. He approaches the podium, where he is flanked by two teleprompters.

This is to be a serious speech, not one of the extemporaneous improvised barn-burners that had characterized earlier phases of his campaign.

He looks wearily at the audience; he looks, and sounds, weary in general, and slightly hoarse, though his voice is somewhat improved since the morning.

"Today I want to talk about how to grow the African-American middle class, and provide a new deal for black America," Trump begins. He lays out three "pillars" for the "new deal"—"safe communities, great education, and high-paying jobs"—and one basic principle: "America first."

That controversial Charles Lindbergh–vintage term, which is also the main theme of his foreign policy, refers in this context to the idea that African Americans should come before illegal immigrants in the distribution of opportunities and benefits.

As he continues speaking, it becomes clear that his fatigue, far from alienating his audience, is drawing them in, creating a sense of intimacy and an air of authenticity.

Something shifts in the atmosphere in the room. The crowd senses it, and he does, too.

He warms up, his tone brightening, his voice smoothing out. The audience begins interjecting, applauding, chanting. "Drain the swamp!" someone shouts, a reference to his latest slogan about corruption.

What looked at first like a pedestrian address that might fail to hit its mark suddenly has the hallmarks of something more significant. A revival. This is a great speech—not quite historic, perhaps, but memorable.

This has been, after all, the first Republican campaign to speak clearly in favor of gay rights—and to inspire the party to applaud, as it did at the Republican National Convention in July.

And now Trump is the first modern Republican to make a pitch to black voters in a serious, sustained way, as if their votes mattered— because, this time, for Trump's presidential bid, they do. They can make a difference.

In Charlotte, Trump seems to be rediscovering the idea that he could win. He still seems haunted by the prospect of losing—win or lose, he jokes, he'll be on Pennsylvania Avenue anyway, thanks to the hotel he has just opened that morning—but winning doesn't seem to be out of the question.

Today there are state polls heading back in the right direction. There are some good national polls, too.

And now there is this moment, whatever it is, when he leans toward a room of strangers, and they lift him.

■　■　■

Landing—hard—at twilight, in Kinston, North Carolina. A rural place, known for a crop that a good portion of America wishes would disappear. These tobacco farms are not like the neat Cartesian checker-board cornfields of Iowa: they are a patchwork of divergent paths and ditches, of rivers and groves, of nature meeting history.

It is also a place that had been flooded, just a few weeks before, by Hurricane Matthew—and not for the first time. Kinston knows devastation and renewal.

The plane taxis toward the crowd, several thousand strong. Many people wave, mistaking the press plane for a campaign plane. They can be forgiven for the confusion: the plane does say "Trump Pence: Make America Great Again." But there's a moment of awkwardness as the journalists—many hostile to Trump, and suspicious that his supporters are "deplorable" xenophobes, rubes, and racists—stumble out of the plane and decline to return the greeting.

Embarrassed, I manage a brief wave to the crowd before taking a few pictures with my smartphone and melting into the throng, notebook in hand, looking for people who might be willing to speak with me. My credentials, such as they are, simply identify me as part of the media—not Breitbart News specifically. I am simply a journalist.

There are children everywhere, perched high on their parents' shoulders in the still-warm night air. The accents are heavy, as Southern as they come.

I talk to an insurance broker still in his dress shirt from the office; I nearly bump into a stay-at-home mom with flaxen hair and more political opinions than she is willing to admit at first.

The people are warm, open, excited to be a part of the drama gripping the nation. They scan the sky; every aircraft is mistaken for Trump's plane.

Finally, a bright light appears to the west and dips gracefully toward the horizon. The music on the PA system, previously a medley of the Rolling Stones, switches to something far more dramatic: the theme from *Air Force One.*

The airplane lands and coasts to a stop as the crowd cheers, the children waving their flags madly. It is a moving scene, and my throat catches; it is almost too evocative, the simple folk of the countryside greeting the big city billionaire hero.

Eventually, Trump emerges and waves.

He has sounded tired the entire day, delivering his words in a strained voice. Now, somehow, his voice is bright again, and he is back to the charismatic Trump of the primary, albeit flipping back to the teleprompter now and then to make sure he ticks off all his talking points.

The crowd loves the show; they have seen it on television, and they chime in with the right cheers at the appropriate moments: "Lock her up!" for Hillary, "Drain the swamp!" for corruption in general.

At the edge of the crowd there are pizza slices, candy bars, and refreshments for sale. The journalists huddle at long tables at the back, cursing the poor internet signal near the hangar: the Secret Service is jamming wireless communications near Trump's plane, the better to mask what his precise location will be, once airborne, from anyone inclined to fire a shoulder-mounted missile, assuming they have one.

Meanwhile, Trump is delivering his stump speech with glee.

"We are going to bring back your jobs, and we are not going to allow these companies to go to Mexico and take your jobs with them," he says, to cheers. Are there jobs missing in Kinston? Regardless, this is the kind of thing one simply must not say, and which one does not hear—which is exactly why the crowd loves it.

There are boos for Obamacare and for "Crooked Hillary" Clinton. There are jeers for the FBI, which botched the Clinton investigation, and for the "dishonest" media, flown in partially at the campaign's expense.

This is the Trump of old—and he seems to have endless time for the crowd, as he moves on past economics and corruption and into foreign policy. He says early voting is going well in Florida; he promises victory in North Carolina; he reminds them to go to the polls.

Then he waves, they cheer, and he is back inside his sky fortress, and away.

■ ■ ■

We are on the press plane now. What happens here is off the record—strictly.

I am the only member of the alternative media on the press plane. Everyone else is employed by a major network or a well-established outlet.

In the mainstream institutional media, the campaign plane is a rite of passage, a form of paying your dues. In four years, perhaps, you're off the trail and in the comfortable studio. Each individual story matters less than the experience accumulated in the time spent on the road.

I have to work hard. In the alternative media, we still think in terms of individual stories. It's not generally worth traveling, except for short stints. Every trip has to defray its own costs. Every single story matters.

The Secret Service has knocked out our wireless internet—we follow Trump, you see, so our signal is just as dangerous as his. The Chicago Cubs, the hometown team I grew up with in the northern Chicago suburb of Skokie, are comfortably ahead of the Cleveland Indians in Game 2 when we lift off the tarmac and my cell phone loses contact with the ground.

I catch an hour of sleep before we land at La Guardia and board the bus into the cavernous, cold city. I check the news again, confirm that the Cubs won, tying the series 1–1, and find myself amused at the day's headlines.

The Drudge Report is calling Trump's speech at the Washington hotel his "best speech" ever. Another headline touts the speech in Charlotte—accurately—as Trump's "New Deal" for African Americans.

Elsewhere, the polls are up and down. Trump has a small lead in Florida; he is behind in national polls he previously led; but one expert says he is guaranteed to win. The *Washington Post* is apparently convinced he will lose, telling supporters to give up now.

On my Twitter timeline, several Trump skeptics chime in, telling me that a close-up shot of what I called a "massive" crowd in Kinston proves the audience was small, because only a dozen people are visible in the frame. I took the photo from that angle to capture the twilight, not to provide a crowd estimate. I reply that it always amazes me how much more people know about an event when they weren't actually there.

I'm only half joking. Reality on social media seems to count for more than the old-fashioned kind, these days.

On my personal Facebook page, an old friend is so upset by the sight of the Trump press plane in one of my photographs that she dismisses me as a "bottom-feeder." Me, I suppose, and the *New York Times*, and CNN, and every other liberal network on the flight with me.

We will be up at sunrise tomorrow to catch the next leg. We can barely manage it, in our twenties, thirties, forties. Trump is doing it every day, and he is seventy years old.

The city is quiet; the diners are closed early. Something of New York's sheen has slipped away over the past few years, the bold spontaneity that it used to boast in the late 1990s and that had re-emerged even after the horror of 9/11, once the trauma was behind. The wide streets of Midtown are impassable at 11:00 p.m., blocked by buses and police and construction and debris.

We pass near Trump Tower, still gleaming in Midtown. We reach the hotel; I take the subway downtown. On foot, in the East Village, I hear voices call out for help from doorways; pots of soup steam in basements along St. Mark's Place, where the karaoke bars are open but empty. Winter seems to have arrived early, before anyone was ready, and everyone is hunkering down, waiting for the cold snap to pass.

That is how millions—certainly the journalists on the trail—seem to feel about the election. Let this bitterness pass. Let it end as it usually does. Let us hope for better when it's over.

CHAPTER THREE

How We "Renegade Deplorables" Saw Trump Could Win–Back in the Summer of 2015

Larry Schweikart

By the time Joel was seeing the last weeks of the 2016 presidential campaign from his ringside seat in the Donald Trump press corps, a group of amateur politicos who would come to be known as the basket of "Renegade Deplorables" had been predicting a Trump victory for sixteen months. Our analysis and data stood in stark contrast to the rather dire predictions for the Trump campaign that Joel encountered almost everywhere, to the point that the so-called "conservative press" bought it hook, line, and sinker. It all started for me in July of 2015, when I was on vacation in Phoenix, Arizona. Joel would join the campaign from the inside; this is our story from the "outside."

Donald Trump, who had thrown his hat in the ring as a candidate for the Republican nomination for president in June, was speaking in Phoenix when I happened to be in the Valley of the Sun on vacation. As I watched the television in my hotel room, I knew I was seeing something unusual for any presidential campaign—let alone a primary campaign. This was a dark horse candidate with no previous political experience speaking to an overflow crowd that had had to be moved to a new venue to accommodate the thousands who wanted to attend. Trump had announced he would give a speech at the Arizona Biltmore Resort on July 11, but within hours the response from people wanting to attend was so overwhelming that the venue had moved to the Phoenix Convention Center. The Biltmore could accommodate only fifteen hundred people. The initial responses showed that thirty-five hundred would be showing up at the Convention Center. But by the time Trump got to the event, there were just under five thousand there by official count, and an attendee with commercial real estate experience calculated the number was almost triple that.[1] Thousands more waited outside, unable to get in. Seeing all this—it made quite a splash on local television—I sat up as if struck by lightning.

A Candidate Who Will Fight

And watching Trump, I saw him do something unusual. He stepped aside in the middle of his own speech to ask a crime victim to speak. Jamiel Shaw Sr., a resident of Southern California, took the microphone to describe how his seventeen-year-old son had been shot and killed in 2008 by an illegal alien.[2] Shaw had seen Trump on television and heard what Donald Trump had to say about immigration and the failed policies of the Obama administration. Shaw made comments to a news team, and when Trump, in turn, heard Shaw on television, he said "this guy's mentioning my name." He turned up the TV to hear Shaw say, "The only man who is sticking up for us is Donald Trump."[3] So he invited him to speak at Phoenix.

"This guy is different," I thought. "He is what the Tea Party, what Rush Limbaugh, what conservatives have been praying for for more than eight years—someone who will fight back." Almost immediately, I engaged in a Twitter bet with a Democrat that neither Jeb Bush nor Hillary Clinton would be their party's nominee. (Well, I was half right!) I concluded Trump would be the Republican nominee, based entirely on his elevation of illegal immigration as an issue and his willingness to stand his ground. (Later, pundits would lampoon the "He Fights!" mantra—without ever actually trying to understand what it meant to the rest of us.) In the less than thirty-day period since the announcement of his candidacy, Trump had emerged as someone who would actually fight for *us*, and that was—to quote Trump himself—YUGE!

As the headline on The Blaze, Glenn Beck's web-based network, said, "The Silent Majority is Back!"[4] (This would prove ironic, as Beck would soon become one of Trump's most rabid enemies, even going on a fast to try to stop Trump.)

Thousands of potential voters may have felt that Trump was speaking for them. But critics were shocked. They were horrified at Trump's blunt comments that many illegals were "rapists," and many were "criminals" (which, of course, all of them were by virtue of breaking immigration law—not to mention any fraud and perjury they may have committed by lying on subsequent welfare, hospital, and education forms). Referring to the Mexican government, Trump thundered "They're killing us at the border and killing us on trade."[5]

At that time, I did not even know Richard Baris, the pollster from People's Pundit Daily or "Deplorable Greg," the amateur politico with the inside information about the voting game on the ground in Florida, or some of the other people who would play key roles in the story. (Indeed, Hillary's "basket of deplorables" comment was still almost a year away.) So I didn't have access to their data and spot-on analysis at that point. But having written on American history and politics as a professional historian for over thirty years, I thought I could spot a historical trend when I saw one.

This was definitely a historic event!

Like Ann Coulter—one of the first to state that Trump would win the nomination and the presidency—I sensed early that Trump would appeal to the vast conservative base that was, yes, angry. They were angry at having been used by the elected political class for over eight years, strung along with promises that those they put in office would actually try to oppose the Democrats, only to find they were betrayed again and again. They were the "forgotten men" and women, whom Obama deliberately and publicly wrote off in 2012 in his reelection campaign. And they were not just Republicans, but millions of Democrats who had been abandoned as well. To me, Trump's appeal to those voters was obvious.

Trump had only been in the race since June 16, when he had announced that "Sadly, the American dream is dead," but "I will bring it back bigger and better and stronger than ever before."[6] With his slogan, "Make America Great Again!" ("MAGA"), Trump tapped into a festering concern about how two midterm elections had sent supposedly conservative Republicans to Washington to stop President Barack Obama's policies and yet for six years, nothing had happened, despite polling that consistently showed Americans thought the country was on the wrong track and that Obama's signature "health care" policy, "Obamacare," was anywhere from a bad law to a disaster. The Republicans had repeatedly refused to fight back.[7] Insurance premiums had risen, insurance companies had pulled out of the Obamacare co-ops, and more Americans than ever were without health coverage or insurance policies. This was all quite predictable from a free-market standpoint, and indeed Republicans had harped on that very point to get elected—twice—yet steadfastly refused to address it effectively in Congress.

As talk show host Rush Limbaugh pointed out, this reluctance on the part of Republicans to fight had two main causes. The first was the lesson Republicans took away from the 1995 budget fight between the Newt Gingrich–led Republican Congress and then-President Bill Clinton. When the GOP, alarmed by out-of-control spending by the federal government, refused to pass new spending bills and allowed the government to shut down non-essential services, the media—the willing allies of the Democratic Party—portrayed Gingrich as "the Gingrich who Stole Christmas." Republicans were blamed for starving old people, closing schools, and a myriad of other disasters that in fact had not happened. Nevertheless, Gingrich and the Republicans were humbled, the non-essential services were restored, and from that point on the GOP was gun-shy about "shutting down government"—or, in other words, actually taking responsibility for the power of the purse that the Constitution gives them. Apparently Americans had grown too reliant on a large federal bureaucracy to live without it.

The second and more debilitating factor that prevented the Republicans (in their own minds) from seriously contesting Obama was his race. No Republican was willing to be called a racist, and therefore none were willing to methodically and effectively oppose his agenda. Republicans had handcuffed themselves—and broken their campaign promises. When President Obama flaunted his unconstitutional actions—ruling by executive order, making recess appointments when the Senate was not in recess, changing immigration law by selective enforcement—they would not bring him to account. Their only two constitutional tools—impeachment and closing the purse—were off the table.

Suddenly Trump exploded onto the national scene—as much as that can be said of any individual who stars in a popular weekly television show, first *The Apprentice* and then *All-Star Celebrity Apprentice* (which by 2010 still had 4.5 million average viewers and which had boasted 28 million viewers for the season one finale). Pundits dismissed his campaign as a sideshow or a publicity stunt, and came out against it with fangs bared. Of course liberal sites fired with both barrels, but so-called conservative observers, including Fox's *The Five*, savaged Trump too. Pundits on that show were frequently heard to say that Trump could not win the nomination. When Eric Bolling insisted Trump needed to be taken seriously, his co-host, Dana Perino, flipped out and attacked Bolling. Later, on the same show, Geraldo Rivera spread the lie that Trump had said "all immigrants" were rapists and that "all Mexicans" were engaged in criminal activities. Perino, viewed as a supporter of Trump's opponent Jeb Bush on account of her connections with the George W. Bush administration as White House press secretary, asked "on what planet" Trump's "absurd" claims were actually true.[8]

The obsessive hostility to Trump expressed by Perino, a de facto spokeswoman for the Bush camp, revealed the deep concern that the GOP establishment (often referred to by conservatives as the GOPe, with the small e standing for "establishment") had about Trump. While on the surface they insisted he was unelectable and even a "rodeo clown" (in the words of Fox's Charles Krauthammer), in private they knew they had a problem. Trump was outspoken—like a lot of people. The really unusual thing about him, especially for a Republican candidate, was that he had the guts not to back off a comment or apologize for it. This constituted a major political shift for the GOP, which had gotten along for almost ten years by being subservient to the Democrats. Typically, if a Republican made a comment that anyone in the mainstream media or the Democratic Party found offensive, an apology would be immediately forthcoming. Then, instead of the issue going away, it—along with the Republican's apology—now became part of the material used to keep him perpetually on the defensive. Often, such violators of the media-enforced narrative simply slinked away, driven from office or from a campaign. But not Trump.

Trump quickly showed that his approach was to hit back, hard. His campaign constituted the effective first counter-assault on Political Correctness (PC) in recent memory. For thirty years, liberals had used PC in the universities and the public square to censor all debate and critical discourse about everything from race to "climate change." Unwilling to take on PC and shackled by the GOPe leadership's "go-along-to-get-along" tactics, Republicans had simply surrendered the debate stage on almost every issue. Not Trump. He challenged not just the individual candidates who opposed him, but the entire PC climate itself and the tyranny of liberal thought-silencing. Trump's approach and tactics went even beyond that, threatening to undermine the entire Washington system that had allowed the Democrats to advance their agenda for decades *whether or not they had the majority in either house of Congress or the presidency.* (Recall how in the George W. Bush years Tom Daschle was treated as the de facto majority leader of the Senate…even when he was in the minority!)

Pundits, still in the denial stage of grief, insisted that Trump's campaign wasn't real, that he would not file the financial reports as required by U.S. election laws. To their shock, he filed those before the ink of their columns had dried. The information in them suggested that he had a personal fortune worth anywhere from $3 billion to as much as $10 billion. His wealth meant that for the first time in recent history a candidate would not be obliged to rich donors and lobbyists—another feather in his cap, as far as supporters go. It also meant that, when Trump won, he would be the wealthiest individual ever to hold the office of president.

Waiting for Him to Implode

Trump's unwillingness to play the game, his position as the "outsider," and his independence from the GOP donor class all gave his campaign a strength that mystified the prognosticators and columnists. They searched obsessively for signs that Trump had "peaked" and uttered almost daily predictions that his campaign was foundering. Perhaps the moment at which the political class was most certain Trump's campaign was finished came during his visit to Ames, Iowa, to speak to the Family Leadership Conference, when he responded to a comment by Senator McCain that he had gone to Arizona and "stirred up the crazies."[9] When Frank Luntz interrupted Trump's monologue against John McCain to note that McCain was a prisoner of war and a hero, Trump said McCain was "a war hero because he was captured.... I like people that weren't captured." He went on to say that McCain had not done nearly enough for America's veterans.[10] Immediately Twitter exploded, saying, "Trump is finished." The conventional wisdom was that he could never survive criticizing a POW, let alone a war hero. "Did Donald Trump Just Strangle Himself with McCain 'War Hero' Comment?" asked the *Legal Insurrection* blog.[11] "Trump Crosses One Red Line Too Many," blared Hot Air.[12] And yet...

In typical Trump style, far from apologizing, the candidate renewed his attack, insisting that McCain had done little for veterans and that he, Trump, would do far more. Veterans' groups began to weigh in, most of them condemning The Donald, but many agreeing with his claim that McCain was ineffective on veterans' issues.

Like the media, the other candidates thought that the "war hero" comment would doom Trump. Florida Senator Marco Rubio said Trump's comment should be "a disqualifier as commander in chief."[13] Before long, however, researchers had dug up jibes of leftist comedians, such as Chris Rock, attacking McCain on the very same grounds. "He was a war hero that got *captured*," Rock had said. "There's a lot of guys in jail that got captured. I don't want to vote for nobody that got captured. I want to vote for the motherf**er that got away."[14] Within a week, new polls were out. By July 26, CNN (to its great chagrin) found Trump *leading* Republican candidates. He was three points ahead of Bush and eight points ahead of Wisconsin governor Scott Walker.[15] Rubio's support was in the single digits.

Meanwhile news was spreading of a beautiful thirty-two-year-old Californian woman, Kathryn ("Kate") Steinle, who had been shot to death on July 1 in San Francisco by an illegal alien. Trump cited her story in his criticism of border policy on July 8, and while he did not address her death at length in his Phoenix speech, choosing instead to focus on Jamiel Shaw, soon her name was brought into every Trump discussion of immigration. More important, it was learned that Steinle's killer had been deported *five times* and had returned to San Francisco because as a sanctuary city it was "safe."[16] The Kate Steinle story gave Trump ammunition against the hostility of the press and the accusations of xenophobia and racism. Events had made Trump's case as powerfully as he could have himself. A national debate about sanctuary cities erupted, with several Republicans calling for an end to all federal subsidies given to any sanctuary city. This topic had been in the news from time to time for years, but it was Trump's campaign that gave it legs.

Attackers from the Chamber of Commerce–supported amnesty crowd jumped all over Trump. Former Clinton administration insider George Stephanopoulos, using his position as a supposedly objective journalist on ABC News' *This Week*, grilled him on his remarks, and CNN's Don Lemon talked about press stories of illegal immigrant women coming across the Mexican border and being raped, but then denied that criminals were coming across the border. "Well," Trump replied, "somebody's doing the raping.... Who's doing the raping?"[17] Lemon had no response. Beltway insiders and media pundits who had ignored the river of illegal aliens coming in for years now had to at least cover the issue, if only to contradict Trump. And their attacks only made him stronger. Trump's immigration message connected, while the McCain comments faded.

By July 20 the *Washington Post* admitted that "even with the drop in support" immediately after the "war hero" reference, Trump had surged into a lead for the GOP 2016 nomination.[18] More surprising, presumptive nominee Jeb Bush was struggling in many polls, with his support hovering in the low teens. Indeed, Bush and fellow Floridian Rubio merely seemed to be swapping votes with each other. One could see the "seven stages of grief" working their way out among the punditry. Initially the majority of the news stories had been full of shock and denial. Jonathan Bernstein said in Bloomberg news that Trump could not win (he would be just one of an army to do so) without "party endorsements."[19] *Politico*'s Jack Shafer included Trump among the "Candidates who Can't" and gave him a "nonexistent chance" of winning.[20] *Vox*, admitting the undeniable—"Donald Trump Is Surging in the Polls"— nevertheless reassured its readers: "Here's Why He Won't Win."[21] Political scientists John Sides and Lynn Vavreck insisted there were three stages of poll surges, "discovery, scrutiny, and decline."[22] And *Vox* predicted, "Decline is in Trump's future."[23] *Salon* admitted that Trump was "winning all the battles" but claimed he was still "losing the war."[24]

All these left-wing sources were singing the song, but Republicans knew the tune and eagerly joined the chorus. Former Republican campaign strategist and Fox News commentator Karl Rove declared "Trump won't win [his] party's nomination."[25] Venerable conservative icon George Will, who later would threaten to vote for Hillary Clinton, predicted that Trump would fold at the debate: "Picture him on stage.... He says something hideously inflammatory—which is all he knows how to say—and then what do the other nine people on stage do? Do they either become complicit...by their silence, or do they all have to attack him?"[26]

Republicans, especially, took solace in the prospect of the upcoming debates, where they thought Trump's lack of political experience would cause him to "implode" (a word used *ad nauseam* by Trump's opponents). Only the top ten candidates—based on their poll standings—would be on the debate stage. And as the top-polling contender, Trump would be fielding the first question. Leading up to the debate, talk show host Rush Limbaugh asked if the GOP establishment had rigged the game against Trump, whether some or all of the candidates had been given orders to "take Trump out"? On August 6, the day of the first debate, Rush told his audience that there was a "Giant psyops underway against Trump," citing a headline from "DC Whispers": "Big Donors Warn Candidates on Eve of Debate: 'Take Trump Out.'"[27] Limbaugh informed his listeners that the "big money people have told Rubio and Jeb and some of the others that you've got to get rid of Trump tonight.... We're pulling your strings and you take Trump out tonight."[28]

There were two separate events that night. The first, called the "Happy Hour Debate" (because it started at 5:00 Eastern Standard Time), featured the seven candidates ranked lowest in the polls. These included former governors Rick Perry of Texas, George Pataki of New York, and Jim Gilmore of Virginia, Governor Bobby Jindal of Louisiana, former Hewlett-Packard CEO Carly Fiorina, U.S. Senator Lindsey Graham from South Carolina, and former Senator Rick Santorum of Pennsylvania. Although NPR claimed there wasn't a breakthrough for any of those candidates, in fact Fiorina jumped almost eight points in the polls.[29] At first her rise in popularity was chalked up to her debate performance alone, but before long the surge in her numbers was being put in the context of gains by other "outsiders," including non-politicians Dr. Ben Carson and Trump and the anti-establishment U.S. Senator Ted Cruz of Texas. Fiorina took aim at Trump, saying, "I didn't get a phone call from Bill Clinton before I jumped in the race." She was referring to a report that Clinton had called Trump and urged him to run.[30]

As for the main event, the moderators from Fox News had already announced in advance that they had a secret plan to deal with Trump "in the event that he doesn't follow the rules."[31] When the ten candidates walked on stage, Trump was placed in the middle, right next to Jeb Bush. He was blindsided by the first question, which asked all the candidates to raise their hands to commit to supporting the eventual Republican nominee. Trump simply shrugged—to scattered boos from the pre-selected audience at Cleveland's Quicken Loans Arena—and said he wasn't giving up any leverage he had with the Republican Party. The question had been designed to isolate Trump from the rest of the Republican field as an "unserious" candidate. (Ironically, it would later backfire against Cruz and Kasich, who refused to give Trump their immediate and wholehearted support when he finally won the nomination.) After the litmus test "support" question, Fox's Megyn Kelly fired off a direct attack on Trump in the form of a question about a long list of names he had called women in the past including "fat pigs," "dogs," and "disgusting animals." Trump said, "Only Rosie O'Donnell," to audience laugher, but Kelly insisted it was others. From then on, the three moderators took turns pitching "gotcha" questions to Trump. Kelly asked about his changed views on abortion and "When did you become a Republican?"

Trump's claim during the debate that he had brought the issue of illegal immigration to the fore was ridiculed on social media. But the "PEORIA Project," which traced presidential campaign conversations across all news and social media from 100,000 online outlets and all 900 channels on television (though not AM radio) found that "Trump's claim during the debate that 'You wouldn't be talking about illegal immigration if it wasn't for me' has some factual justification."[32] Before Trump's entry into the presidential race, the topic of immigration had been brought up 205,089 times per day. After Trump's remarks in Phoenix, the mentions more than doubled, to 443,045.[33] Trump had single-handedly shifted the candidates from seeking "immigration reform" to "fixing the border," and had put the subject of building a fence on the table—and now none of them could win by opposing it.

The real stars dominating (or hijacking) the debate were, in fact, the moderators from Fox News, all antagonistic to Trump. They consumed a whopping thirty-two minutes of speaking time. Trump had the most time of any candidate (10:32 minutes to Jeb Bush's 8:31).[34] Outrage at Megyn Kelly for her "gotcha" questions caused more than 15,000 people to un-follow her on Facebook, and Fox arranged for her to have a convenient vacation. But before she left, Trump fired another salvo, telling CNN's Don Lemon that Kelly was "unprofessional" and that "she had blood coming out of her eyes, out of her…whatever." That sparked another media explosion, with pundits claiming Trump was referring to menstrual blood (Trump claimed that never occurred to him, and that he had been thinking of her nose or ears). Once again, pundits predicted Trump was finished. Erick Erickson, the driving force behind the *RedState* blog, who was holding an event for all the Republican candidates, disinvited Trump after the comments, saying he wouldn't want his children to hear references like that. But it turned out that Erickson himself had referred to former U.S. Supreme Court Justice David Souter as "the only goat f---ing child molester ever to serve on the Supreme Court."[35] Erickson had not only alienated many fans of *RedState* but once again inadvertently managed to hand the news cycle to Trump.

It began to dawn on a few (but only a few, including Rush Limbaugh and Scott Adams, who had caught on immediately to Trump's methods) that Trump's dominance of the news cycle, whether with good or bad news, was tactical genius. Trump spent no money, yet he controlled the discourse, ensuring that almost 100 percent of Americans knew his name. Ironically, *Salon*, a bastion of leftism, was one of the first sites to appreciate what had happened in the week following the debate. Jack Mirkinson admitted he had been wrong: while the reports about a war between Fox's Roger Ailes and Trump were impossible to untangle, it appeared that Ailes had "met his match" in Trump.[36] Most media outlets, however, continued to ignore the implications of the old show biz bromide that any news—even bad news—is good news.

Clueless Conservatives

At that point the second stage of grief, pain, set in. And soon it was giving way to anger—emanating mainly from the ideological purists who saw Trump as insufficiently conservative and used their daily rants to instruct the ignorant among the flock. Jonah Goldberg and Jim Geraghty of National Review Online, along with bloggers Jay Cost and Ben

Shapiro, pummeled Trump for his previous comments on various subjects and for campaign donations to Democrats. Trump had a reasonable excuse, noting that as a businessman in New York he had had to donate to both parties. Rich Lowry, editor of the conservative *National Review*, attacked Trump on his inconsistencies on the issues, calling him a "loudmouth mogul." Trump, Lowry claimed, spoke the language of conservatism "as if he needs help from a translator."[37] Maybe. But the elites, including conservative intellectuals like Lowry, were clearly showing that they needed a translator to speak mainstream American. Lowry was only one of the many establishment journalists—including a half-dozen "conservative" writers—who seemed to be on a mission to stop Trump. *National Review* featured at least one anti-Trump piece a day and peppered Twitter with Trump attacks; Fox News talk shows routinely criticized Trump (but not any of his opponents). Yet it soon became apparent that voters did not see ideological purity as essential for a Republican candidate.[38] Indeed, while the pundits seemed oblivious to the ineffectiveness of the ideological purity argument, ordinary people concerned with America's deteriorating position embraced Trump's practical solutions.

Reince Priebus, the chairman of the Republican Party, said that Trump would not be the party's nominee: "Donald Trump is his own brand, and it's not the Republican brand."[39] (Priebus should have checked with Republicans first—who soon overwhelmingly selected him to represent their "brand.") Priebus's comments were astounding, given that while many had expected The Donald's poll numbers to fall after the debate, by the time Priebus made the statement Trump was still leading in almost every national and state poll. Priebus's remarks only confirmed Trump's concern that he would not receive fair treatment from the national GOP.

Trump's staying power was surprising, but even more incomprehensible was the conservative intelligentsia's cluelessness about what was fueling it. He outraged intellectuals on the Right, such as Charles Krauthammer and George Will, less because he was ideologically impure than because he refused to grovel at the feet of the reigning power. And he didn't quote the appropriate William F. Buckley, Milton Friedman, or Russell Kirk lines. Quite the contrary. Trump symbolized voters "giving the finger" to the party establishment and the Washington–New York elites. And that was exactly what they loved about him. Conservative intellectuals were fundamentally misunderstanding what the voters were saying, just as they had fundamentally misunderstood what voters were saying in 2008 with the election of Barack Obama. Then conservative commentators had carpet-bombed the airwaves and newsprint with examples of how liberal Obama was, how his training, family life, background, and education had all woven together profound threads of anti-Americanism, anti-colonialism, anti-imperialism, and class warfare. Rush Limbaugh maintained that Obama "has a chip on his shoulder," and many argued that Obama's "fundamental transformation" of the United States aimed at a socialist Third World end product. Their warnings were correct—and utterly irrelevant to the majority of American voters. Those voters were determined to demonstrate (however useless and indeed dangerous that gesture would later be shown to be) that they were not racists, that large majorities of whites would vote for a black presidential candidate, and then reelect him.

There were certainly other issues in 2008—voters resented the George W. Bush administration over the Iraq War, and blamed him for the sharp economic downturn that year. But the real engine that propelled Obama to victory, then and again in 2012, was race. As the first black president, Obama offered a way for millions of Americans—they thought—to atone, once and for all, for the sin of slavery and for America's racist past. There was nothing the Republicans could possibly have offered in either election to match that appeal. Obama was *sui generis*, as Hillary Clinton was about to find out. No other president—even another black president, even another black liberal president—will ever reap as much good will.

With the events in Ferguson, Missouri, in August 2014—when Michael Brown charged a police officer, who shot and killed him, leading to riots and massive urban racial turmoil—Americans realized that their attempt to put racial issues behind them by electing Obama had failed. Race relations had only become worse. Obama's Justice Department did nothing to dampen the incendiary situation in Ferguson, even suggesting that the police force was poorly trained. Early in Obama's first term, his Justice Department had refused to police the new Black Panther Party and its intimidation of voters in Philadelphia. So his administration had a history of siding with thugs against police.

Shortly after Ferguson, another episode of alleged "police brutality" followed in New York, and then there was a third in Baltimore. Each prompted riots and racial discord. Again Obama's administration, at best, did nothing to quell the unrest and, at worst, fanned the fires with its rhetoric. What Americans had thought they were voting for with Obama—racial reconciliation and tolerance—was not what they got. But even then, Obama continued to be insulated from criticism by his race.

Voters didn't want to reject the first black president—at least not personally. But they weren't happy with his policies. That should have been clear from the results of the 2010 midterm elections, with the rise of the Tea ("Taxed Enough Already") Party. The Tea Party, which was mostly conservative but had a large strain of Libertarian-minded Democrats, led Republicans to victory in 2010, and again in 2014. Voters put a Republican majority in the House in 2010, and in the Senate as well in 2014. Democrats across the nation lost thousands of state and local offices. The Tea Party message was clear: STOP OBAMA. But the Republican Party hierarchy made the mistake of viewing this as an endorsement of the Republican Party. In fact, voters were willing to validate the GOP only *if* the Republicans were successful in negating or turning back programs and policies such as Obamacare, Obama's disastrous foreign policy, his unwillingness to stop radical Islam, and his regulatory overreach. Unfortunately, the GOP elites and chattering classes saw it only as a transfer of power—especially the power of the purse—and reveled in their new committee chairmanships and party invitations.

The Ruling Class vs. the Country Class

So after two elections with virtually no subsequent action, anger against the ruling classes mounted. Even before the first midterm elections under the Obama presidency, Angelo Codevilla had captured the mood in an insightful article called "America's Ruling Class—and the Perils of Revolution."[40] Codevilla noted that public opinion was overwhelmingly (three or four to one, depending on the poll) against the $700 billion bank bailout bill in 2008, but the Bush administration, and *both* presidential contenders, Barack Obama and John McCain, supported it. The political insiders, Codevilla observed, "think, look, and act as a class." No prominent Republican opposed the basic premises of the "ruling class," and its "denigration of the American people as irritable children who must learn their place"—and they still would not, even after two elections had put them in power to do just that.

"Today's ruling class," Codevilla wrote, "from Boston to San Diego, was formed by an educational system that exposed them to the same ideas and gave them remarkably uniform guidance, as well as tastes and habits."[41] The trends Codevilla was tapping into would be analyzed by sociologist Charles Murray in a book published in 2013: *Coming Apart: The State of White America.* Murray found that there were "Super Zips"—zip codes he identified by wealth and average IQ as measured by the source of residents' university degrees—where aside from a street vendor or coffee shop server, a person might not *ever* interact with someone who had not graduated from an Ivy League school.[42] There were some 882 "Super Zips" in America, and 44 percent of all Harvard-Princeton-Yale graduates lived in those zip codes. Worse, the highest-scoring zip codes were clustered around Washington, D.C., where it was possible "to go from Ellicott City in the north to Springfield in the south without setting foot outside Super Zips."[43]

Moreover, many who lived in these "Super Zips" had never had a *single* non-government job, and the others had often come to government from "Non-Governmental Organizations" or from a very brief career in law. Only a handful had ever owned—or even run—a business. For example, excluding speeches, Hillary Clinton had never received a paycheck from the private sector, and the same could be said of former Treasury Secretary Timothy Geithner and hundreds—perhaps thousands—of others within the D.C. beltway. Congressman Mike Turner of Ohio's 10th District was a lawyer before becoming mayor of Dayton, Ohio, in 1993, then, after a 2001 defeat, sat out only a year before winning the seat as an Ohio congressman.[44] He had served in government for twenty-two years with only a single one-year interruption. Yet Turner was a rookie compared to some in Washington. As of 2015, five of the one hundred senators had already served more than thirty-five total years in government. Twenty Americans, the overwhelming number of them Democrats, had served more than forty-four years in either the House or the Senate.[45]

As Codevilla noted, it is possible "to be an official of a major corporation or a member of the U.S. Supreme Court [Justice Clarence Thomas], or even president (Ronald Reagan), and not be taken seriously by the ruling class."[46] The ruling class shares a fraternity-like similarity of interests, of views, and of social networks—and of friends and enemies. Murray took the argument even further, noting that the similarly minded Ivy League graduates who share similar earnings and wealth find it all but impossible to empathize with ordinary businesspeople or to even understand the struggles of non-wealthy families. They see *themselves* and their own careers as the solution to whatever problem the others confront. And anyone who doesn't share their values and appreciate their solutions is de facto a threat and must be marginalized, if not destroyed.

So the Republicans, who have been in the minority in both the House and the Senate for most of the time since 1932, have contracted a case of learned helplessness. They go along to get along.

Ronald Reagan upset that apple cart. He ran against the elites of the Republican Party and won, then beat incumbent Jimmy Carter in an election that astonished the experts. Reagan beat the "ruling class," largely because of his ability to go over the heads of the dominant media and directly to the people (thanks in part to his experience as an actor). But he also had the advantage of policies that worked well on almost every front. By the time he became entangled in the Iran-Contra Affair, his successes elsewhere insulated him, and in any case it was too late for the ruling class to "get" him.

His successor, George H. W. Bush, ran as a third term for Reagan, but quickly abandoned Reaganomics for a tax increase to solve the problem of the deficit (which somehow never seemed to be a problem when Democrats were in office). Bush betrayed his base and broke his "Read My Lips: No New Taxes" pledge, then was caught between "New Democrat" Governor Bill Clinton of Arkansas and independent candidate and businessman Ross Perot. Historians agree that Perot took votes evenly from both candidates (at one time he led both in the polls), but more damage was done to Bush because a disproportionate amount of Perot's criticism was aimed at him, not Clinton. It became a two-on-one campaign.[47] Moreover, Perot cited as his reason for discontinuing his campaign in July 1992 the "revitalization of the *Democratic Party*" [emphasis mine], indicating the value he placed on defeating George H. W. Bush.[48] Yet it was *Bush*, not Clinton, who insisted that Perot participate in the debates when he restarted his campaign in October 1992.[49] (Ironically, focus groups conducted prior to the election showed that the first alternative to those unhappy with Bush was Perot, not Clinton.)[50]

Neither Perot's nor any other third party movement did anything to upset the elite regime that had reasserted its control over the American political scene after Reagan. Any hope that Perot's Reform Party—to which Trump's 2016 presidential run would erroneously be compared—would hang around, much less reform anything, faded with Perot's exit from the political scene. Ralph Nader briefly tried with the Green Party in 2000, taking enough votes from Vice President Al Gore to hand the election to Texas governor George W. Bush, but his 2004 run proved far less significant; Bush won reelection without Nader's help. The Libertarian Party has traditionally siphoned votes from the Republicans, most notably in tight Senate and House elections, but it has never played a key role in a presidential race. None of these efforts posed even the remotest of threats to the ruling class, which ironically achieved truly dominant status only after 1994, when the Republicans won control of the U.S. House of Representatives for the first time in forty years, ousting thirty-seven Democrat incumbents. The new class of Republicans included Steve Largent, a former NFL star wide receiver, J. C. Watts, the black former quarterback of the Oklahoma University football team, former rock singer Sonny Bono, and Ben Nighthorse Campbell, only the second American Indian elected to the House or Senate.[51]

Buoyed by their shocking victory, the Republicans under Speaker Newt Gingrich aimed high and achieved much, fulfilling the promise in their "Contract with America" to bring ten agenda items up for a vote. They succeeded in passing nine of them, and the Senate voted on six. The Supreme Court struck down term limits, but Gingrich's House passed an impressive welfare reform act (Clinton eventually signed it) and the "Freedom to Farm Act," which also became law. But at that point the Gingrich-led majority went a bridge too far, shutting down the government over a budget fight with Clinton. The Republicans had vastly underestimated the hostility that would come their way from the mainstream media (soon labeled the "drive-by" media by radio commentator Rush Limbaugh because of their penchant for igniting a crisis, reporting it, then moving on to the next "shooting"). Gingrich and the Republicans were swamped by a tidal wave of bad publicity and had to back down. While eventually Clinton was permanently damaged by his affair with Monica Lewinsky and his subsequent false testimony under oath, which led to his impeachment, the Republicans never recovered either. The fact that they lost only a few seats in the House in the elections of 1996 and 1998 was small consolation for Bob Dole's crushing defeat at Clinton's hands in the 1996 presidential election. It was significant that the GOP establishment had dictated the nomination of another moderate "inside-the-club" candidate. Bob Dole's candidacy seemed more like George H. W. Bush's than Ronald Reagan's; the general impression was that Dole had received the nomination because it was "his turn."

But the defeat of the Gingrich Revolution was far more devastating to America's political system than either Clinton's sexual misconduct and law-breaking or Dole's stinging loss, for it marked the entrenchment of a Republican political class that could now crush those of what Codevilla would call the "country class"—the rest of America, outside Charles Murray's Super Zips—with impunity. Dole was a longtime D.C. insider, as was his wife Elizabeth, who was elected a senator from North Carolina in 2002.

Gingrich was one of the last of the "country class" to threaten the GOP. George W. Bush, a Texan at heart, nevertheless de facto sided with the establishment on the advice of Karl Rove, who hoped to take the "high road" and avoid a bloody combat with the Democrats. Rove's political strategy was to aim for a majority of big-government Republicans. But then, in 2003, Bush decided to eliminate Saddam Hussein over concerns that the Iraqi dictator had weapons of mass destruction (WMDs). It was Rove's strategy to ignore the relentless Democrat propaganda offensive against Bush that followed, and the result was an unchallenged and unending cascade of attacks on Bush for the next five years that drove his popularity into the twenties. Rove later admitted that not responding to the critics was a terrible mistake. "Our weak response in defense of the president and in setting the record straight [was] one of the biggest mistakes of the Bush years. When the pattern of Democratic attacks became apparent in July 2003, we should have countered in a forceful and overwhelming way.... We should have seen it for what it was: a poison-tipped dagger aimed at the heart of the Bush presidency."[52]

Whether or not one considered George W. Bush part of the "ruling class," in 2006 and 2008 his administration's "don't fight" strategy ensured the sweeping victory of Democrats who certainly were. The 2006 race saw Republicans swept out of the House and Senate. Then in the 2008 presidential election, a political phenomenon burst onto the scene—a little-known U.S. senator from Illinois with no previous political accomplishments finalized the Democrat takeover of the government. Barack Hussein Obama surged to victory over Hillary Clinton—the presumptive nominee until Obama came along—then handily defeated John McCain (yet another Republican establishment candidate) in the general election. As the first serious black candidate for the presidency, Obama had the full and unwavering support of the media. (Former CBS reporter Bernard Goldberg referred to the media coverage of Obama as a "slobbering love affair.")[53] But even more important, Obama had nearly universal good will from the American people, who wished him success because of his race. Rush Limbaugh was nearly alone in his lack of enthusiasm: when asked for his views on the Obama presidency in 2009, he stated flatly, "I hope he fails." While nearly every other Republican was trying to appear non-partisan and open to the nation's first "black president," the talk show host saw that Obama was a radical whose presidency would damage America badly if it was successful. Limbaugh was prescient.

Over the next six years, it became virtually impossible to criticize Obama *or* his policies without risking charges of racism. In fact Obama was very much a "ruling class" president, having attended an Ivy League college, and having received special considerations and favors throughout his career because of his race. He had very little in common with the millions of Americans who worked forty-hour-a-week jobs or ran their own small businesses, or who served in the military. And once in Washington, with a veto-proof Democrat majority in Congress, Obama implemented the most radical "transformation" (as he called it) of America since the New Deal, pushing through a national health insurance plan that the majority of the public opposed (Obamacare), withdrawing American forces from Iraq despite a destabilizing situation there, and at the same time seeking to destabilize Libya and Syria. He signed off on a massive economic stimulus bill that merely lined the pockets of his supporters and negotiated a nuclear weapons "deal" with Iran that all but assured the rogue state would, in fact, produce them eventually.

Obama succeeded in almost everything he desired, except, perhaps, amnesty for illegal aliens. And, predictably, America failed. Obama's policies were a disaster from the get-go, whether from an economic, domestic, or foreign policy perspective. More American adults were out of work than any time in our history; more people were on food stamps than ever; and abroad, our enemies, from the Middle East to Russia, were on the march. The percentage of people thinking the United States was on the "wrong track" was higher than ever.

Donald Trump had expressed support for Obama in 2008—hoping, as most Americans did, that he would be a genuine American—but in 2015 Trump reversed course and tapped into the seething discontent. Trump's opposition to Obama immediately put him on the side of the "country class," as did the fact that he was actually a businessman who, while residing in a Super Zip, nevertheless interacted on a *daily* basis with his employees, middle class customers at his resorts, and union people. (There is a wonderful YouTube video of Trump doing the jobs of many of his hotel employees, from walking dogs to room service to making beds.)[54] In a sign of the complete unity of the ruling class, neither of Obama's opponents—John McCain nor Mitt Romney—had seriously engaged in criticism of Obama or even his policies, out of fear of being labeled a racist. Now that unified elite stood in total opposition to Trump. Mainstream politicians of the ruling class were content to manage the destruction that Obama had set in motion. Even the Republican elites didn't offer much more than a possibility of slowing America's decline. But merely rearranging the deck chairs on the *Titanic* held no interest for Donald Trump, and he didn't care which senators had chairmanships.

It was opposition to illegal immigration that in one fell swoop moved the liberal billionaire from the ranks of the "ruling class" into the "country class" and made him an existential threat to the elites of both parties. Trump had intended his campaign to be about the economy, but intuitively he tied illegal immigration and the economy together. Immigration was one side of the coin, and the other was the employment situation—as Trump raised concerns about the unemployment rate, the record number of Americans not even seeking jobs, and the jobs that were going overseas.

It wasn't the classic Republican—let alone conservative—pitch. But the Republican Party and the conservative establishment had utterly failed. They had failed to win elections, losing twice to the hardest-left candidate ever to run on a major party ticket despite his deeply unpopular policies. And when they had won, they had failed to fulfill their promises, squandering the mandate the voters had given them. It was time for something—or someone—very different. And to the amateur election observers and analysts who would come to be called the "Renegade Deplorables," it looked like that someone was going to be Donald Trump.

CHAPTER FOUR

On the Campaign Trail:
Ohio, New Hampshire, Nevada, Colorado, and New Mexico

Joel Pollak

October 27, 2016

Thursday begins cold, gray, and wet in Manhattan. Journalists stumble into the press van, still half asleep at 8:00 a.m. We have less than two weeks to go before Election Day.

Three stops await today, all in Ohio. No Republican has ever won the White House without winning Ohio. The moment Donald Trump seemed to take the lead there, journalists began reporting that Hillary Clinton could win without it.[1]

But the state is one Trump must win—and one where his message on trade has resonated.

Trump will also, no doubt, repeat his message on Obamacare today— that the president's vaunted health care plan has been a "disaster" for patients and for the system as a whole.

Premiums are skyrocketing because not enough young, healthy people are enrolling to subsidize the older, sicker individuals who incur more health expenses. To keep the system solvent, those who remain in the system have to pay more. More of them will then drop out, leading to a "death spiral."

The press is calling the sudden price shocks an "October surprise" for Trump. But there is no surprise here. Republicans had warned Americans for years that the premiums were bound to go up, even back when President Barack Obama was selling Obamacare with the promise that families would save $2,500.

The text of the Obamacare statute provides that the new premium increases take effect November 1—one week before Election Day. It's no surprise; it's a feature, and not a bug, of Obamacare. Perhaps Obama hoped that voters would receive a timely reminder before Election Day that the federal government was responsible for providing their health care. With the prices skyrocketing, that ploy has backfired, spectacularly.

The White House had deferred some of the bill's more obnoxious effects until after previous elections, often by executive fiat, in defiance of the text of the statute—an early sign of the sloppiness of the gargantuan legislation that few had bothered to read, and also of Obama's willingness to overstep his executive authority under the Constitution.

The latter, as much as any anticipated price increase, is what drives conservative opposition to the law.

■   ■   ■

Amidst these reflections, we land in Dayton—a place both familiar and dear to me from many summer vacations and Thanksgiving weekends spent there with my cousins. But my family is not here any more: all of them have now moved west to Arizona and California.

We are actually heading half an hour east of the city, to the town of Springfield and the Clark County fairgrounds. There, on the dung-and-dirt floor of the Champion Expo, thousands of Trump supporters are already eagerly waiting for their candidate.

The journalists kick the manure and file dutifully into the press pen, where they occupy rows of tables in front of and behind the riser where television cameras are mounted.

I divert into the crowd instead, seeing no point in wasting hours checking email or messing about on Twitter. I stroll around the audience, looking for interesting signs and people. The mood, as at other Trump events, is upbeat.

In one corner there are about half a dozen black kids, who look like they are in their late teens or early twenties. I shake hands and ask if they are Trump supporters; they look at me oddly. Several tell me they are not voting for anyone.

"I don't care about neither of them racists," one tells me. Another tells me he is voting for Clinton: "Donald Trump could get it done, but he's helping people who have businesses. Hillary is trying to help everybody." I don't argue.

Still another tells me he cannot vote for either, and his reasoning is a recapitulation of charges, valid and otherwise, that both campaigns have thrown at each other through the media. Hillary, he says, criticizes Trump's conduct toward women, but has her own husband's behavior with which to reckon. Trump, meanwhile, is too "crazy" to be president, and he holds violent rallies. (The revelations that much of that "violence" was deliberately provoked by Democrats have passed him by.)

A black pastor opens the meeting, telling the crowd that he is proof "black people support Donald Trump." The campaign frequently turns to black clergy, it seems, for precisely this reason.

A man in a "Trump" winter hat holds aloft a homemade sign with black lettering on white poster board: "Drain The Swamp." Every rally seems to have one or two of these informal "Drain the Swamp" signs, and Trump likes to point them out from the stage, inviting the crowd to chant the slogan with him.

Each warm-up speaker hits Obamacare, which the campaign has evidently decided is its winning message this week. But Ohio Representative Jim Jordan, the somewhat diminutive shirt-sleeved Republican brawler of innumerable House investigative committees, focuses on the Benghazi terror attacks. Hillary Clinton disqualified herself in Libya, he says, and especially when she lied to the families of the victims of Benghazi about why they had died.

There are long delays, now. Trump is backstage, we are told, doing interviews with local media. The crowd groans at each new warm-up speaker.

General Mike Flynn, a foreign policy advisor and frequent media surrogate, appears at the podium. He stumbles and says that there are twenty-one days left in the campaign, then catches himself and says there are only twelve, a correction that the weary journalists seem very glad to hear.

To them, this is not a drama but a death march; the outcome is certain. The Breitbart News team, meanwhile, has just sent me an alert message about a Bloomberg News story that landed while I was still in the air with the traveling press. An "unnamed" Trump official has told Bloomberg News about the campaign's high-tech "voter suppression" efforts, which sound like an effort to stop people from voting. In reality it is an effort to promote negative news stories about Hillary Clinton on social media, where her likely voters will see them. "Voter depression" might be more accurate.

Both campaigns do it, whether simply by spinning the opponent's remarks in the worst possible way, or with specific, targeted campaigns.

As a Jewish voter, for example, I am subjected to near-daily email blasts by anti-Trump journalists who tell me that Trump is the next Hitler. Though I see through the hype, the barrage has the desired depressive effect, even on me. Even if you disagree, you begin to doubt your own judgment, and feel lonely and ineffectual in your dissenting opinion.

Still, it seems like only Republicans are ever taken to task for the tactic. The Democrats and the media have gone into overdrive, describing the Trump campaign's efforts as a naked attempt to stop black people from voting.

Whatever happens at the rally—however many thousands of people attend, whatever the message of the speech or the energy in the room— the media could negate everything with a bad story like that.

Worse, a photograph of a sign that someone evidently has brought to the rally depicting Hillary Clinton's face on a rifle range target is circulating on Twitter.

Whether the culprit was a Democratic plant looking to stir up trouble—as, thanks to James O'Keefe, we now know they did—or a crazy Trump supporter who thinks it is cute to imagine shooting Hillary, the photo could trash the whole event and trigger a new campaign crisis. Trump, it seems, is always only one news cycle away from disaster.

Trump eventually shows up. He is high-energy now. The hoarseness is gone from his voice; he has a message on Obamacare that is succeeding with crowds, and—best of all—the Ohio polls are positive.

He informs the crowd of a "breaking" poll (really, it broke the day before) showing him with a four-point lead in the state. He is smooth, ad libbing when he should, sticking to the script for the key points. One protester is ejected by police; everyone else has a raucous good time.

Onward.

■   ■   ■

Another hard landing, this time in Toledo, under the persistent layer of cloud that seems to have taken over the entire northeastern quadrant of the country.

The motorcade races into the center of the city, to a large indoor convention space. It is only half-full, the one Trump rally on this journey that is packed to anything less than capacity. This looks more like the events I had seen with Hillary Clinton or other politicians, with the crowd and the bleachers arranged strategically for television, so that the empty spaces in the hall are obscured.

There is a man proudly holding up a sign that says, "Trump That Bitch: Before It's Too Late." The rest of the media do not appear to have noticed him, until General Flynn actually points him out from the podium, in a somewhat positive way (without reading his sign aloud).

The crowd actually likes the sign: several people, including women, come over to snap selfies with it. But I can already imagine the cable news discussions about Trump's misogynistic supporters.

On the other side of the hall, attracting no attention whatsoever, are two young women, one of whom is wearing a shirt that reads, in cursive: "Don't fucking touch me."

I suspect they are protesters, and I am right. They tell me that Trump's comments about women are "unacceptable." One complains that she has already been harassed at the rally by a man who tried to touch her on the shoulder with his finger, trying to provoke a laugh.

"Sexual assault is not a joke," she says.

Trump arrives and begins delivering his stump speech, with a few improvised flourishes. He commits a few flubs and mispronunciations, jumbling "Dixon Ticonderoga," and saying "Lee-ma" instead of "Lai-ma" for the nearby town of "Lima." He toys with the words, and has fun with his own mistakes.

Toward the end, somehow, Trump refers to poor, inner city black neighborhoods, to which he has been making an earnest policy pitch in recent speeches, by the term "ghetto."

Social media erupts in howls of derision—though it is not clear why. "Ghetto," Trump's critics in the media seem to believe, is clearly a loaded term, or must be. As the press departs the arena and boards the bus back to the airport, I tweet a link to a video of an Elvis Presley song, "In the Ghetto." I also write a story about the media being "triggered" by the term, and post it quickly—and the story causes an uproar in the press corps because, although it does not quote anyone in the traveling press, it reports that they scrambled to write up Trump's remark. Later, I will agree to remove that part of the description, so as not to antagonize the people with whom I will be traveling for the next two weeks.

But I will continue to wonder: How does one correct media bias, if one witnesses it and cannot talk about it?

I win back some goodwill with my colleagues in the press—or so I imagine—by finding another journalist's lost cell phone. And I avoid an open confrontation with a Buzzfeed reporter who had seemed, prior to this trip, to have made it his personal mission to make my career as difficult as possible—even resorting to publishing a false story that I would be offered a job as a Donald Trump speechwriter, based on a single dubious source.

My nerves and temper begin to settle as we land in Cleveland.

■ ■ ■

Our motorcade races eastward, to the suburban town of Geneva. En route, we learn from news reports that one of the other aircraft in the Trump-Pence charter fleet, the one carrying Pence and his press corps, has skidded off the runway at La Guardia.

The weather in New York is rainy, but not unusually bad, and the runway, while notoriously short and close to the water, is one that hundreds of aircraft use every day. No one knows exactly what happened, but everyone is reported safe, thankfully.

We reach the venue in Geneva, an indoor sports training facility. Here the crowd is larger, some several thousand strong, nearly filling the venue. General Flynn is warming up the crowd again; some are already restless, and I overhear some young Trump fans saying that they have been there for four hours. The crowd, again, is mostly white, but there are people of all ages—and many in their teens and twenties, more than I have seen at previous Trump campaign events.

Trump is not long in coming; he knows he needs to speak soon to have a chance of making the evening news. This is the same stump speech, more or less, that we have heard throughout the state today. But it is more boisterous, and Trump is improving his delivery, even improving his improvised jokes. He has learned to bounce off the teleprompters, using them to lay out his basic arguments and then interjecting with comments about the audience or digs at the media. Trump closes by reassuring the audience that his running mate is doing fine after the mishap with the airplane.

We file out a side door and board the bus again, as hundreds of fans gather at the barrier to watch the motorcade roll away. This is a big country, I think, but it seems much smaller and more manageable when you have a police escort and a private plane.

I work quickly to file my story, making sure to include a quote from a yarmulke-wearing Orthodox Jew at the rally, who dismisses accusations that Trump and his supporters are anti-Semitic as a "stereotype."

Trump's critics in conservative Jewish circles—among my own religious peers, in other words—have bought into the notion that he is fanning anti-Semitism. It is a charge at which I take personal offense, and which, I freely admit, I look for opportunities to dispel.

■ ■ ■

At the *Washington Examiner*, the conservative columnist Byron York—like Peggy Noonan and Conrad Black, one of the more circumspect and insightful chroniclers of the cycle—has a sobering column: "Donald Trump's Great Big, Beautiful Missed Opportunity."[2]

York argues, based on observing a focus group of "late deciders," that Trump lost potential supporters, especially women, around the time of the political conventions in July. Two things happened then: one, Hillary Clinton became her party's nominee; two, Trump got bogged down in petty squabbles with Khizr Khan, the father of an American soldier killed in Iraq—the first of several such skirmishes that the Clinton team had skillfully planned, knowing how to get under Trump's skin and elicit overly defensive reactions.

Reflecting on York's argument, I disagree with his conclusion that the leaked *Access Hollywood* tape and the subsequent slew of accusations did not do the decisive damage to Trump. I would point to rising poll numbers from August to October—before the tape's release—and argue that it did.

But otherwise I see a great deal of merit in York's case. Trump's rhetorical reactions, fairly or unfairly, were seen as a preview of how he would behave as president. The answer: he would be just like one of us.

That is exactly what a president cannot do. When he is attacked, he has to look beyond his personal feelings and consider, always, the national interest and the national image. Obama, to his credit, kept his cool (and, to his enduring demerit, often failed to stir himself when decisive action was needed).

When he looks back, Trump may regret failing to commit himself, completely, to the role. It cannot be worth losing the presidency to defend one's dignity in tabloid-style fights no one will remember.

October 28, 2016

There's just a bit of light behind the clouds as the reporters gather in Midtown New York for the drive to Newark. Our outbound flight has been re-routed to take off from the New Jersey airport, thanks to the mishap with the Pence plane.

The Manhattan skyline appears in the distance across the wetlands and the industrial jumble. Thoughts of fall foliage in New Hampshire brighten the mood ahead of a marathon day, covering five states across three time zones.

We land in New Hampshire in driving rain. Bright leaves still cling to the trees amidst the wind. We reach the Manchester Radisson, and there is a long line to enter—an impressive turnout, given the weather.

We go through the routine Secret Service checks and are ushered into the Armory Ballroom, an older structure with a high wooden ceiling supported by steel beams atop brick walls.

The crowd is broad-shouldered, full of rough-and-ready, live-free-or-die New Englanders. Flannel shirts and Boston Red Sox gear compete with "Make America Great Again" hats and various Trump t-shirts. There is a feeling of excitement in the air. These Trump fans haven't given up yet.

The "media pen" is lightly guarded here, and more of the journalists venture out into the crowd than usual. They seem happy to talk to the locals here, who seem happy to share their views with the reporters. Local TV crews from Boston, enjoying the chance to cover some national news, stage set-up shots.

I make my way through the crowd, starting with an attractive forty-something blonde wearing pink Halloween devil's horns and a

#BigLeague button on her belt above her rear. She tells me that she has wanted Trump to run for president since 2012—back when he briefly led polls of Republican voters, fresh off his crusade to force President Barack Obama to produce his "long-form" birth certificate. She wants a businessman in the White House because the U.S. is a "failing business." She adds, "He's liberty-minded, a free-thinker, not owned by the establishment. I like him because he has the 'Live Free or Die' mentality."

I talk to a family that has driven three hours from Vermont to attend. They have also pulled their kids out of school for the journey; the fourteen-year-old girl was told she would have to miss her school dance if she was absent, and she still came along. Her younger brother is wearing a custom t-shirt: "Common Snore: No More Common Core / Michelle Obama Ruined My Lunch." The father of the family says he's seeing little support from Hillary Clinton in his otherwise liberal state.

Perhaps my most impressive interview of the week comes next. I talk to a Chinese immigrant and real estate broker from Boston, who has also made the drive to attend the rally. She sounds like any other Trump fan: she likes his positions on terrorism, immigration, and renegotiating NAFTA. I ask her how she feels when Trump talks about being tougher on China, especially on trade. She tells me: "I don't look at where I'm coming from. I look at what's good for America."

What a refreshing idea—that you embrace the country you have chosen to join, rather than the one you chose to leave.

That sort of sentiment seems less common nowadays, especially with identity politics rampant, with politicians pandering to new immigrant populations by flattering their differences rather than speaking to them as fellow Americans.

I'm so impressed by her response that I tweet it, with a photograph. It is retweeted quickly by well over one hundred people.

■ ■ ■

There is something different about this crowd. They are more responsive to the warm-up speakers. Perhaps it's the shape of the room; perhaps it's the way the sound resonates off the solid wood ceiling and floors. But they're cheering lustily, and loudly, even for local politicians.

Maybe it's a bit of the old Yankee spirit. These are people who know hardship, and know how to look past it. And perhaps the Red Sox fans know what it's like to come back from a deficit.

Then a familiar—if somewhat unlikely—speaker takes the stage: John Sununu, the Bush veteran who was an ubiquitous surrogate for Mitt Romney during the 2012 campaign.

Romney tried to burn Trump, badly, in a speech in March at the University of Utah. "Donald Trump is a phony, a fraud," he said. He predicted that nominating Trump would guarantee Hillary Clinton the presidency. Romney did not support any of Trump's rivals; he just knifed the man himself.[3]

Sununu has already said before that he would support Trump, but it is a surprise to see him do so onstage—and even more surprising that he is such an effective speaker for the candidate.

The jolly elder statesman turns out to be quite a crowd favorite, drawing applause and laughter as he rips into Clinton. He even manages to elicit some polite clapping (and a few boos) when he tells the crowd to set differences aside and reelect struggling Senator Kelly Ayotte, who has distanced herself from Trump.

Then, as Sununu wraps up, a message appears on my computer: Representative Jason Chaffetz, a Republican from Utah who had withdrawn his support for Trump, then inched back into the fold, has released a letter that FBI director James Comey has sent to both Democrats and Republicans on the House oversight committee: in light of the discovery of new emails containing classified information, the bureau will be re-opening its investigation into Hillary Clinton's private server.

The word begins to spread. A Trump campaign staffer approaches me, his face barely containing his excitement. "Did you hear?" I have heard, and now the question is whether Trump will mention the news.

We are already an hour past the official start time of the rally. The crowd begins to stir; some will undoubtedly have seen the news as it spreads on social media. General Flynn appears at the podium to warm them up. He keeps it short; he introduces Trump.

Trump appears onstage. "I need to open with a critical breaking news announcement," he says, to wild cheers.

"The FBI [cheers] has just sent a letter to Congress informing them that they have discovered new emails [cheers] pertaining to the former Secretary of State, Hillary Clinton's, investigation [cheers, chants of "Lock her up!"], and they are reopening the case into her criminal and illegal conduct that threatens the security of the United States of America.

"Hillary Clinton's corruption is on a scale we have never seen before. We must not let her take her criminal scheme into the Oval Office.

"I have great respect for the fact that the FBI and the Department of Justice are now willing to have the courage to right the horrible mistake that they made. This was a grave miscarriage of justice that the American people fully understood and it is everybody's hope that it is about to be corrected." More cheers and applause, throughout.

As the cheering subsides, Trump jokes, "The rest of my speech was going to be so boring. Should I even make the speech?"

And he does, hitting many of the now-familiar points: Obamacare, immigration, terrorism, trade, foreign policy. But he has a new confidence in his voice, and in truth it is a new campaign.

Trump now has the best of all closing arguments: you cannot elect a candidate to the presidency who is under criminal investigation.

■   ■   ■

What is really strange about the story is the way the FBI found those emails: during an investigation of Anthony Weiner, the former congressman and estranged husband of Hillary Clinton's closest aide, Huma Abedin.

Weiner had been pushed off the Clinton bus several months earlier, when new racy photos that he had sent to a strange woman emerged.

Some of the photos contained his young son. And one of his online paramours turned out to be an underage teenage girl.

In searching through Weiner's laptop, the FBI found thousands of emails that Abedin had sent to Clinton. They were problematic for two reasons: one, they were new emails that the FBI had not yet searched when Comey announced that he would not recommend Clinton be prosecuted; two, Abedin had testified under oath that she had turned over "all the devices that may have any of my State Department work on it and returned" them to the State Department, via her lawyers.[4]

The Clinton camp takes a long time to respond—and for good reason: they were in midair when the news came. Their wifi was cut off, just as ours has been in the Trump traveling air convoy, to prevent the flight from being tracked.[5]

When they do respond, they are shocked and deeply aggrieved. "It boggles the mind why this step was taken with just 11 days to go," says Brian Fallon, the well-groomed spokesman for the Clinton campaign, asserting Clinton's innocence.[6]

The Obama administration is evidently not pleased, either. "Comey's decision to make public new evidence that may raise additional legal questions about Clinton was contrary to the views of the Attorney General [Loretta Lynch], according to a well-informed Administration official," the *New Yorker* reports.[7]

Democrats had praised Comey just days before, when he announced the decision not to prosecute Hillary. Now they are attacking him, suggesting he has buckled under political pressure, or perhaps is acting to sabotage Clinton.

Clinton raises some of those suspicions herself.

"I'm sure that some of you may have heard about a letter that the FBI director sent out yesterday," she tells a rally in Daytona Beach, Florida, the next day. "Well, if you're like me, you probably have a few questions about it," she said. "It is pretty strange. It's pretty strange to put something like that out with such little information right before an election. In fact, it's not just strange, it's unprecedented and it is deeply troubling."[8]

As *National Review* editor Rich Lowry points out, it was also unprecedented to nominate someone suspected of criminal conduct, as Clinton is.[9]

Comey tries to explain himself in a letter to FBI staff: "Of course, we don't ordinarily tell Congress about ongoing investigations, but here I feel an obligation to do so given that I testified repeatedly in recent months that our investigation was completed. I also think it would be misleading to the American people were we not to supplement the record....

"At the same time, however, given that we don't know the significance of this newly discovered collection of emails, I don't want to create a misleading impression. In trying to strike that balance, in a brief letter and in the middle of an election season, there is significant risk of being misunderstood, but I wanted you to hear directly from me about it."[10]

As he had done in July when he announced Clinton would not be prosecuted, Comey has tried to pacify both sides. And as in July, he has just stoked the controversy.

The new revelation does not guarantee that Trump will win, or even that Clinton will face any charges. But it creates a new expectation that the FBI will investigate until the truth is completely known.

That is an expectation Trump will exploit to the fullest. And as reports trickle in that some early voters want to change their votes, it means that the race is wide open. A fifty-fifty contest, in my estimation. And the momentum is suddenly with Trump.

■　■　■

So the Clinton camp has had its "October surprise," with the pre-planned Miss Universe saga, the *Access Hollywood* video, and a slew of women suddenly coming forward to accuse Trump of inappropriate sexual conduct. And the Trump camp has had its surprises, too.

There were James O'Keefe's videos showing that much of the widely condemned violence at Trump rallies had been incited by Democrat operatives and super PACs, apparently coordinating illegally with the campaign.

Then there was the bad news about Obamacare price increases—not really a "surprise," since it had long been anticipated, but certainly a shock to consumers.

And now there is the FBI's bombshell. It will not shake the support of committed Clinton supporters: by this point, they are clearly comfortable ignoring evidence of Clinton's dubious behavior. But it may shift late deciders, bring some Trump skeptics back into the fold, and energize depressed Trump supporters.

The 2016 election is now down to its essence. On the one side, there is a candidate who represents the status quo: slow economic growth, a managed decline in foreign affairs, deep corruption at the highest level, and continued deconstruction of the country's traditional norms. It is a situation with which very few people are satisfied—nearly two-thirds of Americans tell pollsters they believe the country is on the wrong track—but which might still be tolerable.

On the other side, there is a candidate who represents a complete shake-up of the political system, who speaks about ideas long shunted to the margins, who has a reputation for business success, who stands up to all the things and the people who have long since exhausted the patience of millions of Americans, but whose vise-like grip on the handles of power it has seemed impossible ever to break.

But that same candidate is also untested, and erratic, and "thin-skinned," as the Clinton camp likes to say. He could make America great again—or hasten collapse.

■　■　■

After Manchester, I take a bus south to Boston to stay with friends in Cambridge for the Jewish Sabbath. I watch and listen to the news unfold for as long as I can, then switch it off at sundown.

I think of my media colleagues, en route to Maine, then to Iowa, then to Colorado. They have been doing this for months. I have just been doing it for three days, and I am exhausted. I look forward to having a chance to pray, to eat, to see friends—and, especially, to sleep.

But at dinner, I find myself surrounded by young people eager to talk about the election. One wants to know whether I think Trump is destroying conservatism. One wants to know what sort of people actually support

Trump. One tells me that he has no friends who are backing Trump, and since I said I am voting for him, he wants to know why.

I explain, over the course of several hours, speaking until well after midnight—good, respectful conversations.

The next day, I pay a visit to my old Harvard dorm, Dunster House—one of a dozen upperclass houses at Harvard—which, like Yale, has an imitation of the college system of Oxford and Cambridge. The "masters" of the houses have recently been renamed "faculty deans," thanks to protest by the easily-triggered left-wing students on campus, who found the very word evoked memories of slavery, though Harvard was at the center of abolitionism and its students fought bravely for the Union.

I meet a friend to discuss our shared misgivings about this election. The campus, like the country, is ripping itself apart, and no one seems to know how to reconcile. We both support Trump, with greater or lesser degrees of enthusiasm.

At bottom, neither of us fears a Trump presidency; both of us trust the Constitution to provide a basis for opposition. And we hope that—just maybe—a Trump victory might teach people they can survive being offended.

October 30, 2016

We're back in Las Vegas. It's the early morning, and a few bleary-eyed, costumed partiers stumble across the grounds of the Venetian casino.

I arrived late at night on the last flight out of Boston, finding my way through the traffic on the Strip to the hotel, where the casino tables were crowded and bachelorette parties roamed the floor provocatively. Today Trump is heading on a four-state trip, modified to include New Mexico, a typically Democratic state the campaign now hopes to win.

The venue for the Las Vegas event is an interesting choice. Past Trump rallies have been at the Westgate, off the Strip, and at the Treasure Island nearby. But this is the first rally at the casino owned by Republican mega donor Sheldon Adelson himself.

Adelson was an early supporter of former Florida governor Jeb Bush. But he cooled to Bush after long-time family confidant James T. Baker—notoriously unfriendly toward Israel—was appointed as an advisor to the Bush campaign.

Adelson and his wife, Dr. Miriam Adelson, a psychologist from Israel, were then thought to be deciding—like many conservatives—between Senators Marco Rubio of Florida and Ted Cruz of Texas, both of whom were hawkish on foreign policy and claimed Latino heritage.

But Cruz was never able to expand beyond his conservative base, Rubio had a disastrous debate in New Hampshire, and neither of them would yield to the other, allowing Trump to dominate the field.

So Adelson was left with Trump, whom he endorsed—an important sign, given that a small army of bloggers, left and right, seemed committed to portraying Trump as "bad for the Jews." Having a major campaign event at the Venetian is a clear sign of an alliance—and a quiet rebuke to those in the Jewish community's liberal establishment who are still determined to drive a wedge between Trump and what has been, for several elections, a growing Jewish Republican electorate.

The rally is being held in one of the largest ballrooms at the Venetian—a risky choice. What if an audience big enough to fill it fails to turn up?

But turn up they do—first, two, three, five, and then some seven thousand people. A phalanx of women, mostly middle-aged, faces the media pen with pink "Women for Trump" signs proudly held aloft. "We're facing you because we think you ignore us. No matter how many people," one tells me. "We're alive and well!" says another.

This is my first rally since the news about the FBI broke, and the mood is more upbeat and intense than I have seen in months—perhaps more excited than any rally I have seen since I began covering the presidential campaign more than a year ago. The speakers, too, are somewhat bolder.

Talk show host Wayne Allyn Root—who has been stumping for Trump in Nevada—gives a particularly aggressive address, declaring, "We will never accept defeat . . . I will give you my country when you pry it from my cold, dead hands." Root leads the crowd in chants of "Lock her up!"

Danny Tarkanian—son of the late UNLV coach Jerry Tarkanian, and now a candidate for Congress—has an even better idea: "I've got something better…why don't we just vote her down?"

Then General Flynn takes the stage, and finally Trump, as the crowd goes wild. Trump rips into Hillary Clinton, Attorney General Loretta Lynch, and corruption. He adds, for laughs, "We never thought we were going to say 'thank you' to Anthony Weiner."

A woman in front holds up a sign: "Latinas for Trump." The candidate holds up her sign, then invites her onstage to explain herself. She is wearing an attractive off-the-shoulder black dress and a red "Make America Great Again" hat. She says she is from Mexico—and the crowd cheers. She is for Trump, she says, because he is for "law and order." And she wants people to come to the country legally.

More applause, boos for the media, happy faces. The mood has turned, for now.

■　■　■

We approach Fort Collins, Colorado, from the south in stiff headwinds, the snow-covered peaks of the Front Range of the Rockies on our left, the reddish brown agricultural plain to our right.

Colorado is not only a swing state, but a key ideological battleground between the two halves of the country. Once a staunchly conservative Western state, in recent years it has attracted more liberal residents, thanks to its universities and outdoor lifestyle—and also a large Latino population.

In 2006, Colorado voters approved an amendment to the state constitution defining marriage as between a man and a woman, in a referendum that was a response to a 2003 decision by the Supreme Court of Massachusetts legalizing gay marriage. Social conservatives, rejecting the idea that unelected judges should make a sweeping cultural decision for society as a whole, turned to the popular referendum. "Progressives" in Colorado decided to respond, and—thanks to wealthy activist donors—built a network of organizations devoted to creating a new ideological foundation for the state's politics. The strategy bore fruit in 2008, when Colorado went to Barack Obama, and again in 2012.

But pockets of conservatism remained. New gun restrictions passed after a mass shooting in a movie theater in Aurora in 2012 resulted in the recall of two legislators who voted for them.

Such was the consternation among the more conservative northern parts of the state about the left-ward drift that there has been discussion of eleven counties seceding from Colorado. That was the portion of the Colorado electorate that Trump would be targeting in an address at the University of Northern Colorado in Greeley (though the local county, Weld, had voted against secession). Trump's strategy appears to be to shift the state into the Republican column by turning out the conservative north, where levels of frustration with politics as usual are high.

We leave the plane in a hurry, go through the routine Secret Service search, and board the bus from Fort Collins airport to Greeley, twenty miles due east. The sky is as big as advertised, the dry landscape stark and beautiful.

We enter the Bank of Colorado Arena, which is filled to capacity. General Flynn is already being introduced, which means we have little time to wait for the candidate himself. Cowboy hats and Denver Broncos jerseys are in appearance throughout the audience, as are children on parents' shoulders.

Trump emerges, holding—of all things—a rainbow flag with the words "LGBTs for Trump" on it. Everyone cheers. This is something new for Republicans—not only that the party's nominee would proudly claim solidarity with the gay community, but that conservative voters would applaud him. It is an achievement for which Trump will receive almost no credit, with the Democrats still accusing him of homophobia just because he supports traditional marriage and opposes some overly-broad federal anti-discrimination protections.

The nominee praises the crowd for turning out in the middle of a Denver Broncos football game. The defending Super Bowl champions are beating San Diego, 17–7, in the middle of the third quarter. Trump offers to shorten his speech. "No!" is the resounding reply.

He modifies his stump speech to announce more breaking news: the FBI is seeking a warrant for 650,000 emails found on Anthony Weiner's computer. (By the end of the rally, the Justice Department has obtained one.)

Trump has new poll results to report, too—and this time, he's not exaggerating. New polls are all moving in the right direction in the swing states, and most of the numbers do not even take the latest developments into account.

By the time James Comey's letter to Congress is factored in, Trump could be on something like a path to victory. Unless something changes, that is—which, in this election, it almost always does. And it's kitchen-sink time, time for all weapons to be fired.

To that end, Trump spends some time quoting WikiLeaks, in particular some of the negative things that Hillary's campaign chair and longtime political general John Podesta has said about her. He also quotes Barack Obama from the 2008 campaign: "Hillary will say anything, and change nothing."[11]

Then he moves on to local issues. His mention of mining, both in Colorado and in neighboring Wyoming, draws a cheer from several dozen people.

There is an impressive degree of advance research in Trump's speeches—including, in each state, a local example of someone murdered by an illegal alien, to drive home both the "law and order" and "build a wall" points.

The energy in the room in Ft. Collins is positive. There are no outbursts. Perhaps the Secret Service is keeping disruptive protesters away. Or perhaps James O'Keefe's exposé has suspended the Left's "bird-dogging" operation indefinitely.

We rush out before the end of the speech, as usual. The mood among the reporters is excited, now. The idea that the race is once again competitive seems to have given some of them, at least, a new interest in what is happening on the campaign trail.

I admit I would have thought the journalists would be disappointed by Trump's improving fortunes, and perhaps some are. But they are thrilling to the chase, to the chance to be part of a real contest, and perhaps even to be front-row witnesses to history.

■ ■ ■

We have a quick transition to the flight, driving west as the sun begins to set over the Rockies. I file my story on the rally, typing furiously while I take advantage of the last few minutes of a fast, reliable internet connection.

We watch the sky redden over the starboard side of the plane and we descend, banking deeply, to Albuquerque. The runway lights approach far too quickly—and we land with a severe thud, but everything seems fine.

We file out of the 737 and walk in front of the plane toward a hangar where an enormous crowd is waiting. Bright lights shine from the roof onto the tarmac; the brilliant yellow of the New Mexico state flag flutters in the breeze, next to a row of American flags.

The Secret Service agents rifle through our bags and wave us down with wands again as Trump's plane lands. It taxis behind our plane, then moves again, to where it will make a grand entrance in front of the hangar.

It's an amazing spectacle that never quite seems to wear thin. And it seems, as we walk toward the hangar, that there is something indomitable about that airplane. The Republican nominee for president has a private plane, and he knows how to use it. The lights, the music, the choreography of landing and coming to rest in front of the hangar—it's almost comical in its stylized heroism. One wants very much not to be taken in by it. And yet it is arresting, impressive, even moving.

While the plane slows on the runway, I talk to people in the crowd. There are a larger than usual number of Hispanic Trump supporters here, reflecting the demography of the state. One tells me that Trump was not her first choice; she didn't even like him when he was on *The Apprentice*. She sees herself as more conservative than Trump.

And yet, challenged by her liberal friends to defend him, she refused to back down. And she's "stuck with it" ever since.

Inside the hangar, the noise is deafening as the jet appears, the word "TRUMP" emblazoned in white near the nose. When the candidate does not appear right away, the crowd chants, "We want Trump!"

And soon a staircase is rolled up to the aircraft, and the door opens, and he appears, waving. It's pandemonium in the hangar. This is a campaign Coloradans did not expect, that nobody could have anticipated. For two elections, talk of expanding the map has been just talk. Now Trump is trying for it.

He rifles off a list of polls in states where he has suddenly regained the lead. Florida is one. Ohio is another. He promises to win in Ohio and Colorado. And then he pauses—this is not good, he tells the audience— we are only tied in New Mexico. They boo. He promises to win in New Mexico. They cheer.

He asks who has voted early. More cheers. In that case, he says, there's no point in a rally—you've already voted. "To hell with you," he jokes. More cheers.

A scuffle breaks out just a few yards away from where I am sitting in the media tent. This is the first major protest effort we have seen in a week. Two young men have unfurled banners. One of them reads, "Get him outta here." The people around begin chanting: "Trump! Trump!"

Trump keeps speaking over the commotion—he has learned not to goad the instigators. The police arrive and pull the protesters out. It is unclear what organization they are from.

He continues with his stump speech. By now I have heard it a dozen times. Once again, the advance team has done good work planting local variations inside the body of the main text. But the substance is the same. And I suspect the crowd has heard it before, as well. They know every chant and cue: "Drain the swamp!"; "Build the wall!"; "Lock her up!" And, of course, there is Trump's ritual jeering of the media: "the worst people"; "the biggest liars in the world."

As familiar as it is, this time Trump's speech has an edge of excitement. This is not a reliably conservative state. This is New Mexico.

Trump is not even supposed to be here. But he just kept fighting, and started to regain momentum just in time for the FBI revelation—and now it looks like he may just have a chance at winning.

The fact that he is spending time and money to be here is a sign itself. The polls may not show it, but he is surging. To his fans, anyway, he is winning.

There are a few odd moments. One young man is carrying a crumpled Confederate flag. I see him hovering near the media pen. I wonder if he is going to unfurl it in front of the cameras. He may be a Democrat plant—a provocateur.

I call him over and ask to interview him. He says he is a "Southern boy"—from southern Illinois, anyway. I ask him what the connection is between the flag and Trump. There isn't one, he explains. "I carry it because I believe in it," he says.

But the people around him have begun to notice him, and somehow the Southern boy from Illinois loses his nerve, and leaves the flag alone.

Trump finishes his speech and boards the plane, which taxis away. The crowd files out, and we leave for our own plane.

We are exhausted, and we have another flight to go—this time, to Michigan, where Trump will try to expand the map again tomorrow, to a state that Republican presidential candidates have coveted, election after election, in vain.

Hillary Clinton does nothing like this. She does not pack every possible moment with events, or fly across the country. Covering Clinton is a much easier assignment, and also a more boring one. There's not much to do, not much access to anything, and no sense of drama or adventure.

Despite their continued skepticism about the man, the journalists—doomed to play the Washington Generals to his Harlem Globetrotters, several shows a day, every day, until the election—seem to be enjoying the sudden shift in mood.

We board the plane, which is about to become a lot more crowded.

CHAPTER FIVE

The Wild Ride: Primary Season 2015

Larry Schweikart

Joel's dash through Ohio and New Hampshire in October of 2016 seemed light years away from the primary season that had started more than a year before. But the themes were the same: "Trump can't win," "Trump keeps putting his foot in his mouth," and "Trump can't appeal to women." What is unusual is not that these nostrums were wrong, but that they were wrong for over a year. As we will see, the very same negative prognostications accompanied Trump's entire primary race.

Back in the summer of 2015, the primary campaign continued to roll on, with some polls showing Trump up two to one over his nearest rival. Significantly the elites' anointed candidates—Bush, Rubio, and Walker—were getting battered. On August 17, one of the biggest polls after the second debate, from Fox, found that Trump's support had barely moved; it was down just one point (within the margin of error). Those who had moved up were all non-establishment candidates—

Ben Carson, Carly Fiorina, and Ted Cruz. Bush had dropped to third place (and, in some polls, fourth), in single digits.[1]

Let's See Some Meat

On August 16, after critics complained that Trump's proposals had no policy specifics, the candidate had offered an Immigration Reform Plan "that will make America great again."[2] Labeling the Schumer-Rubio immigration bill (normally referred to as the "Gang of Eight" bill after the four Democrats and four Republicans who had drafted it) as "nothing more than a giveaway to the corporate patrons who run both parties," Trump proposed a wall across the southern border, and the defunding of "sanctuary cities" that refused to enforce U.S. deportation laws. He also had a plan to make Mexico pay for the wall through increases on fees at all border crossings, increases on NAFTA worker visas from Mexico, and the impounding of all remittance payments derived from illegal wages. In addition, Trump promised to triple the number of Immigration and Control (ICE) agents, impose a national e-verify system for employers to check the legal status of employees, and end "catch-and-release" policies. Trump demanded the deportation of all criminal aliens and—his most controversial point—an end to "birthright citizenship," whereby women crossed the border to have "anchor babies" whose American citizenship would enable the "chain migration" of their families.

Trump's plan stated flatly that "A nation without borders is not a nation," that "A nation without laws is not a nation" and that "A nation that does not serve its own citizens is not a nation."[3] The proposal, drafted with the advice of Republican Senator Jeff Sessions of Alabama, referred to a "blood trail" associated with criminal elements that were pouring across the border of Mexico.

It was a startlingly bold plan, causing amnesty proponents to screech to the heavens. One blogger called it "hardcore porn for nativists."[4] But it had a more important effect—it immediately drove other Republican candidates, such as Scott Walker, to issue their own similar plans. As well they should: a Rasmussen poll taken just three days after Trump announced his plan found that voters overall—not just Republicans—favored building a wall and 80 percent favored deporting all illegal aliens convicted of a felony.[5] Trump had outflanked all his GOP opponents, appealing over the heads of the entire "ruling class"—which, Democrat or Republican alike, was unified in its support for amnesty-based immigration "reform"—to the American people. Especially noticeable was the continued fall of the original presumed nominee Jeb Bush, whose slide in the polls started to concern even his big donors.

Evidence that the final stage of grief—acceptance—was already setting in came when Bloomberg Politics managing editor Mark Halperin (an establishment journalist if there ever was one) admitted that Trump had reached "a turning point" where "establishment candidates" thought he could win Iowa, and "most" believed he could win the nomination. Halperin even went so far as to conclude that "a significant number think he could win the White House."[6] Henry Gomez, writing on Cleveland.com, admitted "Donald Trump Proves Us Wrong," saying, "maybe this Donald Trump thing is for real."[7] On August 19 a CNN/ORC poll showed Trump "competitive" with Hillary Clinton, down only six points to the presumptive Democrat nominee, when he had previously trailed by sixteen.[8] Soon, he would tie her, then lead. And the polls, as we'll see below, were already being generously sauced with pixie dust. Trump was probably further ahead of Clinton than the mainstream pollsters were reporting.

Social Media Monster

Another factor was that, though few had noticed, Trump had built an astonishing social media network that dwarfed those of his rivals, including Clinton. Many in the media who should have learned from the power of Obama's social media campaign in 2008 failed to appreciate that Trump had not only mastered the art of campaigning on social media but broken new ground for a Republican. In 2008, Obama had 2.3 million Facebook followers and McCain, 622,000; Obama's website had four times as many visitors as McCain's; and the Obama campaign posted six times as many campaign-originated videos to YouTube as McCain. Most important, Obama's videos had garnered 300 *million* more views than McCain's. Obama had 125,000 Twitter followers in contrast to McCain's 5,300. In the number of online references to the campaign's voter contact operation, Obama had a lead of 479,000 to 125! Obama's appearances on Oprah Winfrey's talk show and the selection of his book by her powerful book club were estimated to have added one million votes to his election.[9]

By the third week in August 2015, Trump had 3.7 million Twitter followers. His closest GOP rival? Marco Rubio had 816,000, while Rand Paul came in at 669,000. Establishment favorite Jeb Bush had 266,000. Trump had more Twitter followers than Ben Carson, Carly Fiorina, Marco Rubio, Ted Cruz, Jeb Bush, Rand Paul, and Scott Walker *put together.* He had added 320,000 in one week, three times as many as Carson (his nearest competitor) and more than ten times as many as Bush had added (26,000). Trump's *weekly Twitter growth* exceeded the entire Twitter accounts of Mike Huckabee, Chris Christie, John Kasich, and Scott Walker combined.[10]

The astounding dominance of Trump in social media stung reporters, who could have taken solace in Hillary Clinton's 4 million Twitter followers…except that an April 2015 audit showed that Clinton had purchased followers on both Twitter and Facebook in an attempt to seem hip. The *Daily Mail* reported that more than half of Hillary's then 3.6 million Twitter followers were either "fake or completely inactive." An audit conducted by "Status People" showed that 15 percent of her followers were fictional, while only 44 percent were people who actively used Twitter.[11] Trump critics claimed that most of his Twitter followers had joined him before he became seriously involved in politics—largely as a result of *The Apprentice* (something that was true enough)—and that that fact indicated that his followers were not following him because of political interest (which was false). His rapid growth (often over 200,000 a week) since he had announced his candidacy constituted an audience almost entirely concerned with his political aspirations.[12] The *Washington Examiner* had claimed on August 14, 2015, that under 40 percent of Trump's online followers were "members of the voting-age population." But since the article was written, Trump had expanded that number by 300,000—meaning that even if only 40 percent of them were eligible to vote, he still had more voting-age followers than Hillary Clinton and every Republican in the race—by a two-to-one margin! By late August, he was gaining almost 400,000 followers a week and rapidly approaching Clinton's faux numbers.

Bull in a China Shop

It started to dawn on some of the GOP insiders that Trump actually had a strategy and was not, as some liked to categorize him, a bull in a China shop. After an "audacious spectacle" in Mobile, Alabama, where the candidate conducted a fly-over in his "Trump Force One" black jet, he was greeted by up to 30,000 supporters for a rally. The *Washington Post* admitted that the South would prove key to Trump's nomination. "We're going to be strong in Iowa, New Hampshire, and the other states that start it out," said his campaign manager Corey Lewandowski, but he added, "Then comes the South. That's the path to the nomination."[13] At the time Lewandowski uttered those words, Trump was actually leading in all three of the states "that start it out"—Iowa, New Hampshire, and South Carolina. By Super Tuesday, when seven Southern states have their primaries (Alabama, Arkansas, Georgia, North Carolina, Tennessee, Texas, and Virginia), along with Vermont, Massachusetts, plus caucuses in Colorado and Minnesota, the delegate count could be all but decided. Within two weeks after that, other states where Trump had a sizeable lead—Michigan, Florida, and Missouri—would be coming up. By March 22, when Arizona (another state Trump led as of August) voted, it would be difficult for any candidate to assemble the needed delegates to overcome his lead, even if the race was in doubt. Only in Louisiana (where Governor Bobby Jindal was a favorite son) and Ohio (where Governor John Kasich led in one poll) did it seem that Trump would not almost automatically be the top vote getter.

The other candidates continued to founder, impotently attacking Trump's "lack of conservatism." George Will, labeled by one blogger "Guardian of the GOP Establishment," continued to complain that anyone supporting Trump could not be a Republican, that they must "share his aversion to facts."[14] Will called Trump "incorrigibly vulgar," complained he was "coarsening...civic life," and referred to his "squalid performance." (Unlike anybody else's, it was a winning performance.) Oddly, Will had not found Barack Obama's assault on America's prosperity, international prestige, family values, and character "squalid," "vulgar," or "coarsening." He reserved those terms for a Republican who challenged his elite status as "opinion maker." RinoTracker responded by pointing out "Will's consuming arrogance" and his assessment of small-town America as a "crude place where mindless loudmouths congregate at the local bars to parade their ignorance."[15]

The polling continued to roll in. On Trump's immigration policies, a CNN/ORC poll found that his numbers among Hispanics were not hurt and that he actually did better in a head-to-head matchup with Hillary Clinton than did Jeb Bush, who was assumed to be pro-amnesty.[16] In a line that had to be painful for the *Washington Post* reporter to type, "Trump's position among non-white voters improved" after his comments. At a press conference in Iowa, Trump took questions from everyone. (It is worth noting that Hillary Clinton, the presumptive Democrat candidate, rarely took questions from the press and never allowed hostile follow-up questions.) As Trump began to call on reporters, Jorge Ramos, the face of Univision—the Spanish-language station in Los Angeles—bullied his way in and interrupted when Trump had called on a different reporter. Trump instructed him to "Sit down. You haven't been called." When Ramos continued to talk, Trump had him removed. (Ramos was let back in later.) As Jeffrey Lord wrote, "the incident was a perfect metaphor for the illegal immigration issue. Ramos jumped the press conference rules and was sent back— only welcomed back inside when he agreed to live by the same rules" as the other reporters.[17] Once again, an incident that would have sent other candidates scurrying for the hills or apologizing only boosted Trump's standing as someone who wouldn't back down from a confrontation.

RINOs Unraveling

Meanwhile, the candidacy of his presumed major opponent, former Florida Governor Jeb Bush, continued to unravel. In late August three of Bush's top fundraisers left, and he issued orders to his campaign staff to begin tightening their belts. Reports that "donors aren't worried…yet" began to appear with regularity, indicating, of course, that donors were *very* concerned. Bush took a further beating—partly in Trump's Tweets—for speaking Spanish at an event. Trump immediately blasted him for not setting a good example, then, in a September 2 press conference, added that speaking English was essential to getting ahead economically in the United States.

In late August, policy issues began to take a back seat to increased concerns, fanned by the GOP establishment, that Trump still entertained notions of running as a third party candidate if he did not win the primaries. They renewed their demand that Trump pledge to support the eventual Republican candidate. On September 2, Trump met with RNC head Reince Priebus and emerged to deliver a statement saying he had signed such a pledge—then held it up. In reality, as talk show host Rush Limbaugh pointed out, Trump had very likely hoodwinked the Republican establishment into promising to support *him*. At that time he was not trailing in a single national Republican primary poll (often, he was leading by double digits and in fact since July had only trailed in the RealClearPolitics average of polls one time, and then only for a week, to Ben Carson).[18] At the state level, he showed amazing stamina as well: he only trailed in three state-level polls, once each (behind Walker in Iowa and Wisconsin and behind Kasich in Ohio). None of the expected front-runners, including Rubio, Bush, or Walker, were coming remotely close to him in national polls.

By late August, Trump had regained the lead over Walker in Iowa and was trailing only the sitting governors in Wisconsin and Ohio. All the non-traditional, non-establishment candidates continued to gain momentum. Ben Carson tied Trump in one state poll, generating a phenomenal amount of media buzz ("has Trump peaked?"), and gained significantly in late-August national polls, routinely coming in second.

Fiorina managed to boost her poll numbers enough to gain a lectern on the national debate stage for the second Republican debate. And outsider Ted Cruz generated consistent headlines, although his popularity remained anemic compared to Carson's. Of the establishment politicians, only Walker consistently ranked in the top four (usually at the bottom). Still, by early September 2015, as he topped 30 percent in a still crowded field in a Monmouth poll, it looked like a long shot for any of the candidates to derail Trump.[19]

By the time of the second debate on September 16, Trump had begun holding often massive rallies. He attracted between 20,000 and 30,000 in Mobile, Alabama, and 20,000 and a full arena in Dallas, Texas; he spoke to a large crowd on the deck of the battleship USS *Iowa* in California; even on quick, "in-and-out" stops such as the Iowa State Fair he was mobbed. His appearance on *The Tonight Show*, where "Trump" (Jimmy Fallon in a blond wig) interviewed himself in a mirror, was generally considered a hit. Stories emerged that other candidates were being recruited to take The Donald out in the second debate. In fact, most had already tried.

Almost every candidate except Cruz had gone after Trump personally and often viciously. Rick Perry, who had dropped out early in September, was just the first. Carly Fiorina sniped at Trump, even after he supported putting her in the second debate despite her lower poll numbers. Weeks before the debate, stories had surfaced that the GOP establishment was beginning to support Carson as a kind of Trump "firewall." As the debate neared, both Rand Paul and Fiorina were reported to be ready to "take Trump out."[20]

Almost every early question the second debate touched on was phrased to allow the candidates to attack Trump, and every one of the candidates save Cruz took their shots, but the most damaging exchange appeared to be with Fiorina. She was asked about a comment that Trump had made on his plane when she came on the TV screen. Trump had reportedly said, "Look at that face! Would anyone vote for that? Can you imagine that? The face of our next president."[21] Asked if she would feel comfortable with Trump's finger on the nuclear codes, Fiorina called

Trump a "wonderful man" and said that all the candidates' capabilities would be revealed "over time and under pressure." But in response to the comment about her looks, she said, "women all over this country heard very clearly what Mr. Trump said."[22] The stacked audience, which scarcely cheered for Trump at any time—even when he propounded positions that were overwhelmingly supported in the polls—gave her "raucous cheers and applause." Pundits, once again, raced to microphones and Twitter to insist Trump was "finished."

Yet within a week it had become clear that once again Donald Trump had been playing chess when everyone else was playing checkers. Or a more appropriate analogy might be poker, for Trump played the man (or the woman) not the hand. His closest competitor going into the race, Carson—the "firewall"—had closed to within a few points of Trump in one national poll, and actually had tied Trump in a Michigan poll, not released until the day after the debate. Fiorina was well back in the pack with the other single-digit candidates. Trump had kept his focus on Carson. He didn't knock Carson out—and he didn't need to. The brilliant surgeon was shut out of the early questioning by the moderator, then looked tired, distracted, and without energy for much of the debate. After the debate he slipped considerably in the polls. By a week later, Carson had fallen back almost to the bottom. Fiorina gained, but only very briefly. By September 22, the Morning Consult poll had Trump back to 32 percent (he had a high in one poll of 39 percent) and with a lead of twenty percentage points.

Increasingly, the anti-Trump establishment commentators had to resort to claiming the polls were simply wrong, although soon, in the general election (when Clinton led), they would be back to assuming that the polls were right. American pollsters engaging in foreign polling had badly missed on elections in Israel—as they would on the Brexit vote in England in June of 2016. They had also underestimated the extent of the GOP victories in the past two off year elections, although they got the direction of those races right. But their early polling showing Trump's rise in popularity was fairly accurate. That was about to change—and, as we shall see, not because Trump was getting less popular.

In the meantime, Trump came out with his second major policy paper—following up on the immigration proposals he had released in August—on guns. On September 21, Trump announced his gun rights plan, which featured a national "right-to-carry" provision and an end to bans of the right to carry on military bases and recruiting centers. Trump insisted, "the government has no business dictating what types of firearms good, honest people are allowed to own," and vowed to fix the "broken mental health system" which was the root cause of so much gun violence.[23]

By rolling out major policy pieces step by step—and with the help of such intellectual heavyweights as Sessions on immigration and (later) Steve Forbes on taxation—Trump was indicating that by election time he planned to announce detailed and well-grounded policies on every major issue confronting the nation. More important, as the content of his plans showed, *he had steadily moved to the Right* from his previous, off-the-cuff policy pronouncements. It was as if Trump, faced with the challenge of actually making policy, was boning up on each issue and arriving at a much more conservative stance than he previously held. Critics, particularly those in the National Review Online attack cue, claimed he really didn't mean it—that he was just pandering. But surely no one could believe that his controversial immigration policy was pandering.

Owning the News Cycle

Equally important, by producing policy papers once a month, Trump ensured that he would continue to control the news cycle for the better part of a year. His tax policy paper, which was released on September 28, was as close to revolutionary as any plan since Ronald Reagan's. He outlined four points: Single people earning less than $35,000 and married people earning less than $50,000 would owe no taxes at all, amounting to savings of about $1,000. For all other taxpayers, four brackets—0, 10, 20, and 25 percent—would replace the current seven, and the Alternative Minimum Tax and the marriage penalty would be eliminated.

Corporate taxes would drop to 15 percent, making "America's tax rate one of the best in the world." And Trump would eliminate the death tax. His tax savings would be fully paid for by a one-time repatriation of corporate cash abroad (at least $2 trillion, according to a 2014 Credit Suisse report) at a 10 percent rate and a cap on the deductibility of business interest expenses.[24]

After the buzz about the Republican debate died down, the popularity of Carly Fiorina—whom the pundits had hailed as "winning" the debate—flattened, then began to sink, hitting a new low of 6 percent in a Public Policy Polling survey in early October. Carson had stubbornly held on to second place in most polls—even tying Trump in one Pennsylvania survey. But national head-to-head polls in a number of key states, including Iowa and Florida, were starting to show that Trump could win the general election—usually by less margin than the favored GOPe candidates, but still defeating Hillary. In many states, including Ohio, Michigan, Virginia, and Pennsylvania, he was trailing by only the margin of error. Other early general election polls, such as a Quinnipiac poll of Connecticut, showed him losing to Hillary forty-seven to forty (twenty points ahead of Carson). Mitt Romney had lost the 2012 vote in Connecticut by the same margin, and in 2008 McCain had been crushed by twenty-two points in 2008 there. Before he had even won the nomination, Trump was equaling or strongly surpassing the performance of the previous two GOP candidates.

No question Trump's bluntness meant he could generate bad news for himself as fast as good news. The drive-by media jumped on his comment that "if [polls] changed, and that went in a different direction, and if I thought that I wasn't going to win…I would certainly want to get out…I'm not a masochist"[25] as a sign that Trump was not serious about staying in the race. A story in the *New York Times* called "From Donald Trump, Hints of a Campaign Exit Strategy" claimed that Trump had "started to articulate a way out of the presidential race: a verbal parachute that makes clear he has contemplated the factors that would cause him to end his bid."[26] Other media outlets joined in the chorus. But Trump crushed the media trial balloon instantly, saying on *Morning Joe,*

"I'm never getting out." Later, on CNN, he told Chris Cuomo, "I'm going all the way."[27] At about the same time, when Ted Cruz, one of the few candidates not to have criticized Trump, claimed that Trump wouldn't be the nominee, he would, Trump responded that this made perfect sense: "What else can he say?"

And in another key area—financing—Trump was making his opponents look silly while positioning himself as the fiscally responsible candidate. In early October, Trump announced that he had spent less than $2 million on his campaign so far, most of which had been paid to his own company for use of his airplane (according to federal election rules). It was entirely possible that through September Trump had not actually spent any money at all on the campaign while Bush and Cruz had gone through more than $5 million each and Walker and Perry had been driven from the race broke. While at an event in Georgia, Trump admitted that he had begun with an initial budget of $20 million, but had not spent much of it—nothing at all on ads. He said his campaign had prepared some and "might" run them, or might not. He still steadfastly refused lobbyist money and "big donors," but he had opened up his site to take small donations.

The Anointing of Hillary Clinton

While a great deal of attention was focused on Trump, the Democrats had an unfolding story of their own. Vermont Senator Bernie Sanders had begun to attract massive crowds and started to raise money on a level approaching that of Clinton. Naturally, as they had with Trump, the drive-by media discounted any chance Sanders might have of winning the nomination. Still, the Clinton-controlled DNC, headed by Debbie Wasserman Schultz, took no chances. The first Democrat debate was scheduled for October 13, a Thursday night opposite a National Football League game. Observers such as Rush Limbaugh argued that such scheduling was deliberate to "hide" Hillary from the public, as her poll numbers seemed to fall the more people saw her and heard her speak. Trump wanted to ensure that people watched, so he announced he would live tweet the event. And his tweets probably drew a larger audience than the debate itself. They were, in general, hardly inflammatory, but he did note that no one on stage was presidential: "Sorry, there is no STAR on the stage tonight!" Nevertheless, his Twitter following gained 60,000 during the debate.[28]

Hillary Clinton emerged unscathed from the debate, as Sanders—a self-admitted socialist who had only switched parties to the Democrats to run for president—refused to challenge her on her ongoing email scandal, saying "the American people are sick and tired of hearing about your damn emails." By his unwillingness to address Clinton's biggest weakness, he effectively eliminated himself as a serious candidate. Vice President Joe Biden, who had seemed poised to enter the race before the debate—at one time CNN had considered putting a lectern up for Biden should he choose to appear on stage—suddenly backed out, convinced he couldn't beat Clinton. In an October 21 Rose Garden announcement, Biden said that the time was not right for him to run. (Many thought Trump's most potent challenger had just recused himself.) And so, despite Sanders's poll numbers and large crowds, Clinton found herself with no serious primary challenger. She had already begun securing the "super-delegates" to her nomination.

Thinking the Unthinkable

While it is doubtful the Democratic debate itself played any role in the media's reassessment of the Republican primary race, it was clear that by the third week of October 2015 that some of the political observers were coming around to the notion that Trump would likely be the nominee. Philip Bump at the *Washington Post* asked, "Is it time to concede that Donald Trump is likely to win the GOP nomination?"[29] National Review Online, home to some of Trump's most vicious and persistent critics, published a piece headlined, "The Establishment Thinks the Unthinkable: Trump Could Win the Nomination."[30] Ed Rollins, a campaign officer for Reagan, called Trump "a serious player for the nomination," and Steve Schmidt, John McCain's 2008 presidential campaign manager, agreed, "Trump has sustained a lead for longer than there are days left [until the beginning of the caucus and primary season]."[31] Yet NRO could not report the story without taking a jab at Trump, quoting Bush press secretary Ari Fleischer comparing Trump to a car accident. The "risk for the party is he tarnishes everybody," he complained. Polls suddenly showed that Republican voters saw Trump as the "most likely" to win the nomination.[32] Even so, by October, there were more than thirty predictions in major media outlets of the business mogul's collapse, and well into November prognosticators would occasionally announce the "end of Trump" over something outrageous that he said.

But a flap involving Trump's response to Jeb Bush's comment that his brother had "kept America safe" had no effect on Trump's position in the polls. Trump had responded that 9/11 occurred while George W. Bush was president. To some, that suggested he was blaming Bush for 9/11—long a leftist and "9/11 truther" position. At a South Carolina rally, Trump said that "They knew an attack was coming.... George Tenet, the CIA director, knew there would be an attack, and he said so to the president and said so to everybody who would listen." But, Trump claimed, the agencies were not communicating—"they had a lot of problems getting along—and that's leadership."[33] While Trump said he did not "blame Bush," he reiterated that the attack had happened while Bush was president. The exchange tied the establishment candidate to the unpopular administration of his brother.

George W. Bush might have gone down as a top tier president had he stepped down in 2004. The Iraq War, while far from won, had not yet turned sour as it would in 2005, when Hurricane Katrina would also badly damage Bush's reputation. All it took was the mortgage crisis of 2007 (mostly brought about by Democratic policies) and the stock market and banking collapse of 2008 to finish off Bush's popularity as he left office. For Jeb to have any chance, he had to avoid being seen as the third term of George W. Bush. Trump did not waste any time when Bush's campaign announced it had to cut payroll and lay off staffers. "Bush has no money," he said at a Florida campaign rally. "He's meeting today with Mommy and Daddy, and they're working on their campaign."[34] "Here's a guy," Trump said, "who wants to run our country, and he can't even run his own campaign."

Increasingly, Bush seemed not to have any chance at all. Slowly, calls for him to drop out began to surface. Ben Carson, rather than the erstwhile establishment candidate, seemed to be the most unshakeable opponent behind Trump. He had steadily ranked second in almost all polls, national and state, and by the end of October had actually overtaken Trump in two separate Iowa polls among registered caucus-goers, suggesting that Trump might not win the first electoral test of the campaign. Carson had run a dedicated Facebook campaign, responding daily to three questions at the site, and the perception of him as a more "religious" candidate appealed to evangelical Iowa voters. His peaceful demeanor and lack of combativeness appealed to many who "just wanted to get along." And his campaign was surging: those Iowa polls were followed by a poll in Texas showing Carson ahead, and a national CBS poll giving Carson a slight lead.

Nevertheless, Carson had the "Clinton problem," namely, the more he spoke and the more people saw him, the less popular he became. He continued to commit gaffes that—had Trump not already survived similar missteps—might have sunk other candidates. Carson, for example, had said that a Muslim should not be president, before clarifying that he had meant that a Muslim who accepted Sharia law could not be president because of the conflict between the presidential oath to the Constitution and the requirements of Sharia law. Trump, meanwhile, speaking on the issue of terrorism, said that it might be necessary to close certain mosques.

Now that he was leading in some polls, it would have been expected that Carson would receive the bulk of the attention in the third Republican debate, in Boulder, Colorado, on CNBC. Instead, he was nearly frozen out, asked an early sarcastic question about his "ten-year relationship" with a company called Mannatech, when in fact Carson had only made paid speeches for them. After a follow-up question, the audience loudly booed moderator Carl Quintanilla.[35] By the time the questioners addressed Ted Cruz with a similarly "gotcha" question about why he opposed the budget deal (after all, how could he possibly lead if he didn't support something they saw as great?), the senator launched into a two-minute takedown of the entire drive-by media. Accusing the moderators of treating the debate like a "cage match," Cruz said the questions "asked so far in this debate illustrate why the American people don't trust the media."[36] He contrasted the tone of the questions asked of Republicans to those at the Democratic debate, "where every fawning question from the media was, 'Which of you is more handsome, and why?'" Cruz's explosive attack carried the night, but he soon got assistance from Marco Rubio, Mike Huckabee, and Chris Christie. Trump had his own zinger—"Do you write this stuff?" directed at the moderators—but it was clearly a Cruz night.

Even so, Trump had done what he needed to do, namely not make a major mistake. And his deconstruction of John Kasich perhaps finished the Ohio governor's campaign, although Kasich would slog on a while longer in the low single digits. Kasich had touted his state's economic record, but Trump pointed out that Ohio had the good fortune of having fracking come into the state, implying that Kasich had nothing to do with Ohio's recovery.

The "Cruz missile" that had been launched in the debate set off a conservative media frenzy, but the fact was that little in the race had changed. Trump remained the only candidate committed unequivocally to not only border security but deportation; his was the only gun plan involving a national right to carry; and while Cruz's flat tax plan was more appealing in many respects, it did not contain the one-time repatriation of American money overseas that promised to bring in almost $2 trillion.[37]

Despite the Carson surge, Trump continued to lead in most states. On Thursday, November 12, Trump gave a speech at Fort Dodge, Iowa, where he launched into an attack on Carson and asked "how stupid are the people of Iowa…to believe this crap [the things Carson wrote in his book]?"[38] Trump was referring to Carson's own admission that he had had a "pathological temper" in his youth. Trump said that pathologies were "incurable" and likened Carson's anger issues to child molesting. Had Trump not been quoting embarrassing admissions from Carson's book, his charge might have damaged himself more; the fact that Carson had written what he did softened the blows. Still, once again the media and the anti-Trump GOPe establishment bloggers raced to proclaim Trump's campaign over. Twitter was ablaze with obituaries, and talk show host Rush Limbaugh played clips, including nearly a dozen news reporters using almost identical language about Trump having gone on a "tirade." Combined with the Iowa polls and the handful of national polls that Carson led, it seemed to many that Trump had—once again—finally "peaked."

Instead, he bounced back yet again.

Until We Figure Out What's Going On

And on November 13, world-changing events shook the campaign. Islamic radicals, some with direct ties to the terrorist group ISIS, struck at five different targets in Paris, including a soccer stadium and a heavy metal rock concert (ironically, with an American band) at the Bataclan Theater, leaving nearly 120 dead and another 80 badly wounded.[39] Trump immediately tied the attack to the French gun laws, tweeting that if a handful of people inside the theater had possessed guns, the story would have been much different. The event also provided Trump the opportunity to raise the issue of terrorism and the threat of ISIS (the Islamic State of Iraq and Syria, which Obama constantly referred to by its *less* used name, the Islamic State of Iraq and the Levant, or "ISIL") again.

In June earlier that year large numbers of Middle Eastern immigrants began arriving in Europe. At first, these were identified as "refugees" seeking "asylum." Over time, the numbers swelled to 180,000 and began to overwhelm nations on the fringe of Europe, so that those nations soon began funneling the migrants straight through to other nations. Italy and Greece "appear to be acting simply as a gateway to more attractive parts of Europe, including Britain," the head of Britain's UKIP Party warned.[40]

Sweden slammed shut its open-door policy to immigrants, announcing, "We simply can't do any more."[41] Hungary built a fence—exactly the same prescription that Trump had been demanding for America's southern border. Poland strongly resisted taking any refugees, accepting only 115 Syrians in all of 2014. But those policies were responsive to public opinion across Europe. Other European governments ignored their constituencies and admitted the immigrants anyway. By the fall of 2015, armies of immigrants—consisting largely of military-aged males— poured into southern and central Europe, overrunning towns, overwhelming police resistance, and pushing into France and Germany. Fears spread that these "refugees" included ISIS infiltrators.

The GOP establishment thought that finally the issues had turned against Trump and that voters would seek candidates who had "more experience." In fact, with terrorism on Americans' minds again, and Obama insisting the United States take vast numbers of Syrian "refugees," Trump's message resonated all the more strongly than ever.

He raised the issue of the allegiance of Muslim immigrants by telling his rallies that on 9/11 there were "thousands" of Muslims cheering in New Jersey. Once again, the media and political establishment were aghast. But then it turned out that a 2001 *Washington Post* article had reported that "authorities detained and questioned a number of people who were allegedly seen celebrating the attacks and holding tailgate-style parties on rooftops while they watched the devastation on the other side of the river."[42] While the reporter used the word "allegedly," and while there was no mention of "thousands," the report seemed to give at least some support to Trump's claim. Over the next few weeks, hundreds of bloggers and users of Twitter would confirm that as individuals they had seen Muslims cheering.

In their haste to discredit Trump, the media had unwittingly stumbled into a hornet's nest of suppressed memories about 9/11. People began recalling many unpleasant facts that had been buried in the intervening fourteen years. While it is unlikely that Trump saw "thousands" of Muslims celebrating *in New Jersey*, he probably saw some, and conflated those with the, yes, "thousands" being shown on television celebrating in Palestine, Egypt, and throughout the Middle East.

What made this issue all the more serious—and all the more to Trump's advantage—was that the media had deliberately downplayed those celebrations in an effort to portray the majority of Muslims as "peaceful" and "just like us." Trump had done what no other politician was willing to do, namely raise the issue of whether Islamic immigrants truly wanted to become Americans. Critics would scream "xenophobia," but in fact there is reason for concern about the nature of Islam, and about whether it can be successfully assimilated into Western, Christian nations. In other words, Trump's 9/11 comments had uncovered a key concern Americans had secretly suppressed for nearly a decade and a half, as they were continually told that to express such concerns was hateful and paranoid. And once again, Trump had not only taken on the issue itself but the poisonous political correctness that forbade even *discussing* the issue.

The issue of the "thousands" of Muslims celebrating revealed another aspect of Trump's appeal. As Salena Zito pointed out in the *Atlantic*, his critics always took Trump literally but never took him seriously. And his supporters took him seriously and rarely took him literally.[43] Whether there were "thousands" of Muslims celebrating *in New Jersey*, there were in fact enough reports of Muslims celebrating in America and multiple thousands celebrating around the world that Trump's comments were *taken very seriously* by large numbers of people.

The media and the GOP establishment, as usual, failed to latch onto what Trump was really expressing. In a speech in Columbus, Ohio, on November 23, Trump talked about the 9/11 attacks and seeing the second plane come in from his apartment window. He noted that he could see people jumping from over eighty stories up to keep from burning to death. Again, media "fact-checkers" and GOPe bloggers raced to discredit the claim. Trump's apartment was four miles away, they noted. But he had not said he saw the jumpers with his naked eye. He had a telescope, and the news was on his television. Like any normal person, he shifted from his naked eye to the TV news. Once again, the media and the GOP establishment had stumbled into suppressed memories: images of the "jumpers" had been censored and edited from any 9/11 coverage for many years (though they did appear in many historical videos, such as HBO's excellent *9/11: In Memoriam, New York City*). By disputing Trump's claim, his opponents had merely resurrected another set of disturbing images from 9/11 that the politically correct crowd had been trying to purge for over a decade. Once again, in their attempt to damage Trump, they only underscored his point.

Trump wanted a ban on immigration from Muslim countries "Until our country's representatives figure out what is going on." Combined with the threat of ISIS in the Middle East, the images of armies of Muslim men sweeping across Europe, and the Paris shooting, Trump's message vaulted him to the top of the GOP field on the issue of national security—where supposedly he should have been badly beaten by Rubio or even Bush. In a December Miami, Florida, poll, an astonishing 70.5 percent of GOP voters either "strongly agreed" or "somewhat agreed" that there should be a ban on new immigration by Muslims.[44] Fox News found that when Trump's name was disassociated with the ban, the level of support actually went up by 5 percent.

In late November, Carson started to drift off the political stage, at which point Texan Ted Cruz, who undoubtedly on a litmus test of issues was far more conservative than Trump, made his move. Especially in Iowa, Cruz had seeded the ground for months with staffers and operatives, and his religious appeal resonated. He seemed poised to score an early victory. Cruz's chances were up considerably in an early December *Des Moines Register* poll ("the gold standard") showing him with a 31–21 lead over Trump.[45] Immediately, Cruz supporters claimed that their candidate was "surging," and that Trump's earlier criticism of him ("he was somewhat of a maniac in the Senate") had backfired.

What was even more interesting was the blizzard of articles in the establishment media lavishing praise on Cruz, often re-tweeted by the GOPe bloggers.[46] Even uber-liberal sites like MSNBC ran stories like "How Ted Cruz Could Win the GOP Nomination."[47] Of course, many of these writers utterly hated Cruz—possibly as much as they did The Donald—but saw him as a roadblock to Trump that could be conveniently eliminated once Trump was out of the picture. At that point, the remaining establishment candidate, Marco Rubio, would step in. To his credit, Cruz performed brilliantly in the fifth debate, but in a faceoff with Rubio about immigration and national security, Cruz allowed himself to be dragged into the weeds of policy votes (which *no* senator can ever win, given the nature of strategic votes for early versions of bills so they can kill them later, and the politics of voting for something to attach a poison-pill amendment to it that will ensure its later defeat). A full week after the debate, Cruz and Rubio were still enmeshed in a back and forth over whether or not either or both had supported "amnesty" and increasing H-1B visas, and whose record on national security was more believable—meaning neither was catching up to Trump.

But there was no question that by late November or early December Carson voters were (at least temporarily) abandoning Carson for Cruz, who shot into second place in almost every poll. That became a story, but the more important story was that Trump still dominated almost every state and national poll. And increasingly, some polls, including the USC/Dornsife poll and some state data, began to surface showing support for Trump among minorities. In a Miami, Florida, survey, 39 percent of black Republicans supported Trump, and in a Landmark, Georgia, poll, the number was 56 percent.[48] These were the very voters that the GOP supposedly needed to reach out to, according to the establishment, and yet when a candidate came along who appealed to them, the GOPe opposed him. Some of us were already seeing Trump's crossover appeal and were bringing it up whenever possible. But to paraphrase *Star Wars*, the stupid was strong with the GOPe, and its minions refused to even contemplate that Donald J. Trump might be the best "big tent" candidate the Republicans ever had, including the Gipper.

CHAPTER SIX

On the Campaign Trail:
Michigan, Pennsylvania, Wisconsin, and Florida

Joel Pollak

October 31, 2016

Just eight days left on the countdown clock to the election.

The sun rises late in Michigan, and so do we. Granted a blessed reprieve from the usual 8:15 a.m. "call time," we're grateful that our day will not begin until 10:30. But I do need to wake up at 7:00—4:00 a.m. in my Pacific Daylight Time brain.

It's still dark outside when I finally stir, after several false tries, at 7:30. Lots to do this morning, as there is every morning. I am still editing the California portion of the news website, even though I am assigned to follow Trump on the campaign trail.

Grand Rapids is picturesque, the fall colors magnificent on a clear if cold Halloween morning. After five days away from home, today is the day I miss my family the most. We don't really make a big deal about Halloween—we stick to the Jewish holidays and the patriotic ones—but our children enjoy the spectacle of the holiday in Santa Monica. The neighborhood just to the north of us is famous across Los Angeles for its decorations, costumes, and street parties.

The other journalists have been away so much longer. Most are young, single people. A few have families, and miss them terribly. They love what they do, but it is hard to be away from those they love.

I try not to dwell on those feelings. After finishing my initial tasks, a quick workout at the hotel gym, and a conference call, I find a local hair salon, where the stylists are amused to see me. For the past few days, I have been looking more Appalachian Trail than campaign trail.

The press meets at the hotel, and we head to a local arena for the next Trump rally. After the usual security process, we are inside the DeltaPlex arena, capacity 6,200. It is Halloween, and a few of the Trump supporters in attendance are dressed in costume. There is Abraham Lincoln with his wife, Mary Todd; there is the customary Hillary Clinton in prison garb; and there is a woman outside dressed as a bottle of ketchup, with a sign imploring Michigan to "ketchup" and support Trump.

One woman is dressed as the Statue of Liberty. She is attractive, articulate, and in demand by the TV crews. When it is my turn to interview her, I ask what motivates her support for Trump. She tells me she cannot tolerate Hillary Clinton's views on abortion. I follow up with a question about Trump's remarks about women.

She pauses for a moment. She tells me that she grew up with boys, and knows that the "locker-room talk" Trump referenced in his defense is a real thing.

As she continues, passion seems to enter her voice. She is a mother of two children, a small business owner, a committed Catholic, and a college-educated woman who has traveled the world.

And she is proud, she says, to be voting for Trump. He loves women, she says, and he is trying to do the right thing for them and the country. There is no adult human being who hasn't used foul language, and she tries to judge people by the good they do, not just their failings.

It is a response that comes from the heart—and I hear similar passion from other women in the room.

A group of middle-aged women, seeing that I am a journalist, accost me from behind. They are furious that we—the media—keep saying that college-educated women do not support Trump. They are college-educated—bachelor's, master's, and associate's degrees between them. And they are tired of being told they are stupid if they are voting for Trump.

There are many women in the room—and children, too, pulled out of school for the occasion. There seems to be a shortage of the pink "Women for Trump" signs that have been ubiquitous at every other rally, so people have scrawled "WOMEN FOR" on the regular Trump signs.

They disagree with Hillary on the issues—but their motivation, now, seems to come from somewhere else: they are tired of being told there is one way to think, believe, and vote if they are female.

In the midst of the gathering crowd, I spot two yarmulkes—one, an olive-green knitted kippah with "Israel" in yellow Hebrew and English letters; the other, made out of red leather and with "Donald Trump" written on it in Hebrew, right to left. I have been noticing the Jews in the crowd more keenly lately, ever since an incident in which a crazed man shouting "Jew-S-A!" at the media at a Saturday rally was written up by journalists as clear evidence of anti-Semitic tendencies in the Trump camp.

I ask the two Jewish men about their support for Trump. One tells me that he recently returned from Israel, where everyone he met who was in the Israel Defense Forces (IDF) supported Trump and could not fathom how Israel would survive with four more years of "Obama-like policies."

He adds that he is asked by fellow members of the community how he can support Trump if he is so smart. His reply: he asks them how they can support Hillary Clinton if they claim to be moral.

Trump rally crowds do tend to be mostly white, older, and Christian—in short, representative of the traditional American majority. But there are certainly people of different backgrounds—black, young, Jewish, gay, and so forth—on hand, and they seem eager to show that they, too, support Trump.

The display of diversity—most of it spontaneous—feels different from the typical, stilted, showy "coalition"-style politics of previous GOP campaigns. A woman who writes "Latinas for Trump" on a pasteboard is not trying to be a community organizer. She is making a statement of defiance, at considerable personal risk from the Left.

Trump is late today, which either means he has had trouble leaving Chicago—where he stayed at his home there, one of many he has scattered around the country—or it means that he is doing interviews with local television stations.

That takes time, but it is the best way to reach a local media market. After all, if people don't attend the rally in person and don't watch cable news obsessively, they are unlikely to hear about it, or have any exposure to the candidate.

Finally, General Flynn appears onstage—the usual cue that Trump himself is about to appear—and informs the crowd that he has one more person to introduce, before Trump comes to the podium.

That turns out to be Bobby Knight, the famous—and infamous—Indiana University basketball coach. His endorsement in the primary helped Trump not just carry but sweep the Hoosier State—a state whose socially conservative profile meant that it was probably a much better fit for Ted Cruz.

He has something to say about the nominee: "Donald Trump is a tough son-of-a-bitch," he says, to roars from the crowd.

He brings Trump on, and the candidate receives an ecstatic welcome from the arena, now filled with about 8,000 people. They linger there together, before Trump launches into his usual stump speech, adjusted for the state he is in today. He emphasizes one line in particular, however—one he has used before, but perhaps too rarely: "This is your one chance," he says, to put things right.

He then brings up the latest news from WikiLeaks. It turns out that Donna Brazile, the hyper-partisan CNN contributor who became acting chair of the Democratic National Committee after an earlier round of WikiLeaks had exposed secret collusion with the Clinton campaign and forced several resignations, had secretly leaked CNN debate questions to Clinton during the primary, on multiple occasions. By the time Trump takes the stage, CNN has already fired Brazile.

But that's not the point, Trump explains. The issue is that Hillary Clinton didn't report Brazile at the time. In other words, she cheated. If I did the same, he says, I'd get "the electric chair."

At that point there's an interruption from Bobby Knight, who returns to the stage to make a point: "In a Donald Trump administration, there will be no bullshit!"

The crowd loves it; the employees of the television and radio networks carrying the event live may not have felt the same way, however. It's that kind of campaign, and that kind of year.

■ ■ ■

We pile into the vans and head to the Gerald Ford airport. The Grand Rapids rally has run so late that we have to almost sprint to the plane.

We take off and fly east, over gorgeous autumn countryside, and land in Detroit. Working furiously from the moment we land, I miss what I am later told is a spectacular view of the main Trump plane touching down on the runway. We have a prize angle of the jet way after it stops; the journalists crowd to one side of the bus for photos. Trump descends, and his son-in-law, Jared Kushner. Then my old boss, Steve Bannon, who is something of a mysterious object of fascination for the journalists, many of whom ask me if I really know him.

The drive from Detroit south to Warren, Michigan, is a long one—and the police have to clear a path the entire way. In spots, irate commuters have to shift over into the two right-hand lanes. One intrepid motorist, frustrated, actually joins the motorcade, changing lanes to cross right in front of our bus. An officer on a motorcycle roars into action, pulling up next to the car, pointing at the driver, even smacking the window angrily. The Secret Service agent on our bus, next to the driver, shrugs: this is Detroit.

We arrive at a high school gym in Warren. A large overflow crowd is gathered outside; the journalists, who on the campaign trail have seen almost everything, are impressed. The place is packed, the bleachers decorated with tall hand-painted letters in the back: "VOTE TRUMP" in blue and "AMERICA FIRST" in red.

There are more Halloween costumes—one couple dressed as Rosie the Riveter and Uncle Sam. But there is little time for interviews, and the media pen is tight.

The speech is a shorter version of the earlier one, Bobby Knight just as profane, the crowd just as boisterous. Trump adds a new comment on the WikiLeaks scandal: "If they [CNN] fired Donna Brazile, why aren't they firing Hillary Clinton?" There is a protester this time, quickly surrounded by Trump supporters chanting "Trump!" and "U-S-A!" until the infiltrator is removed. Trump jokes that he is probably being paid to protest and cause violence, as others have been. He is really enjoying himself, now.

In fact, Trump is at his most upbeat in days—perhaps ever. His voice is strong and confident, not hoarse and plaintive, as it was on the day he opened his hotel. Just five days ago, he seemed a man contemplating defeat, and what it would mean for his life, and for history.

Now, tantalizingly, he seems to be savoring the prospect of victory.

He knows winning, and this is what winning feels like. The people at the rally seem to sense it, too—they are excited, happy, optimistic.

Perhaps it is all a bubble. Some polls have tightened since last week: a new poll out from New Hampshire, for example, shows Trump ahead of Clinton—though within the margin of error. The poll was taken before the big news from Comey, and the visit to the state, on Friday. What's more, the poll shows Republican Senator Kelly Ayotte pulling ahead of her challenger, Democratic Governor Mary Hassan, as Hassan, who had latched onto Clinton in the hope that a presidential landslide would propel her to victory, is finding the Democratic presidential candidate a drag.

Several mainstream media news organizations present early polling data that suggest there has been little shift in Clinton's support or her lead over Trump. One poll has her up three points, just as she was before the email scandal expanded. Another has her up six points, which is less than her prior lead, but still comfortable enough to make it through

Election Day with a victory. It may be that the new spirit at Trump rallies is just a snapshot of a newly excited base, not an expansion.

But Trump has a closing argument, and Clinton does not. His claim is that it would be risky, to the point of irresponsibility, to elect someone who could face prosecution and who had placed the national security interests of the country behind her own.

Her claim is that Trump is not the kind of person we would want teaching manners to our children.

It is not clear, yet, which is the most effective argument. But it is certainly clear which of the arguments feels most powerful.

■ ■ ■

We land back in New York at 8:30 p.m.—which feels like a mercifully early hour, leaving a few hours to relax and catch up on sleep. Tomorrow, the final week of campaigning will begin.

It is only Monday night, but it already feels like Wednesday. That is how busy we have been, how far we have moved across the country. Trump's energy is exhausting the rest of us. This is partly why the rest of the campaign traveling press has been counting down the days until they are done.

Theoretically, I should go to bed early and maximize sleep. Practically, of course, things work out differently.

I arrive at my friend's apartment in the East Village to find myself catching the tail end of a dinner party—leftovers from a celebratory dinner for a newlywed couple the night before. (The newlyweds have long since retired for the night: whether to sleep or to make love, a wise decision.) The rest of us, including some old friends and some new ones, stay to eat and chat.

Inevitably, the subject turns to politics. Three of us are pro-Trump. Three of us are not. We pour glasses of wine and sparkling water and rehearse the same arguments that have consumed the country for months, even years now.

Hillary Clinton has the qualifications and record to do the job—but no actual achievements. Trump promises to disrupt the system and end the smothering tyranny of political correctness. Aren't we afraid that Trump would commit abuses of power? Aren't his many outbursts symptoms of a deeper instability? There are no guarantees—but I believe that even if Trump were to "crash" the presidency, he would be held in check by Congress and the media. Perhaps, finally, Democrats would rediscover the checks-and-balances they had neglected for eight long years under Obama.

■ ■ ■

It is now 1:30 a.m., and the others retire. I still have work to do, laundry to wash, bills to pay. I resolve that I will be done with political arguments for the next seven days. They simply take up too much energy. And I need my rest.

The next week will be grueling—except for the Jewish Sabbath, that blessed day that makes all other days possible, that allows me to work late into the night and gives me the energy to be ready for the day's tasks at otherwise absurd hours.

I consider the conventional wisdom. Trump should lose. He is still behind in the polls, even though the momentum is shifting in his direction. The alternative possibility depends on the notion that there is a "silent majority" that will turn out at the polls and make the difference.

I find it hard to believe in that silent majority. I believed in it in 2008, the election I really did feel was the most important. It failed to turn up—or when it did, that silent majority voted for the candidate who promised change.

The conservative side has not learned the lesson of the defeats of 2008 and 2012, it seems to me. It still relies on faith—while the party of government plods along with its mundane organizational style of politics, assisted by technology but still fundamentally the same as it has always been: approaching the voters, each one as an individual, and asking for their support.

Trump makes his pitch to crowds—huge crowds, big and beautiful crowds. Crowds do not vote, and faith alone does not win battles, or elections. That is what I think. That seems the smart opinion, the right view.

And yet the energy of the crowds I have felt over the past several days is telling me that something really is different. This time doesn't have the almost morbid, bitter-end feeling of the dying days of the McCain campaign. The mood is very different from the awkward over-confidence of the Romney campaign, as well.

This feels like the movement that I always wish we conservatives had. The issues are different, the candidate deeply flawed, but the people are there.

If there were ever a chance for faith to triumph, this would be it.

November 1, 2016

The dark before the dawn in New York, exactly one week before Election Day. The press gathers for the drive, through traffic, to La Guardia airport.

On two hours' sleep, I attempt to digest a speech given the day before by venture capitalist Peter Thiel at the National Press Club in Washington, D.C.

Thiel "came out" twice this year—as a gay man to the Republican National Convention, and as a Donald Trump supporter to Silicon Valley. The former applauded him heartily; the latter recoiled in horror.

Thiel's argument is that Trump is the voice of millions of Americans who "judge the leadership of our country to have failed." He notes the intolerance of "louder voices" who "do not intend to tolerate the views of one half of the country." And he predicts, "No matter what happens in this election, what Trump represents is not crazy and it's not going away."

For his trouble, a Silicon Valley columnist urges the tech industry to "attack" Thiel for not being "inclusive" enough.

I consider the state of the election. It all comes down to one week from today. As I was preparing to leave this morning, it had struck me just how improbable a Trump victory would be.

Hillary Clinton has a far better ground game, a turnout machine in which she has invested millions of dollars and the best new technologies that Silicon Valley could devise for the purpose. Trump has his charisma and swagger, coming in on a wing and a prayer. It should be obvious who will win.

And yet. A new poll from ABC News and the *Washington Post* shows Trump taking a one-point lead nationally, 46 to 45 percent. Ten days ago, he was behind by twelve points, 38 to 50 percent.

It may mean nothing—state-by-state results are the ones that matter, and he appears to be losing in North Carolina, where we will make a return visit later this week. But the surest sign that the race is competitive is that the press plane is filling up. There are few empty seats.

This is the show.

■ ■ ■

As we warm up the engines, a rehabilitated Pence plane appears behind the press plane. The two running mates are to appear together in Valley Forge, Pennsylvania, where Trump will give what is billed as a major policy address.

Valley Forge, of course, is where General George Washington retreated for the winter of 1777–78, when the Revolutionary War was going poorly for the Continentals. He regrouped, retrained, and fought again, to victory.

We fly over a red-green countryside and land in Philadelphia, where the Democratic National Convention was held just weeks before but, it seems, a lifetime ago. We rattle in our little bus northwest to the town of King of Prussia, and to the Hilton Doubletree hotel, where a line is already winding down the driveway to enter. This is a "policy speech," not a rally, so there are only a limited number of people on the list to attend. But the people outside are just as excited as at a rally.

The event is staged inside a small ballroom, with seating for about 300. After a greeting from Republican members of Congress who are also physicians, the event kicks off with a speech by Pence, who has experience with health care innovation from his tenure as governor of Indiana. He took the controversial step of accepting the expansion of Medicaid under Obamacare—with some conservative strings attached, such as health savings accounts.

Pence also runs through the Trump-Pence replacement for Obamacare. It is not a very detailed speech; for a "policy address" it is rather thin on numbers and details.

But the purpose of this event is not to make an academic argument; it is to sound a serious tone about a prime issue in the campaign in a potential "pickup" state.

As Pence and Trump discuss Obamacare, Hillary Clinton is planning to appear at a rally in Florida alongside former Miss Universe Alicia Machado. The contrast is key.

Also key is the appearance of the candidate and the running mate on stage together at Valley Forge. The two are always oddly effusive in their praise of one another. Trump often boasts to crowds about his "amazing" running mate, who—if media reports are to be believed—was not among his first choices. Pence talks about how Trump is a great leader and the best for this moment in history—though he certainly kept his admiration to himself during the primaries.

Still, their handshake onstage makes the point: these men will work together, on matters of urgent importance. That display, really, is what we are here to see.

I have a brief moment to rendezvous with one of my Breitbart California colleagues, Michelle Moons, who has been on the Pence plane.

We take a brief selfie, then divide up the work. She will take photos and interview supporters; I will do my best to take down quotes and set the backdrop for the event by looking at Pence's past policies.

Pence introduces Trump, who—for the first time in days—sounds labored, almost subdued in his delivery. It seems deliberate: he is trying to strike a presidential tone.

He has one week left to remind voters that for all the antics at his rallies, for all the one-line put-downs on the debate stage and the 3:00 a.m. tweets, he has the temperament to occupy the Oval Office.

To me, it feels a little bit overdone. Trump's speech is also light on some of the details. But the crowd is delighted and cheers him lustily.

Trump waxes expansive on the problems with Obamacare, which has only become more cumbersome and expensive over the years since it was passed. Alarmingly, he notes, in one-third of Pennsylvania counties the health insurance exchanges set up by the government only have a single insurance provider, including for the city of Philadelphia—"where I went to school," he notes, referring to his days at the Wharton School of Business.

Trump promises to request a "special session" of Congress to "repeal and replace" Obamacare. "Our replacement plan includes Health Savings Accounts, a nationwide insurance market where you can purchase across state lines, and letting states manage Medicaid dollars." He adds, commenting on his own text (as he does so often): "So much better."

He ends with a march through his familiar policy points—trade, jobs, school choice, and increased military spending. The audience applauds, delighted.

Then it is off to the airport, this time in the full motorcade. But half a mile from the hotel we pull off the road. We find ourselves at a gas station, where the lead vehicles—gleaming black SUVs—pull up in front of a Wawa food mart.

And there, quite casually, Trump emerges, along with some members of his family, his campaign manager, and staff. They disappear inside the store. We are left to wonder: What emergency could possibly have been the cause of that?

It transpires that they are buying Tastykakes, a local favorite. The story, once it hits social media, is likely to do just as much for Trump in southeast Pennsylvania as anything he said about Obamacare.

Then we are off again on the highway, bumping along at a speed that the bus was almost certainly never designed to go. Each minor pothole sets off a major earthquake in the back, where I now very much regret sitting. I manage, barely, to file my story.

Soon we are aboard the aircraft. It is becoming quite full now, as more reporters join the caravan. Perhaps they would have joined whether or not Trump's chances were improving, given that the long election is finally entering its last days.

But perhaps there is keener interest because of the way the race is shaping up. Hillary has thrown aside her plan to end on a positive note. She has to slam Trump with everything she's got.

WikiLeaks continues to roll, and the email scandal just keeps going.

■   ■   ■

Our flight to upper Wisconsin—perhaps the least likely of places for a Republican to be campaigning in the last week before Election Day—takes us over a red-brown countryside. Winter starts earlier here, and though the sun is bright and the air temperature is mild, the fall foliage season, just beginning in the mid-Atlantic, is already almost over here, in the Upper Midwest.

Eau Claire is a town of straight streets, humble hills, and a gently flowing river—orderly, decent, and spectacularly beautiful. We are three hours early for the rally. But the scene as we arrive is compelling.

A long line of Trump supporters has already formed outside the Zorn Arena an hour before the doors open. And across the street, separated from the Trump line by police barriers, are about 200 anti-Trump demonstrators, mostly students. They shout and chant at us as our bus arrives—as Trump fans cheer us whenever we are in Trump's motorcade. We are just journalists, folks.

I decide to take photos of the best signs. "The pussy grabs back Nov. 8," one says. Another sign defends Islam: "Stand with Islam: I'm With Her," it reads, referring to Hillary Clinton.

Various posters declare Trump to be a racist, a misogynist, and a homophobe. One poster is a bit racist, itself: "Even white people are sick of white people's bullshit." One accuses Trump of "homophobia"—an odd charge, given Trump's open embrace of gay Republicans.

One young woman has a cryptic, yet vaguely amusing, sign: "Trump deletes tweets." I ask her what it means. She tells me he has a record of trying to erase his most controversial online statements—which is true.

She adds that she meant the slogan as a counterweight to the charge that Hillary Clinton deleted her email. Well and good. She poses for a photograph, which I post to Twitter, as she looks on. I thank her and move along to other photos and interviews.

About half an hour later, she runs into me and asks me to delete the tweet. She realizes the irony, she says, and she's studying journalism, but she's afraid that having that photograph on the internet could hurt her job prospects. I consider the request, but ultimately decide against it.

Meanwhile, shouting matches break out between the protesters and the Trump fans. Some of the protesters' chants seem counterproductive: "Make America Native Again!" is one such.

I speak to a few of the Trump fans. Some have driven several hours from Minnesota to be at the rally. They laugh at the protesters. One woman, a self-described housewife who is proud to tell me she has eleven children, says of the demonstrators, "They don't look too bad. I don't think Hillary paid these ones." She points out that some of the signs are misspelled. A quick look confirms it: someone is holding up a sign accusing Trump of "rasism." On a college campus.

I realize I have devoted most of my attention to the crowd at the protest and very little to the line that has grown over the past hour and a half. I start walking; the line seems never-ending. Two pedicabs appear, and one of the drivers is happy to take me the full length of the line for free. We start at the end and come back to the entrance of the arena. It takes us nearly four-and-a-half minutes, and we cover nearly half a mile. Thousands of people are waiting, patiently.

The last time I saw similar lines was in New Hampshire, in late October 2008, when Governor Sarah Palin was due to speak at a local school. People seemed to be willing to stand in line for miles just for the chance to see her.

She represented something new in American politics: a real person; an outsider mocked by the establishment; a working-class hero who matched career and family and beauty besides. It was love—in a failing cause.

A reminder that crowds don't vote.

But they do make a lot of noise, and the cheers inside the arena are rocking the rafters. It's a star-studded lineup of speakers for such a small venue—capacity, 3,500—former New York mayor Rudy Giuliani; embattled Senator Ron Johnson of Wisconsin; Republican National Committee chair Reince Priebus; Wisconsin Governor Scott Walker; and, yes, Indiana basketball coach Bobby Knight. The only major Wisconsin figure missing is the Speaker of the House, Paul Ryan.

Ryan remains one of the stars of the Republican Party and the conservative movement. But he made a strategic miscalculation that continues to cost him politically. He was a Tea Party hero for standing up to the president directly over the issue of shoddy accounting in Obamacare. He was hailed as a conservative's dream pick when Mitt Romney chose him as his running mate in 2012.

But the loss in that election—which he expected to win—seemed to have affected him. When he returned to Washington in 2013, Ryan felt that the staunch opposition of the previous two years was futile, and he was determined to show that conservatives could govern.

To that end, he sought compromises—on immigration, on budget issues, and on the national debt. And each time, he was burned. Democrats continued to attack him for his entitlement reform proposals and accused him of racism for discussing cultural factors that contribute to inner city poverty.

Meanwhile, he lost the trust of conservatives who wanted him to lead opposition to Obama, not to find common ground. That hostility could not stop him from becoming Speaker, but it greatly complicated his task.

Trump's candidacy presented a new dilemma. Endorsing Trump meant possibly alienating the minority voters that Ryan had worked hard to cultivate. Rejecting him meant alienating the voters who saw Trump as the answer—and dividing the Republican Party.

Twice, Ryan appeared to undercut Trump. The first time was before the Republican National Convention, when Ryan declared he was not yet ready to endorse Trump even though he had promised to back the party's nominee. The second was in early October, after the *Access Hollywood* tape. Ryan called off a "unity" rally scheduled for Wisconsin the next day. Just as that crisis was subsiding, Ryan fueled it again by freeing his caucus not to back the nominee in a widely publicized conference call with House Republicans.

That was the moment Trump declared himself to be "unshackled," free from the constraints of the party leadership, with whom he had been doing an uncomfortable dance for months. "The shackles have been taken off me," he said, mocking Ryan as "weak" and "ineffective."

Trump did not declare total war on the party; he was careful to praise Republican National Committee (RNC) chair Priebus, and sacked a Virginia activist who had organized a protest against the RNC. But he made it clear that now he would run his way.

Yet the Trump onstage in Eau Claire is remarkably disciplined. He jokes and ad-libs, he plays to the crowd and revels in the chanting and the applause, but he mostly sticks to his stump speech.

The one exception: he appeals to Democrats in Wisconsin who have already voted early to change their votes, reminding them that it is legal to do so in the state. He closes, as he always does now, with an appeal to the "dreamers"—a word he has taken back from the Left.

We rush out to the waiting bus and roll through the now-darkened streets of Eau Claire with the motorcade. Hundreds of people are waiting at the airport to cheer Trump as he arrives to board his plane. They cheer the journalists, as well.

Trump may be right: this is a movement, and perhaps an extraordinary one. There is something that has awakened in the country. But what, exactly? And is it enough to defeat the Clinton machine? I refuse to suspend disbelief.

November 2, 2016

We arrive in Miami after midnight and check into our hotel on South Beach at 12:45 a.m. After a hard day of work, I am thrilled to be on South Beach, a place I visited often as a teenager in the 1990s, when the area was just becoming legendary.

I am tired, but I have to head outside. I find an automated bicycle rack and rent a bike for an hour. Some of the clubs are still going strong. I have an orange juice at the News Café, in honor of the late Gianni Versace: it was his last drink.

The next morning, it is still dark at 7:00 a.m. I file a story and send out the day's assignments to my California team, then head out for a run. The stiff breeze that was blowing the night before is just as strong as ever, the blue-green ocean choppy and restless. I dive in and swim through a few waves, dunking my head and letting the ocean wash away the fatigue of the campaign trail. I head back to the hotel, change, apply some bug spray—to avoid the mosquito-borne Zika virus—and board the bus.

The Miami rally is the first of four that Trump will hold in Florida over the course of twenty-four hours. From "expanding the map" over the past three days, he is now returning to "battleground" mode, and will focus on Florida and the other most hotly contested state, North Carolina.

The morning news shows highlighted Hillary Clinton's rally here the day before, which drew a large crowd and featured former Miss Universe Alicia Machado, who complained that Trump "called me names."

Trump's own rally is scheduled to start at noon. It is a sweltering hot day, well into the eighties, and the fans at the Bayfront Park Amphitheater are using campaign signs to provide themselves some shade.

This is a diverse bunch: there are more than the usual number of blacks, Hispanics, and Orthodox Jews among the predominantly white crowd. I talk to a Haitian-American couple who are here because they are furious about the Clintons' long record of corrupt dealings in Haiti.

I spot a young woman in a "Feel the Bern" hat—not a particularly common sight—and ask her why she is at the rally.

"I should be the last person to vote for Donald Trump," she tells me. "I'm a legal immigrant, I'm female, I'm Hispanic, I'm a Bernie supporter. The way that I see it is that Bernie was running for the people, and so is Trump. They're populists. That resonates with me. Trump and Bernie care about people, instead of enriching themselves and their donors."

At the Democratic National Convention in Philadelphia in July, I spent a lot of time interviewing Bernie Sanders supporters. After he folded his tent and endorsed Hillary, some said they might support Trump, while others preferred Green Party candidate Jill Stein. Polls indicated that most had come home to Hillary—partisan identity was decisive, or they had more in common with Clinton than they did with Trump. But this young woman has remained anti-Clinton.

Trump arrives onstage after a few introductory speeches, and he is in his usual fine form. He begins by name-checking all the "ethnic" signs in the audience: "Blacks for Trump!" "Hispanics for Trump!"

There is a real political value to that, because it builds the sense among supporters that they are part of something large and diverse. And because each of these groups is small, their presence will probably go unnoticed by the press unless he specifically points them out.

The speech is the usual stump, modified for local industries, local incidents, and local details. He adds some "breaking news": the Justice Department official who is to oversee the Clinton email inquiry is not only a close associate of Clinton campaign chairman John Podesta—which was known—but also, according to WikiLeaks, actually tipped the campaign off to the fact that questions about the emails might come up at a congressional hearing. More evidence that the "system is rigged."

We are soon whisked away through a back tunnel, where the Secret Service is guarding the press bus and the motorcade. A voice calls out, "Hey, Cubbies."

It's Stephen K. Bannon, executive chairman of Breitbart, on leave. We shake hands and exchange greetings before I retreat to the tunnel. There are plenty of journalists eager to make a story out of a Breitbart reporter talking to the Trump campaign's CEO in anything other than a professional and arm's-length manner.

Then we are down the tunnel, through a side door, into another tunnel, and onto the bus. We head to the airport in the motorcade, and board the plane quickly.

But there is an announcement before takeoff. Thanks to a story that was written about lax procedures on the campaign planes, the Federal Aviation Administration (FAA) is now cracking down on Trump's campaign flights. It is not clear which story triggered the response, though

NBC's Vaughn Hillyard hurried onto MSNBC's *Rachel Maddow Show* to complain about previous hard landings.[1] Now, cell phones must be off; large electronic devices must be stowed. No more fun.

■ ■ ■

We have a short flight to Orlando, but a long ride to the next rally, at the Central Florida Fairgrounds. We have missed the motorcade, thanks in part to our new, slower takeoff process.

Part of me wonders whether the campaign shut the press out of this particular motorcade to send a message: don't look for opportunities to trash the campaign. Blaming a bad landing in New York on poor campaign management, as Hillyard and Maddow had seemed to do, is out of bounds. Or maybe I am just imagining things.

Regardless, the slow motion of the bus eventually overcomes the adrenaline that usually keeps me going, and I nod off to sleep for about twenty minutes. It's always a dangerous thing to do around this bunch of reporters. My nightmare is someone snapping a photo or shooting a video of me sleeping, perhaps snoring. As a conservative and a critic of the media, I cannot let down my guard.

We eventually arrive at the fairgrounds. The arena is an odd one—a stage, a high rise of bleachers behind it, another small set of bleachers off to the side, and an endless open space.

I notice a stunning woman in a beautiful dress going through security. She turns out to be Manasvi Mamgai, a former Miss India who is also a Bollywood actress. She is a voice for Trump in India, working with an American organization called the Republican Hindu Coalition.

There are a number of other versions of "group X for Trump" in Orlando. There are many more "Hispanics for Trump" signs than I have seen anywhere else.

One woman tells me that she supports Trump because she supports "freedom of any kind." She adds, "I'm a born Cuban and I know what the Left can do to you and your country. I hope that people understand that."

On the far side of the crowd is a homemade "Gays for Trump" sign, black marker on fluorescent green.

The gay issue is an emotive one. Earlier this year, an Islamic terrorist whose father immigrated to the United States from Afghanistan murdered nearly fifty people at Pulse, a gay nightclub in Orlando. During the attack, he called police and pledged allegiance to the leader of the Islamic State terror group—a fact that was concealed from the public by the Obama administration for as long as possible. Hillary Clinton tried to make the issue about gun control and denied that "radical Islam" was involved.

Trump addresses the Orlando attack, calling it the "worst attack on the LGBTQ community in our country's history": "Can't let it happen, can't let it happen. Hillary wants to increase by 550% Syrian refugees pouring into our country. [Boos.] Her plan would mean generations of terrorism, radicalism, and extremism spreading in your schools and throughout your communities. When I'm elected president, we will suspend the Syrian refugee program," he says, to loud applause.

"And we will keep radical Islamic terrorists the hell out of your community," he adds. "And we'll build 'safe zones' in Syria. We have to help the people! We're gonna build safe zones—but the Gulf states haven't been doing their thing. And believe me, they have plenty of money. They'll help us, they'll fund it—I'm sure they'll be thrilled."

He also hits the key points of his economic policy, and promises to bring jobs back to Florida—as he has done everywhere on the trail.

A woman, noticing that I am a reporter, grabs my arm. "I'm a woman, and a small business owner," she says, "and we have to put that man in office."

She has the same note of frustration as the women who accosted me in Grand Rapids—that sense of irritation at being ignored, at the conventional wisdom that only a certain kind of woman would support a man like Donald Trump, and that *that* kind of woman is the kind of woman no good woman should ever want to be.

She tells me that the burden of regulations and the cost of insurance are crushing her family business, which is a small manufacturing company producing boxes.

I ask if she believes him when he promises to bring jobs back. "Yes," she says. Her business just needs "a little breathing space" to thrive.

Her daughters, she said, are involved in the business all over the world. She wants to grow her company in the U.S. so that she can bring them back home to work with her.

A young black man is standing nearby. I ask him what motivated him to support Trump. He answers that he has been following Trump's career since before the election. I ask whether Trump's minority outreach efforts have been effective. He is a bit puzzled by the question.

"I don't know. I liked him before that," he says.

Without meaning to be, that answer is a rather devastating critique of my line of inquiry. Can't a black person just like Donald Trump, period?

I look around and see a cross-section of Orlando. A plump, heavily tattooed woman; an older white man in a wheelchair with a "Vietnam veteran" hat; a "soccer mom" type with an Israeli flag cell phone cover.

There are more people to speak with, more photographs to take. But I have ventured far outside the media pen, and if I don't watch what is happening back there, I could be left behind by the motorcade. Sure enough, they have begun to pack up, and so I leave quickly.

We race to the airport, and I type furiously the whole way, hoping to file my story before the flight, where the new rules will not permit me to work as we taxi on the runway.

We arrive on the tarmac and see an enormous array of police motor-cycles parked in rows by the main Trump plane.

Our van heads to the press plane, but the pool photographers head over to the other one: Trump is going to meet the motorcade cops. He spends several minutes with them, then boards.

■ ■ ■

Our flight is again a short one. We arrive in Pensacola as the sun is setting above the pristine white beaches of the barrier islands.

This is a special place to me; my wife was stationed here during her Navy training, and I visited her several times as I set up our new home in California. On one of those visits, our first child, our daughter Maya, was conceived. We gave her that name, which means "water" in Aramaic, in honor of the Navy and the conditions of her creation.

The motorcade roars past familiar landmarks, through the downtown, and along the Pensacola Bay until we arrive at the Maritime Park's Hunter Amphitheater, an ornate stage at the water's edge at the foot of a broad, sloping hill.

The sun has just set, and the twilight glows behind an audience of thousands of people—families, students, old people. In the back a buxom pair of local beauties in tight-fitting "Veterans for Trump" t-shirts sell gear and sign up volunteers.

The far western panhandle of Florida is naturally conservative. It is bordered to the north and west by Alabama; culturally, at least, it is Alabama. The University of Alabama's football team probably has more fans here than the University of Florida's.

Andrew Breitbart, who attended college at nearby Tulane University in New Orleans, used to call Pensacola the "redneck Riviera"—the place where working-class white southerners would go for vacation, if they had one.

I approach a mother who is cradling a newborn in a baby carrier, with other children hopping about. I introduce myself and begin asking questions: Why does she support Trump? She looks at me quizzically. "'Cause we're not idiots," she says.

Her father puts it a bit more clearly: "It's a simple decision: Do we want an honest president, or another dishonest president?" For all of Trump's fibs, flubs, and flip-flops, Hillary Clinton is still seen as the more dishonest of the two.

There isn't much time to interview other people, as the warm-up speakers keep their remarks brief. One, a pastor, talks passionately about Trump's commitment to faith. It might be a tough sell in a different audience, given the well-known facts about his torrid personal life and the damaging accusations that have emerged over the previous several weeks. Yet she points out that Trump is standing up against the religious persecution of Christians. That earns great trust.

Darkness falls, and the crowd continues to grow. Suddenly, Trump is introduced, and appears onstage in a blaze of pyrotechnic fountains, to the tune of Lee Greenwood's "God Bless the U.S.A." He smiles and waves at the crowd. At first he sounds a bit tired, perhaps a bit slow, off his usual pace. It is, after all, the third rally he has addressed today.

But then he seems to find a rhythm, perhaps a feeling for the audience. And the speech acquires a sense of intimacy.

This has been Trump's appeal as a rally speaker from the start. He doesn't try to weave inspiring phrases together. He doesn't exhort the audience to perform a mission. He invites them into his confidence, tells them what he—the celebrity, the billionaire—is really thinking.

His stump speech has an additional section, detailing how he intends to increase military spending, particularly on the Navy and naval aviation—a winning pitch in this Navy town.

As he wraps up, we pack our computers and cameras and move out silently, waiting backstage, by the motorcade, but close enough to see and hear what happens. I see speechwriter Stephen Miller pacing nervously, frowning in his dark suit and black tie. Steve Bannon strolls along, taking it all in. Near us, a man in a green "pyro crew" t-shirt fiddles with some wires. And half a minute later, as Trump says "Make America Great Again," the fireworks erupt over the bay.

We pause to take it all in, then head back to the plane. We check the score in the baseball game: Game Seven of the World Series is tonight, and the Cubs are out to an early 1–0 lead. I am still wearing my Cubs hat, as I have all week, even when the team dropped two straight and fell behind, three games to one. The Cubs fans on the plane gravitate to where I am sitting. We watch as much of the game as we can until we take off. The Cleveland Indians even it, 1–1.

In the air, with a weak internet signal, I watch the Cubs' official Twitter account. First they regain a 3–1 lead. Then 4–1, and then 5–1. And suddenly, a team that looked like it was certain to lose the World Series, that had come so close to the finish only to be denied, was about to pull off one of the most spectacular comebacks in sports history, in one of the biggest games played since baseball had been invented.

Later, the Indians catch up, tying the game in the eighth, sending the game into extra innings. And then the Cubs pull themselves together, and take a two-run lead. The Indians never give up, scoring a run in the bottom of the tenth before the Cubs finally seal the deal and break the curse.

An analogy? The thought has begun to cross my mind.

CHAPTER SEVEN

"When Did You Become a Republican?" From the Birth of the Parties to Trump's Primary Victories

Larry Schweikart

As Trump was blasting from campaign stop to campaign stop with Joel and the rest of the press in tow during the last weeks of the general election, it's critical to remember Megyn Kelly's snarky question to Trump back in the first GOP debate: "When did you become a Republican?" Imbedded in that question was the implication that Trump did not share Republican values or virtues and that all the other candidates on stage did. But just what was Trump supposed to be representing? The #NeverTrump intellectuals and pundits claimed to represent "conservatism." Trump didn't. He wasn't "Republican" enough. Did that mean Trump was, as they feared, about to start a new third party? On the contrary, Kelly's question indicated that neither she nor many of the so-called experts really understood what Republicanism was all about, where the parties came from, or how they got here. In fact Trump harkened back to the party of Abraham Lincoln and before him, the Federalists, in wanting individual liberty, national strength, economic

*growth, and the sanctity of laws. The jump from Joel's campaign press
plane to the 1820s is not so far after all.*

Is Donald Trump inaugurating the third "party system" in American history? Only future events can confirm whether historians will point to the 2016 election as a decisive turning point for our political parties. The signs are that Donald Trump, more out of necessity than deliberate planning, is at least disrupting the regime that has dominated American politics in one form or another since Martin Van Buren created the Democratic Party to elect Andrew Jackson in 1828. (That was the second "party system" in America; the first was Republicans vs. Federalists, beginning in the late years of George Washington's administration.) While Trump's campaign did use some familiar political methods, Trump also pioneered novel tactics for getting his campaign noticed and mobilizing supporters. He knew he had to, because from the outset he was operating out of a fundamental understanding that he was unlikely to be fully embraced by either major party. Wisely, he decided to avoid a doomed third party run like Ross Perot's and instead to create essentially a "party within a party" as a Republican. Realizing that he would be denied the enthusiastic and energetic support of the GOP machine, Trump began to construct a completely separate strategy for winning the primaries.

A Party Created to Protect Slavery
(Hint: It's Not the GOP)

A full understanding of the magnitude of what Trump did requires a little history. When Martin Van Buren created the Democrat Party in 1825 to elect Andrew Jackson president, he introduced a revolution in how political candidates were selected, presented to the American public, and eventually elected. His second American party system was, in his mind, a way to prevent the all-encompassing issue of slavery from producing disunion and, ultimately, civil war. (Of course it failed to prevent a war. Indeed, the self-contradictory structures and mechanisms by which Van Buren's party system operated *all but guaranteed a war* over slavery in the long run.)

The event that inspired Van Buren's design was the passage of the Missouri Compromise in 1820. He feared the prospect that new free soil states carved out of the Louisiana Territory could put their electoral power behind the abolition of slavery, causing slave states to break up the Union. Van Buren's solution was to change the nature of the people holding office, rather than the laws. Under his new Democratic Party structure, members would tacitly agree not to raise slavery as a political issue. But how could the party make anti-slavery members from the North comply with this tacit party rule? Van Buren's answer was a bribe. He greatly expanded the "spoils system" to use political and government jobs as carrots to reward compliant party members. Through an organizational structure of states, counties, districts, wards, and precincts, Jacksonian operatives would turn out the vote, and based on their loyalty and success, be rewarded with a better (often paying) party job, or even jobs in government. The higher up the ladder one went, the larger the political plums.

By stacking the government, including the House and Senate, with party loyalists who would refuse to address the slavery issue, Van Buren had one major component of his scheme to keep the Union together (at the expense of addressing slavery) in place. There were three others: The states had to remain powerful while the federal government was kept weak. The presidency had to remain in the hands of someone favorable to slavery, or at least someone who would acquiesce to it. That meant a "Northern man of Southern principles" or a westerner. (Van Buren had divined that, as the slavery issue increasingly caused the South and the North to grow apart, no one from the slaveholding South could again be president. And in fact, no *true* southerner—a Texan or a Tennessean was counted as a westerner in the nineteenth century—would be elected president again until Jimmy Carter.) Last, a system of propaganda in the form of highly partisan newspapers under tight party control was set up to get the candidates' issues out and to enhance their name recognition. Despite the vicissitudes of history—the emergence of the Whigs as opposition to the

Democrats and their eventual replacement by the Republican Party, a bloody Civil War, civil service reform—the broad outlines of Van Buren's second party system still exist. It is no exaggeration to say that today's modern media is a complete throwback to the days of slavery when the "partisan press" existed solely for the purpose of electing Democrats.

The Frankenstein into which Van Buren had breathed life would quickly grow out of his control, mainly because of the galloping expansion of the spoils system. Government grew with every election, and it grew even faster when a competitor party to the Democrats, the Whigs, arrived in 1832. They, too, had to campaign on the basis of giving away jobs, and the spoils wheels spun even faster. In the meantime, beginning with Andrew Jackson, presidents began to act independently of both the Congress and the courts—Jackson issued more vetoes than all his predecessors put together, and John Tyler annexed Texas on a mere joint resolution of Congress, not a two-thirds senate vote. Van Buren's system did succeed in keeping a "Northern man of Southern principles" or a westerner in the White House...for a while. But then in 1860 came Abraham Lincoln, a Northern man of Northern principles. Suddenly the South realized what terrific power had been acquired by the presidency since 1828, but it was too late to reclaim it. So Southerners opted for secession and war.

The Civil War did not eliminate the spoils system—quite the contrary, it only made it worse by adding tens of thousands of veterans to the rolls of those receiving government benefits through the efforts of the Grand Army of the Republic, a veterans' lobbying group. Matters got so bad that by the time Grover Cleveland became president in 1885, the number of veterans receiving benefits was still growing, even though logically the Civil War veterans should have been dying out!

Not much about the second American party system changed in the twentieth century, with the Republican Party firmly ensconced as the opposition party to the Democrats. Although handing out jobs as political rewards was more difficult after the Pendleton Act for civil service reform, candidates could now promise jobs and benefits to entire sectors and regions of the country, and the government grew even more rapidly.

And up to the time of the 2016 election, the structure of the parties had scarcely changed. They were still hierarchical, based on states, districts, wards, and precincts; they still promoted loyalists who got the job done at a lower level to a higher position; and they still largely controlled the political activities within a state. The parties' power was considered so great that it was often (mistakenly) thought that merely having a governor of one party in place assured that the presidential candidate of that party would win the state in the general election. Controlling access to membership lists—and more important, money—the parties made it difficult if not impossible for an outsider to make inroads into even congressional and senate elections, let alone presidential elections. The "party system" was succeeding just as Martin Van Buren had planned nearly two hundred years before. It perpetuated a venal and corrupt political establishment, more interested in their own positions, rewards, and prestige than in any principle. It kept issues that were critical to the health of the nation off the table indefinitely—and political power out of the hands of the people.

Enter Donald J. Trump.

Trump instinctively knew he would not be welcome as a candidate in the mainstream of the Republican Party, which, by 2015, had degenerated into a shadow, me-too version of the Democrats. (The Republicans had an eerie resemblance to the very Whig Party they had replaced in 1855 because the Whigs had become a me-too party to the Democrats.) Nevertheless, by running as a Republican in the Republican primary—with the constant threat that he might leave and mount a third party run—Trump effectively forced the Republicans to treat him as a "normal" candidate, at least nominally. Still, he knew that he could not expect immediate help from the governors, some of whom (Walker in Wisconsin, Jindal in Louisiana, former governor Pataki in New York, Christie in New Jersey, and Kasich in Ohio) would themselves be running for the office. (As it turned out, he received almost no help at all from Ohio's Kasich, even in the general election, so petty and vindictive was the "son of a mailman.") Even if he became the nominee, many would harbor grudges and be likely to obstruct any official attempts to enlist their assistance. As it happened, a few state-level GOP officials even attempted (unsuccessfully) to deny Trump a position on the primary ballots. Trump found he got little institutional party support in staging rallies, promoting events, or fundraising. In many ways, that was a blessing, for it unshackled him from the party system nearly altogether and further contributed to the inability of the press to understand him and his methods.

Unshackled

But in the end, Trump's independence from the Republican Party establishment proved an advantage. Using Eventbrite, an event-staging website that provided online access to tickets, Trump's campaign began laying out a series of rallies—ostensibly public, but, because controlled by Eventbrite access, essentially private. Moreover, because Trump rented the facilities himself, he could make them private functions, even with 15,000 people present (as he did in Lowell, Massachusetts, in January 2016). Trump embarked on a number of these large rallies, beginning with his initial speech in Phoenix on July 11, 2015, but then increasing to giant venues such as the Dallas rally at the American Airlines Center in September when he had close to 20,000 people in the arena. The "rally" approach gave Trump mass audiences, before which he could practice standard campaign talking points, yet at the same time engage in truly improvisational exchanges with the audiences. While each speech included the basic promises to close the border, be tough on Islamic immigration, and make better deals with China and other trading partners, they differed enough to invoke the aura of a "live concert" in which Trump would veer off into gun control, attacks on Hillary, frequent jabs at the media ("they're so dishonest"), and other extemporaneous comments.[1]

In these events, Trump deliberately stayed away from specific plans or details, not even quoting the specifics he had already laid out on his own website. This was a calculated move, predicated on the notion that such "ten-point plans" were part of what had gotten America into trouble.

Candidates always had detailed plans—which were almost immediately ditched with the first hearing or vote in Congress. Instead, Trump instinctively copied Ronald Reagan, who had focused on only two large issues in his brilliantly successful 1980 campaign: reviving the economy and reestablishing our national defense. Reagan never delved into the details (as Trump opponents Chris Christie and Marco Rubio did) about how many aircraft carrier groups should be added or what the specific strategy to deal with ISIS should be. ("Why tell them our plans?" he repeatedly asked. "I want to be unpredictable.") Reagan had learned from almost a decade of doing speeches and talks on General Electric shop floors to speak everyday English and to connect on just two or three big points. The Gipper kept things in generalities, painting a vision of the bigger picture—as did The Donald.

Of course critics found this maddening, insisting that he had no plan and no strategy, and that being unpredictable was dangerous. The fact is that *no* candidate can predict his or her specific plan even after being sworn in. Trump's frequently expressed desire to "bomb the crap" out of ISIS resonated with enough people that knew his intention: destroy the enemy, by whatever means necessary.

Trump's dramatic reshaping of the established American party system and its pecking order of entitled goodies went well beyond merely using the internet and Twitter as his main source of "new media" communication, and even beyond the private rally approach. As a celebrity, he was already reaching Americans who in other circumstances might not have been likely voters. By January 2016, some insiders had begun to discern Trump's appeal—and his threat to the existing regime. In *Politico* (which talk show king Rush Limbaugh maintained was the favored organ for the GOP establishment's leaks), Scott Bland wrote about "Donald Trump's Big Tent." Bland reported that "a *Politico* review of private and public polling data and interviews with GOP pollsters shows a coalition that certainly begins with conservative, blue-collar men [but which now] extends to pro-choice Republicans, independents and even registered Democrats unnerved, primarily, by illegal immigration." Polls taken by Overtime Politics in Missouri and Florida in early

January showed that Trump was winning the income categories of $45,000–64,000 and above $65,000—a good proxy for "college educated." This kind of news grated on Republican insiders, consultants, and pollsters such as Adrian Gray and Guy Benson, who assured themselves that Trump's appeal was only to the ill-informed and uneducated (by which they meant stupid).[2]

Probably without intending to, Trump had carved out a party within a party from the existing GOP—a new party that crossed all demographics (he was winning the highest percentage of women and blacks in the aforementioned surveys, and trailed only Rubio among Hispanics). And yet, surprisingly to many—especially the keepers of official conservatism such as the pundits at NRO and many supposedly conservative talk-show hosts—Trump continued to lead among those labeling themselves "conservative" and only slightly trailed Ted Cruz among those calling themselves "very conservative." Added together, the two "conservative" demos gave Trump a large lead. He had stolen the GOP's most loyal voters from under their noses.

More important, he appealed to Democrats. A shocking survey of likely voters by Mercury Analytics in early January 2016, using a "dial test" reaction to Trump's first major campaign ad, found that 20 percent of Democrat voters said they could vote for him. Even worse for the Democrats, of those who threatened to cross over, a high percentage of them said they were 100 percent sure of switching.[3]

Stop Trump!

Just before the Iowa caucuses, the flagship of the old line conservative media publications dedicated its entire January 21 issue to stopping the New Yorker. The "Against Trump" issue of *National Review* was written by more than a dozen leading conservatives including economist Thomas Sowell (who would go on to advise a reluctant vote for Trump in the general election) and talk-show host (and Cruz donor-supporter) Glenn Beck (who would remain #NeverTrump to the end). Each one took Trump to task on a different issue or along different lines. Never in

American political history had a leading publication outright rejected the leading figure of its own party. Even at the height of dissatisfaction with Lyndon Johnson, there was nothing comparable: venerable left-wing publications didn't ditch him for Eugene McCarthy or Bobby Kennedy. The *National Review* firing squad was a sign of how incredibly desperate the establishment Republicans had become—and how close they were to irrelevance. Another was how the elites were increasingly willing to align themselves with a man they hated almost as much—Ted Cruz. Until Trump was a serious threat to win the Republican nomination, few had ever praised Cruz—their support had much more frequently been directed at Rubio. As the actual voting began, they were hoping against hope that the polls were wrong.

The first test would be in Iowa on February 1, and Trump seemed to be doing well there. But Emerson College's poll, unlike all others, showed Cruz with a victory there. Iowa is historically an outlier. Very few winners of the Iowa caucus have won the Republican nomination, although Obama won the Democrat caucus and the nomination in 2008. Part of the difficulty with Iowa's caucus system is that partisans gather in large halls or churches or schools and supporters of the candidates are invited to make brief speeches. In many of these, no Trump advocates had been lined up, and the media stigmatizing of Trump—especially among conservatives—worked to dampen down public expressions of support for him. It is a much different setting from a traditional secret primary vote. Cruz's vaunted "ground game" had callers and door-knockers getting out his supporters, and there were speakers for him in every location. The previous week, Trump had won the endorsement of conservative darling and former vice presidential nominee Sarah Palin, who spoke at Trump rallies in Iowa, but it was widely agreed that he had not spent the time or the effort recruiting the ground troops necessary to carry the caucuses. Moreover, the Iowa caucus system, with its small gatherings and process of having a person speak to the little crowds on behalf of each candidate, did not play to Trump's strength. At some locations, he had no one to speak for him, because no one had been recruited.

Even so, on election day, Trump turned out an astounding 38,500 Iowa voters, almost 9,000 more than Rick Santorum had won with four years earlier. But Cruz was supported by a whopping 45,000, shocking the pundits. (Significantly, Republican turnout across the board had spiked from four years earlier.) Equally important, Marco Rubio, who had flopped up to that point, managed to grab an impressive third place. It was a sobering moment for Trump. Observers on his plane afterward described him as contemplative. After immediately congratulating Cruz and then noting that he hadn't taken Iowa seriously enough, Trump promised to work harder in New Hampshire—and noted that he had walked out of Iowa with as many delegates as Cruz.

And he did work harder. After Iowa, Trump became the Energizer bunny. No candidate in either party would work as hard as he did, make more stops, or campaign with nearly as much energy. He left Jeb ("Low Energy") Bush in the dust, and later it would be argued that his relentless series of campaign appearances was bringing on bouts of ill health for Hillary Clinton as she tried to match his pace.[4] No one could. Trump neither smoked nor drank, and seemed to require no sleep at all—in the tradition of Thomas Edison or Napoleon Bonaparte. Iowa merely inspired Trump to work even harder.

Sweet victory for Cruz was short-lived and badly tainted. Early on Iowa caucus night, CNN had broken a story that Ben Carson was returning to Florida, intimating that he was quitting the campaign. Cruz and his people immediately began approaching voters with the news, urging them to change their votes to Cruz if they had planned to vote for Carson. They even re-circulated the CNN tweet, even after Carson denied the news. This perceived "dirty trick" came on the heels of an official-looking mailer from the Cruz campaign publicly shaming Iowans for not voting in previous elections. The dirty tricks tarnished Cruz's night and damaged his reputation as the "Christian conservative" candidate. Cruz, with his dependence on church support and morality, could not just shrug off the shenanigans as politics as usual. The scandal, combined with the establishment's giddiness over Rubio's third-place finish, diminished Cruz's impressive Iowa achievement. And, predictably, the next day, Trump was on the warpath about campaign violations, suggesting that Cruz's actions were "illegal"—and even that his victory should be invalidated by Iowa officials. It wasn't a serious suggestion, of course, but that wasn't the point: less than twenty-four hours after a defeat, Trump had reclaimed the news cycle.

The Ringmaster

By that time, several major themes of the 2016 campaign were becoming clear.

First, Trump was simply no ordinary candidate, and anyone— political opponent or media outlet—treating him as such would meet only with frustration.

Second, Trump understood the news cycle better than anyone in politics, including Obama. He knew how to keep his name in the news, and others' names out. Having talk show hosts talking about Trump, even negatively, meant that they weren't talking about Rubio or Cruz or Kasich. And in a primary season, especially one with more than a dozen candidates, it was essential to attract attention.

Third, Trump understood that traditional campaigns were going the way of the dodo. In the age of the smartphone, phone banks at campaign offices would be less effective than in previous years, and social media would be more powerful than ever. Twitter, a non-factor in Obama's 2008 campaign, had become a major outlet for making and breaking news. Armies of Facebook "friends" meant Trump supporters could reach acquaintances with Trump-friendly news on a personal level, bypassing the gatekeepers in the antagonistic media.

Finally, there were the rallies, which could now be organized in days, not weeks or months. They not only energized supporters and (when the media dared show the crowds) demonstrated Trump's popularity, but also allowed the campaign free penetration into local markets with brief but unfiltered coverage of the events. Trump had brilliantly positioned himself as a ringmaster.

But there was another monumental issue at play in the Iowa caucuses that would have a crucial role in the 2016 election. The media had ignored the pathetic performance of the pollsters in Iowa. In that case, their failures worked against Trump. He had led in all but one or two Iowa polls. Now all of Trump's stunning and continued high poll numbers had to be reevaluated. Polls in New Hampshire, just eight days away, showed him with a solid lead. But Trump was concerned. He met with former Massachusetts Republican Senator Scott Brown, who had scored an incredible coup in 2009 by winning Ted Kennedy's seat in a special election in a stinging rebuke to Obama's policies. He was the first Republican senator from Massachusetts since Edward Brooke (1967–79), and he obviously knew how to campaign in the Northeast. Brown bluntly told The Donald that he needed to beef up his ground game, spending money and engaging callers and door-knockers, and Trump listened. Brown even offered to take on the job of setting up Trump's call centers. ("We had the call centers humming," he cheerfully observed.)

But the fact is that the polls may simply not have captured all the dynamics in Iowa. Some of the blame for Trump's failure can be laid on his decision to skip the final debate the weekend before the caucus. Trump's feud with debate host Fox News and its anchor Megyn Kelly (who had been remarkably rude to Trump in the very first debate) had flared up, and he had tried to strong-arm Fox into removing her as a moderator. Roger Ailes, the head of Fox News, refused. Kelly would stay. (Ironically, Ailes himself would soon be out after charges by Gretchen Carlson and other Fox anchorettes alleging that the Fox executive had sexually harassed them.) Trump pulled out of the debate and held a competing event, raising $6 million for veterans just down the street. (While Fox had good ratings for the Trump-less debate, it didn't match viewership of its earlier event including him.) Many concluded that his absence had hurt him with Iowa voters.

New Hampshire Picks Nominees

Unlike Iowa, which has a poor track record when it comes to choosing the party's nominee, New Hampshire tends to be much more in sync with voters' final selection, and Trump did not miss the debate prior to the New Hampshire vote. That debate proved uneventful for him—but not for Rubio. Early in the evening's questioning, Governor Chris Christie lit into the Floridian, who in turn launched an attack on Barack Obama, saying Obama was not just incompetent but had deliberately directed American decline. At that point Christie (who in 2012 during the Hurricane Sandy relief effort had been pictured with his arm around Obama on a New Jersey beach) challenged Rubio—who strangely repeated his previous statement almost verbatim. He then did the same thing two more times that night, leading Christie to accuse him of being robotic and programmed. The charges stuck. Talk show hosts and Fox news played the clips incessantly. Rubio, coming off his Iowa surge, would fail in New Hampshire on Tuesday night, while Trump emerged unscathed.

Later, many accused Christie of being a set-up man for Trump, of engaging in some sort of corrupt bargain. And in fact the New Jersey governor would soon drop out and become a Trump supporter, although after Trump won the election, Christie would be cut loose on account of charges that he had stacked the Trump transition team with lobbyists.

As the New Hampshire votes came in, the anti-Trump bloggers were noticeably silent, indicating the news for Trump was good. Indeed, it was better than good. Trump walked out of New Hampshire not only the winner, and now the leader in delegates (with seventeen to Cruz's ten), but with a record-setting margin of victory. He had received over 100,000 votes, beating the second place finisher, John Kasich, by almost 55,000 votes. Cruz struggled to come in third, and Jeb Bush, written off as dead months ago, managed a fourth place finish. Rubio sank to fifth, raising questions about his viability as a candidate. (Over the next week, talk show host Rush Limbaugh would appear to be working feverishly to resuscitate Rubio's campaign by insisting he was the only one attacking Obama.)

Trump didn't just win in New Hampshire—he won *every single demographic*, including young, old, different income groups, moderates, conservatives, the educated, and the uneducated. Even more stunning, the New Hampshire GOP turned out a record 212,000 voters, beating the total Democrat number by 3,000 in a state Democrats had won in the last three presidential elections. And the polls were wrong again—but this time in the other direction. The RealClearPolitics polling average for Trump was just over thirty-one, but he won the primary with more than 35 percent. Now, Trump had significantly under-polled.

From New Hampshire, the campaigns headed for South Carolina, where Cruz desperately needed a victory in the exceptionally conservative state with its high evangelical constituency. Cruz had some hope of doing well later, on "Super Tuesday" in the so-called "SEC primaries" (in southern states such as Georgia and Alabama), but if Trump won South Carolina and his ultimate victory came to be viewed as inevitable, Cruz's support would possibly dissipate. The GOPe elites were also desperate. They had positioned Rubio as their roadblock to Trump after Iowa, only to have Christie pull the rug out from under him. Everyone knew that Jeb had no real chance. But Christie and Carly Fiorina dropped out after New Hampshire (Mike Huckabee and Rick Santorum had pulled out after Iowa, as had Rand Paul). That left Trump facing a wounded Rubio, a lackluster Jeb, a fading Carson (who insisted he had not left the race and was in it to the end), Kasich (who had no hope of winning any of the southern primaries), and Cruz, whom the Republican establishment hated and feared almost as much as Trump, and who in any case seemed too weak a candidate to stop their nemesis. Two weeks out, South Carolina polling averages had Trump up by an average of sixteen points over Cruz, with Rubio in third.

A Palmetto Stiletto

A South Carolina debate was scheduled for one week from the primary, on February 13. Having skipped the Iowa debate, Trump was under pressure to attend. According to the GOPe pundits, he had to do well. That afternoon, however, Justice Antonin Scalia, considered the most conservative jurist on the Supreme Court, died in his sleep while on vacation in Texas. Suddenly the Court itself was open to massive restructuring. A single Obama appointee (which, thankfully, he would not get) could have tilted it far left. After all, even with a so-called "conservative majority," two key cases involving homosexual marriage and Obamacare had gone against conservatives. At the beginning of the debate, when Trump was asked about his thoughts on a replacement, he mentioned two conservative federal judges, Diane Sykes and Bill Pryor.[5] After that, however, Trump and Jeb Bush got into another verbal brawl over whether or not George W. Bush had "kept America safe." Trump reiterated his position that 9/11 had occurred on Bush's watch and that the Iraq War was a mistake. GOPe pundits immediately labeled Trump a "9/11 truther" and claimed he was on the same page with Code Pink, the radical left-wing anti-war group.

Throughout the course of the Palmetto debate, Twitter was aflame with GOPe bloggers convinced Trump had had "a meltdown," that he had crashed. They were ecstatic because he had—they thought—finally crossed the line and offended conservatives who (they believed) still "revered" George W. Bush. That was the term Rush Limbaugh used to describe Bush on his talk show the following Monday. Trump's candidacy was over.

Only it wasn't. Trump's verbal jabs at George W. Bush had been a stiletto in Jeb's side. Over the next week, in poll after poll, Trump's numbers either held rock steady or *increased*. He topped 40 in a national Reuters poll and hit 41 in a Michigan poll. In all but one South Carolina poll he was in the mid-30s, a good fifteen points ahead of either Cruz or Rubio. The experts were mystified.

Limbaugh was the first to pick up on the fact that Trump's "meltdown" was really strategic, that he had in one bold move taken one of the biggest general election issues off the table: the Bush administration. Without a Bush in the race, either Hillary Clinton or Bernie Sanders (who remained close on her heels and who actually won New Hampshire by a huge margin, despite being cheated out of delegates by the "superdelegate" system the Democrats had) would have to run on their own records. And that was a problem. The Palmetto Stiletto had in fact killed two birds with one thrust.

By the Wednesday before the South Carolina primary on Saturday, the glumness was apparent on National Review Online and among the

Twitterbirds. A "secret, internal" Bush campaign poll showed Ted Cruz up by two in South Carolina, and the Hart Polling Firm, using a heavily weighted sample of "very conservative" voters, managed a single national ("shock") poll showing Cruz ahead, but these were discounted, even by the establishment. Increasingly their argument was that Trump still hadn't cracked 50 percent, and therefore that *all* the remaining candidates could beat Trump by coalescing around one alternative to Trump—an absurdly unlikely scenario, and one that assumed that absolutely *no* voters from any of the other candidates would go to Trump. That was clearly not the case, as he continually hit new peaks.

The other meme of the day was that Trump could not beat Hillary—he was not doing well against her in some national polls. (This one proved closer to the truth: the general election was in the end a tight race, and Clinton would win the popular vote.) But before the South Carolina vote, a Quinnipiac Poll appeared that showed Trump beating Clinton by three points (admittedly less than some of the other GOP candidates, but it undercut the "can't win" argument). Moreover, buried in the Quinnipiac poll were interesting tidbits that revealed the appeal Trump had, and why Cruz was struggling so badly against him. A new question asked who would be "most likely to change Washington," and Trump won on that question, four to one. The signal was clear: *none* of the existing candidates on either side could run against Trump as a "change" candidate. Rubio, Cruz, and even Kasich could claim "experience," but Americans were seeking something else.

This explained volumes about the Trump phenomenon, and showed why many of the tactics by his competitors had failed. The over one thousand endorsements Ted Cruz had assembled from political insiders and politicians—no matter how conservative those endorsers were—merely made Cruz look like an "establishment" figure. Contrary to what his team had likely thought, these endorsements were killing him. Likewise, when Rubio received the endorsements of Tim Scott, a South Carolina senator with a conservative voting record, and of former Tea Party favorite governor Nikki Haley, who had used her highly-coveted opportunity to respond to Obama's State of the Union to blast Trump as anti-immigrant, it only made Rubio look like another Washington insider.

On the eve of the South Carolina primary, Pope Francis seemed to question Trump's Christian faith, insisting that people who think about building walls instead of bridges are "not Christian." It was an astounding comment, especially given that the pope had not questioned the faith of *any* dictator on the world stage. Nor did the pope bother to mention that the Vatican itself is protected by rather large walls. But instead of dampening Trump's numbers, the pope's statement had the effect of elevating Trump even further—as was demonstrated by his shocking (to some) victory in the South Carolina primary.

Thinning the Herd Mentality

With South Carolina (and the Nevada caucuses, another big Trump victory), a series of primaries and caucuses began to thin the herd. Rick Santorum, Mike Huckabee, Bobby Jindal, Chris Christie, Rand Paul, and Carly Fiorina all dropped out of the race. The mantra from the GOPe bloggers remained that once the vote consolidated, the opposition to Trump would finally bury him. Opponents insisted that he was opposed by 65 percent of the GOP voters. That was an odd argument for them to make, as it meant—seeing that Trump was in the lead by a substantial margin—that every *other* candidate was opposed by 70 or 80 percent of the GOP voters! It also assumed that those who supported all other candidates were doing so to oppose Trump, not because their desired candidate had anything special to offer. In reality, as candidate after candidate dropped out, Trump continued to win.

On March 1, Super Tuesday, the first real test of Trump's widespread appeal produced a resounding endorsement of his candidacy. He took Massachusetts as expected, and southern states where he had led big in the polls (Alabama, Georgia), but also carried Arkansas (which Cruz had contested) and Virginia, adding them to the states already in his column— New Hampshire, South Carolina, and Nevada. Cruz, meanwhile, pulled off two somewhat shocking upsets in Alaska and Oklahoma, and won his home state of Texas (which he was favored to win and which he had led in for much of February). But Cruz won less than a majority of the vote in Texas—though he did take a majority of the delegates—indicating weakness even in his home state.

And after Super Tuesday a new problem confronted the Never-Trumpers. According to Rule 40(b) of the Republican Convention, for a candidate to have his name even placed in the nomination he has to win the majority of delegates in at least eight states. Even if Trump hadn't won enough delegates to sew up the nomination before the convention, would any other candidate, even Cruz, be able to get to eight states and qualify to challenge him there? Many analysts assumed that if the party thought it necessary to stop Trump, they would waive Rule 40(b).

By March 5, caucuses had occurred in Kansas, Maine, and Kentucky, and there was a primary in Louisiana. Before that point, Cruz had won the Texas and Oklahoma primaries, and Trump all the others, but Cruz had dominated the caucuses. In this round of voting, Trump carried Kentucky and Louisiana, while Cruz won the Kansas and Maine caucuses. (The total number who voted in Maine was dwarfed by the number of voters in a single county in Louisiana. In the March 1 Alaska caucus, Cruz had won by a minuscule 600 votes.) For the most part, Trump was still winning primaries, and Cruz caucuses.

Romney's Errant Bomb

On the morning of March 3, Mitt Romney, the 2012 GOP nominee, had given an unprecedented televised speech in which he encouraged Republicans to vote strategically to defeat Trump: Cruz supporters in Florida should pull the lever for Rubio, who was ahead of Cruz in the polls there, and both of those candidates' supporters in Ohio should vote for Kasich. For the former GOP nominee to announce his opposition to the front-runner in the Republican primaries was beyond unheard of. It bordered on party suicide. And Romney's aim proved as inaccurate as that of the rest of the GOPe and media who kept launching grenades at Trump. Subsequent polling showed that Romney's speech had no real impact on Trump, with 17 percent saying it made them less likely to vote for the New Yorker and 15 percent saying it made them *more* likely to vote for Trump. (On March 15, reporter Sheryl Atkisson wrote about "Eight Trump Enemies Helping Him Succeed"—and Romney wasn't even on the list.)[6]

But immediately after Romney's speech, Trump's opponents thought they had him. In the debate, Trump, flanked by Rubio and Cruz ("a joker" and "a liar," as the New Yorker had once referred to them), was attacked relentlessly on the specifics of his positions. He appeared rattled and often did not have sound responses to the criticism. Pundits who (yet again) thought Trump had "imploded" wondered why it had taken Cruz and Rubio so long to dig into the specifics of his proposals.

And yet once again, Trump proved the master of the new political media: before the debate had even ended Trump had "won" the debate in polls on the Drudge Report and *Time*—and every other online poll, as Trump's supporters flocked to the online sites to register their view that Trump was the victor. He had discerned Obama's tactic in 2008 and 2012: use social media to "win" a debate in debate polls *regardless* of what happened on stage.

Still, Trump's team sensed some weakness in their candidate. The split decision Cruz victories in Kansas and Maine, combined with shallow margins for Trump in Tennessee and Louisiana—Cruz actually tied the billionaire in Pelican State delegates by the time the voting was over—had given Cruz a number of delegates. With Rubio's collapse, it appeared that the "consolidation" that the GOP elites hoped to see was occurring, behind Cruz.

Anti-Trump brigades ecstatically noted that Cruz was only one hundred delegates behind Trump. And the Texan thought he had momentum. On March 10, though, Trump slapped Cruz back by winning three of four states (Michigan, Hawaii, Mississippi, and losing only Idaho). Those victories left him with over 462 delegates. The Florida and Ohio winner-take-all races were lining up as the last chance to stop a Trump nomination, and he continued to lead in both states, although Ohio was tightening.

Leading up to the March 10 debate, pressure mounted on Marco Rubio to exit the race and throw his support to Cruz. Instead, the media was treated to the announcement that Trump would be rolling out the endorsement of Dr. Ben Carson the following day. Trump had called Carson's admitted violent behavior as a younger man "pathological," but Carson had also been the victim of the infamous Cruz "Carson is dropping out" Twitter campaign in Iowa, and he still held a grudge. Carson's pending endorsement was used by Trump early in the Thursday night debate, in which both Cruz and Rubio were civil and non-combative, much to the consternation of the #NeverTrump pundits. Trump's numbers with Frank Luntz's focus groups were off the charts, in the 80 and 90 percent range for much of the time Trump spoke, and liberal pundit Mark Halperin gave Trump's performance an "A+." By all accounts, no one had laid a glove on The Donald, who many were saying had looked "presidential." Heading into March 15, the second Super Tuesday, Trump had recaptured all his momentum and was just two states—Ohio and Florida—away from the mantle of inevitability.

Black Lives Apparently Don't Matter If Blacks Take Them

Then came a game changer. On March 11, a Trump event in Chicago was violently disrupted by Black Lives Matter and other George Soros-funded left-wing groups. While some police were present, there were not nearly enough to deal with the thugs. Black Lives Matter had surfaced after the police shooting in Ferguson, Missouri, of Michael Brown, who had rushed a policeman in his car. The propaganda among the activist groups was that Brown had had his hands up saying "Don't shoot." (No security camera footage or any witness confirmed any such thing, and in fact the evidence was that the suspect, as the officer claimed, had forced his way inside the police cruiser and was going for the cop's gun.) Black Lives Matter had no interest whatsoever in all "black lives," only in the relatively small number of blacks killed in police shootings that they could turn into anti-cop propaganda.

As word of the violence reached Trump, he canceled his Chicago event out of concern for the safety of the attendees—but there were already hundreds on scene. Black Lives Matter and other radical groups claimed a victory disrupting and even closing down the event, but the really significant development was GOPe media, bloggers, and other candidates blaming Trump for the violence. Ted Cruz, trying to walk a fine line, said "the responsibility for [violence] lies with the protesters.... But in any campaign responsibility starts at the top.... And when you have a campaign that disrespects the voters, when you have a campaign that affirmatively encourages violence...you create an environment that only encourages this sort of nasty discourse."[7] Yet the conservative site *RedState*, just the previous day, had urged far-left protesters to bring guns to Trump rallies![8] On March 12, at a rally at Vandalia airport near Dayton, Ohio, a left-wing radical charged the stage and got within grabbing range of Trump before Secret Service pounced on him and other officers surrounded Trump. The man was let out on bail later that day. (One wonders if an attack on Hillary Clinton would have resulted in such a hasty bail?)

Cruz paid heavily for his comments, losing over 300,000 Facebook "followers" in twenty-four hours and losing the endorsement of some of his key supporters. But while he continued to drift further back behind Trump in Florida and Missouri, he won the Wyoming caucuses (Trump did not even contest Wyoming), and remained alive in Illinois. And although John Kasich had echoed Cruz's criticism suggesting that Trump was the cause of the violence, Kasich seemed undamaged by his comments. Kasich was tying or even leading Trump in some polls on the eve of the second Super Tuesday voting on March 15. The GOP establishment had frantically urged that Rubio or Kasich drop out in order to consolidate the anti-Trump vote, then abruptly shifted to urging Cruz and Rubio voters in Ohio to back the governor. Even "The Terminator," former actor and California governor Arnold Schwarzenegger, publicly campaigned with Kasich. These feeble, and even comical, efforts to deny Trump the first round victory at the convention increasingly smacked of desperation.

Trump Will "Fall Short" of 1,237

March 15 gave Trump's opponents the breathing room they needed. Trump won Illinois, the Marianas, North Carolina, and Missouri (in a squeaker, within the margin that permitted a recount). In Florida, Trump had one of his most impressive victories, beating Marco Rubio by 400,000 votes and winning every county except Miami-Dade. Trump even took non-Cuban Hispanics in Florida. But in Ohio, John Kasich managed a nine-point thumping of Trump. What went largely un-commented upon was the New Yorker's nearly unanimous victory in the eastern counties bordering Pennsylvania—an area where blue collar and fracking workers were dominant. This would prove an important indicator of Trump's strength in neighboring Pennsylvania in November. Still, the failure to gain Ohio's winner-take-all sixty delegates forestalled Trump's "inevitability." Websites such as Nate Silver's *FiveThirtyEight* were projecting that Trump might fall short of 1,237 or that going forward he would have to win an unusually large number of delegates to secure a first-round nomination. After all, they reasoned, many of the remaining states had proportional voting, including Illinois.[9] Still, Ohio was the only primary or caucus Kasich had won, after being embarrassed in neighboring Michigan. Impervious to reality, the Ohio governor boldly proclaimed that he was now the favorite and that others should unite behind him.

Contrary to the delusions of the NeverTrumpers, Kasich's victory didn't change the basic math. Trump had around 750 delegates. Cruz, in second place, had 465, or only 53 percent of the number he needed to win, and Kasich only had 144. Meanwhile, Cruz operatives moved into Louisiana to the state party apparatus to grab several of the delegates that had been awarded to Trump in his victory there. Reports appeared that Cruz and others in the GOP would seek to pry away delegates already won by Trump before the convention. Whether allowed under the rules or not, Cruz's move infuriated Trump supporters and only reinforced the image of Cruz as a "dirty trickster," stealing delegates that were not his. It may have been smart tactics, but it was strategic stupidity.

Sex Bomb #1

By late March, the GOP had gone from supporting anyone who could outright win the nomination to hoping simply to deny Trump the 1,237 delegates he needed to win the nomination on the first ballot at the convention. They were hoping for an "open convention," at which an alternative to Trump might be able to win on a later ballot. Several GOP spokesmen publicly disavowed Rule 40(b). Since only Trump had won majorities in eight states, GOP elites now held that the rule was no longer valid.

Although Cruz was almost 300 delegates behind Trump—and a number of large-delegate, Trump-friendly states were coming up—it nevertheless appeared that he had some momentum. He was within a few points of Trump in a (questionable) Fox poll (Fox's hostility to Trump had begun to infect its polling arm), and supposedly led Trump in Wisconsin, which was a key state. Then the Cruz sex scandal broke.

Just before Easter, on Wednesday, March 23, the infamous *National Enquirer* ran an article "Shocking Claims: Pervy Ted Cruz Caught Cheating—With 5 Secret Mistresses."[10] After waiting two days, Cruz released a statement on Facebook: "I want to be crystal clear; these attacks are garbage. For Donald J. Trump to enlist his friends at the *National Enquirer* and his political henchmen to do his bidding shows you that there is no low Donald won't go. These smears are completely false, they're offensive to Heidi and me, they're offensive to our daughters, and they're offensive to everyone Donald continues to personally attack. Donald Trump's consistently disgraceful behavior is beneath the office we are seeking and we are not going to follow."

Actually, Cruz had led. Just before the Utah primary, the pro-Cruz "Make America Awesome" SuperPAC had run an ad with a picture from a *GQ* modeling shoot by Trump's wife, Melania, showing her semi-nude on a rug with the caption, "Meet Melania Trump. Your Next First Lady." Trump immediately tweeted "Lyin' Ted Cruz just used a picture of Melania from a G. Q. Shoot in his ad. Be careful, Lyin' Ted, or I will spill the beans on your wife!"[11] Cruz attempted to deflect the charge, saying the PAC was out of his control—legally true, but operationally unlikely. No one knew what Trump's threat to "spill the beans" on Heidi meant; it was likely a reference to her time at Goldman Sachs—a touchy point with many conservatives. But regardless of who had "started it," both wives were now campaign issues.

The *Enquirer* sex bomb story touched off a firestorm. The *Enquirer* had gone from being a joke to having some modicum of credibility with the John Edwards affair, which it reported on almost exclusively until the mainstream media could no longer ignore it. Edwards, considered a leading Democrat presidential contender for 2008, was exposed in a 2007 story in the *Enquirer*, and eventually other news outlets picked up the story—which was in fact true.

Now it was Cruz's turn to feel the *Enquirer*'s heat. Nevertheless, after furious denials from several of the women, the *Enquirer* apparently had nothing else, and the Cruz story died.

Meanwhile, Trump's Twitter thread continued to make news, with critics in the conservative media (led by *National Review*, Ben Shapiro, and Guy Benson), firing off a never-ending stream of articles and tweets consisting of little more than re-hashed polls about Trump's purported unfavorability with women. In fact, Trump's unfavorables were almost identical to those of Ronald Reagan in 1980. And, as would be revealed in the general election, women didn't dislike Trump so much after all. As Rush Limbaugh repeatedly warned the NeverTrumpers on his radio show, none of the attacks would have an impact on the loyalty of Trump's supporters; only the candidate himself could separate them from him.

Cruz's "ground game," combined with complete NeverTrumper radio domination in the state, made Wisconsin a stinging defeat for Trump. He lost every demographic. The loss sparked endless new columns proclaiming the end of Trump's campaign, "Trump has peaked" stories, and more phony math showing that he could not reach the magical 1,237 delegates needed to win on the first ballot at the convention.

Indeed, the Wisconsin loss shook Trump, so much so that in the second week of April he demoted campaign manager Corey Lewandowski behind a new hire, veteran political strategist Paul Manafort. Technically, Manafort was brought in to supervise securing existing delegates, but he immediately acted like the man in charge of the campaign, re-focusing Trump on winning all the New York delegates, then directing the campaign in Indiana, West Virginia, and Pennsylvania, while essentially conceding Colorado, with its odd convention-caucus system, to Cruz.[12] (Indeed, some of the names of Trump delegates listed on the brochure given out in Colorado were wrong.) Manafort also made it clear that he intended to wrap up California for Trump.

The introduction of Manafort caused internal strife, initially pitting him against Lewandowski, and any savvy political operative could see that Trump's original manager was not long destined for the campaign world. Yet in the longer term, rather than sending a message that Trump's camp was in turmoil, the shakeup sent just the opposite signal: Trump is in charge and will not hesitate to replace those who do not perform—at *any* level.

"I would take capable over experienced all day long," Trump once said, but clearly he needed an experienced political hand at the wheel. His tiny campaign (only 94 staffers nationwide when he brought in Manafort) was minuscule compared to Hillary Clinton's 765-person staff. Trump had no internal pollsters or speechwriters at that point, either. And even though a battery charge against Lewandowski by a former Breitbart reporter had been thrown out, it was clear that as the campaign entered a new phase he did not have enough clout or political skill to continue as its head.[13]

Within a week it was abundantly clear that Manafort had righted the ship. But neither he nor Trump was taking the Northeast for granted. Trump was campaigning hard in New York, as well as Rhode Island, Connecticut, Pennsylvania, Delaware, and Maryland. Most observers expected him to walk out with ninety delegates and to hit about 50 percent of the vote in each state, although some thought Pennsylvania might be "in play."

First, on April 19, Trump crushed his opponents in New York, winning every district but one and securing eighty-nine delegates and 60 percent of the vote. (Some had thought he would only win seventy-five to eighty delegates there.) Ted Cruz didn't win a single delegate and came in third to John Kasich. Then, on April 26, the Trump sweep stunned even the most cynical and partisan critics. Trump not only won every state, with his lowest percentage of the vote being 54 percent in Maryland, but he also won *every county save one* in Pennsylvania. By late April, Trump stood just a few delegates short of 1,000, and it was clear to any neutral observer that the upcoming votes in California, New Jersey, New Mexico, West Virginia, and Oregon would hand him the nomination.

Even so, Cruz acted like nothing had happened, and indeed doubled down, trying to lure away Trump delegates to vote for him on the second ballot at the convention. Trump had no intention of letting the convention go to a second ballot, but Cruz's efforts looked shady, like he was "stealing" delegates. (He wasn't: he was merely trying to persuade them to vote for him after they were no longer bound to vote for Trump.) After his shellacking by Trump on the Northeast "Super Tuesday," Cruz named Carly Fiorina as his vice-presidential selection. Not only was this a highly unusual move for someone who wasn't the front-runner, but picking a running mate in *April* smacked of desperation. And while technically an "outsider," Fiorina had by that time been damaged by Trump's assaults on her business record and her connections to Pacific trade deals he labeled as job-killing. Fiorina's selection certainly did not help Cruz. But it was beside the point. By that time, only a Cruz victory in Indiana followed by a sweep of Montana, North Dakota, New Mexico, and a large number California districts could deny Trump the nomination. None of those things would happen, and Fiorina, who had lost a Senate race in California despite spending an all-time record amount of money, would not help Cruz in the Golden State. Even as a woman, she hardly softened Cruz's sharp image.

Cruz knew it was over. Word began to leak that Cruz had begun cutting staff and Kasich already had ended his ad buys in Indiana. When the actual Indiana vote came in, it was a dominating victory for Trump— his seventh in a row—with the final margin of seventeen points obliterating even the polls that had predicted Trump would win. Trump added another 587,000 votes to his total, bringing him to over 11.5 million.

This was an astounding number: as a percentage of the U.S. population, it surpassed the totals George W. Bush had received in 2000 and bested the total Ronald Reagan got in 1980 by 25 percent. Trump had received more primary votes than any candidate in Republican Party history. Moreover, Indiana proved that voters turned out for Trump— but not necessarily anyone else. About 14 percent of the Indianans who voted for Trump did not vote for Governor Mike Pence (who, ironically, would go on to be elected vice president of the United States on a victorious Trump ticket).[14] The split was indicative of how much Trump was drawing from non-traditional voters and how popular he was personally.

Cruz briefly made noises about staying in the race to the convention, but on May 4 he announced he was suspending his candidacy. "We left it all on the field in Indiana," Cruz said. He failed to congratulate Trump, who had beaten him badly in seven consecutive primaries.[15] That same day, John Kasich, having vowed to stay in the race until the end, dropped out. Trump had wrapped up the race that many thought would go to the convention and left prognosticators with egg on their faces...again. Polls in the remaining states shifted overwhelmingly in his favor. One New Jersey poll showed him with 74 percent support, while the first polls out of Nebraska—a state he had been thought likely to lose—suddenly had Trump the undisputed leader.

Trump immediately moved to unify the party against the Never-Trumpers, mostly GOPe stalwarts who were seeing their influence and revenues dry up. Speaker Paul Ryan quickly noted that he was not ready to support Trump as the presumptive nominee "at this time," initiating a Trump-Ryan meeting in the second week of May. Many of the Never-Trumpers, including *Weekly Standard* editor Bill Kristol, were still talking about a third party run by Mitt Romney or another unnamed candidate (eventually the unknown Evan McMullin would throw his hat into the ring), but those were pipe dreams. And whatever losses Trump had from the NeverTrumpers he made up for with crossover voters and what an anonymous pundit named "Sundance" called the "monster vote"—the millions of Americans so disillusioned with politics that they had not voted for years.[16]

There was something to the increased vote Trump was turning out. In Georgia, the increase over 2012 was 44 percent. After Indiana, Trump had received a total of 10.7 million votes (with another 10.3 million going to Cruz, Kasich, and Rubio combined).[17] "Deplorable" Pollster Baris saw early indications of a "monster vote" brewing when his surveys began to turn up large numbers of Trump supporters who had not voted in three or four previous elections.[18] The suspicion that many Trump supporters were "shy voters" reluctant to tell pollsters—or even their own friends and family—how they were going to vote was confirmed after the election, at least anecdotally, in an article about "Trump's Secret Supporters": one retired nurse said "I was guarded" and a retired engineer said "I didn't want to bring [my Trump support] up with anybody else.... I didn't want to have to go through confrontations...."[19]

While total Republican votes were up, Democrat turnout for the competitive primary between Hillary Clinton and Bernie Sanders was down by 3 million. If the same trend held in the general election, the Republicans stood to turn out at least 62 million voters in the general election, 2 million more than Romney had in 2012. Of course, that was before Gary Johnson, the Libertarian candidate, and Jill Stein, the Green candidate, were factored in, and before Evan McMullin siphoned off a handful of votes in key states. By August 2016 the third party candidates threatened to take 13 percent off the top, with Johnson's numbers coming fairly equally from Trump and Clinton and Stein's support entirely from Clinton. Still, there was no guarantee that the huge primary vote would stay with Trump in the general election.

The fun was only beginning.

CHAPTER EIGHT

On the Campaign Trail:
From Florida to North Carolina and New Hampshire (Again)

Joel Pollak

November 3, 2016

We land in Jacksonville: humid air, and overcast skies. It's a long ride to the Equestrian Center—so long that I wonder if anyone else will have bothered to make the trip.

But they have, and they are there by the thousands—over 4,100, fire officials tell me, filling most of the stands and half of the large horse show ring. I meet a colleague who lives nearby in Florida, and we catch up on the latest.

This is "Trump country," he says—but Trump may have turnout problems.

Walking around the arena, I see a few things I expect to see: blonde Southern belles, all smiles and short shorts; Southern men in camouflage "Make America Great Again" hats; even, toward the end, a Confederate flag in the rafters. There is a woman with a glittering homemade sign, "Redheads for Trump," that I briefly mistake for "Rednecks for Trump."

But I also see a few things that surprise me. One is the presence of a Hasidic rabbi, in his black suit and black hat.

He is looking for men who may be Jewish and who would like to put on tefillin, leather boxes and straps Jewish men use in prayers. He holds a sign: "#MakeTefillinGreatAgain." He tells me that he has had two men agree already. We discover that his cousin is a rabbi in my town. He tells me that he would do the same at a Hillary Clinton rally (presumably, with another slogan). What impresses me is that he thought there would be enough Jews here to make it worth his time.

There is also a sign across the arena: "Gays for Trump." The man holding the sign, and the man next to him, have driven down from Savannah, Georgia, to show their support. They tell me that the primary reason they support Trump is the "possibility of Muslim terrorism." Trump's immigration policy is fodder for cable news criticism, but it is aimed at keeping out people—even if they are just a minority of the whole—who reject homosexuality violently, as in the Pulse nightclub shooting.

Trump is looking upbeat. He does not mention the Cubs' World Series win, as I half expect him to do, but does mention the latest report, from the *Wall Street Journal*, that the Clinton Foundation was the subject of a broad investigation by the FBI, which officials from the Department of Justice tried to intervene to stop. One report has suggested that an indictment in the case is likely. Trump summarizes the news, then says that Clinton "shouldn't be allowed" to run for president.

That is the sort of statement that might once have attracted a great deal of attention. But as odd as it is—with possible implications that the executive might interfere with elections—it is not even in the top fifty most bizarre or disturbing things said by either candidate, and certainly not by Trump himself. He could simply mean that she should be facing prosecution instead of an election. Or that she should have been replaced by her party. But he leaves room for doubt.

Yet what Trump says is just the way most people speak. Something, someone, should have prevented her from running. Simple.

Trump's plain speech is often controversial, but connects to the heart of the matter. It is a persuasive rhetorical tactic—and so is the way he structures his speeches, interrupting his prepared text to respond to the audience. It has an effect. People say they feel he cares about them.

More than one person tells me he or she admires Trump because he could have chosen to live his rich life in isolation, but risked it all instead. That is powerful. I will hear it again and again from Trump supporters in the days ahead.

■ ■ ■

The next event is in Concord, North Carolina. We board the plane, which is still growing ever more crowded as the finish line nears and the race tightens.

Hillary Clinton is in North Carolina, too, speaking at two events. While we are in the bus on the way to Trump's rally in Concord, I tune in to hear some of her speech. She brags about the Cubs' win, telling the audience, "I have been a fan all my life." Cubs fans know that is nonsense. She abandoned the Cubs for the Yankees.

Our logistics are somewhat bungled this time. Our plane arrived too late for us to join Trump's motorcade, so we have to drive to the rally the ordinary way, through traffic. Without the adrenaline of reporting to sustain me, I fall asleep. I try sitting up straight, but inevitably find myself leaning against the seat of the woman next to me, a very pleasant reporter from the *Washington Post*. I wake up, apologize, and scramble to find out if I have missed any news of importance.

The traffic isn't too bad, but it is a long way to the venue, and we are still ten minutes away when someone notices a Tweet saying that Trump has already taken the stage. Frantic calls are made to editors, messages and emails are sent asking for backup. If Trump happens to say something new, and we miss it—we've failed at our job.

We arrive about fifteen minutes into the speech and race into the hall. There is zero time now for interviews. Time to make lemons into lemonade.

I look around for interesting people. There are three Hasidic Jews seated behind Trump, with sidelocks and the whole outfit—in the middle of nowhere, North Carolina. One holds a sign: "Democrats for Trump!"

Behind me, a voice suddenly booms: "Truuuuump!" He does it again: "Truuuuump!" His voice resonates throughout the hall, and a few others eventually imitate him. He briefly upstages the man himself—and attracts Secret Service and police, who give him a warning.

That's the only story I manage to squeeze out of the truncated trip before we rush to the motorcade and back to the airport.

Polling guru Nate Silver of *FiveThirtyEight* now says Trump's chances have improved—to one in three. I wonder if the Trump surge is too weak to push him across the finish line ahead of Hillary. Impossible to know.

■ ■ ■

We land in Raleigh at sunset. As we taxi toward the terminal, we see, in the near distance, the Hillary Clinton campaign plane, with her slogan, "Stronger Together," emblazoned on the side. We descend from our plane and board the buses.

Our motorcade loops around, then pauses at Trump's plane. A few hundred yards away, we see Clinton's motorcade at the base of a jetway jutting out from her plane. They pass us by; they have bigger vehicles, and far more of them. Cars and cars and buses and buses and buses, compared to our humble two-van procession.

She heads to a rally in Raleigh, where she will appear with Bernie Sanders and songwriter and performer Pharrell Williams. Democrats can almost always draw on that kind of celebrity firepower. Ronald Reagan had an edge, I muse: he was a star himself.

The drive to Selma, North Carolina, is long and exhausting. I find myself nodding off again on the bus as darkness falls. We arrive, after more than an hour of barreling down highways, side streets, and dirt roads, and reach "The Farm," a large open-air ground in front of a stage at the side of what looks like a corrugated iron shed.

We approach from backstage. A giant American flag is mounted from the raised ladder of a fire engine. Beyond it, a massive field with thousands upon thousands of people, extending almost as far back as one can see, as the crescent moon rises in the mist.

Even the journalists who have been on the trail for months are impressed. This is one of the largest crowds of the campaign, and these people have come from every little town and farm in the surrounding countryside. I guess the crowd at 10,000 strong—perhaps 15,000.

I ask one man why he is there. He tells me he wants to be part of history, part of the movement. He wants to support the man he believes will be the next president of the United States of America.

Selma is near Fort Bragg, and the theme for the evening is strengthening the military and honoring veterans. Before Trump comes onstage, there is a small ceremony honoring Medal of Honor winners, admirals, and generals. The honorees file across the stage and take seats behind the podium.

Then General Flynn comes on, and introduces Donald Trump. And the sound of the crowd is deafening. They wave signs, they wave babies, they chant "U-S-A!"

And Trump picks up his theme, speaking extensively about the sacrifices of the veterans, and his plans to beef up the military.

He strikes a humble tone—one that eluded him in the early August controversy about the Khan family, when he was asked by ABC News' George Stephanopoulos what he had sacrificed and he replied that he had created jobs. Now, he says that he "couldn't have done" what a veteran did. "I'm financially brave. Big deal."

He outlines an ambitious plan to build new ships for the Navy, new aircraft for the Air Force, and new battalions for the Marines. Some of it sounds far-fetched: Where will a country with $20 trillion in debt find the money for a massive military expansion? And how will Trump square that spending with the peacetime military he says he wants, used only to defeat terrorists and for defensive actions?

But to this audience, the fact that anyone wants to expand the military at all is refreshing.

The people are friendly to the journalists; even after Trump does his usual "most dishonest people in the world" routine, they want to talk with me. When we leave, they wish us a safe journey home.

Their faith in their candidate is heart-warming. While I ponder the polls, and wonder about a way forward, they are simply convinced he is going to do it. Maybe that's because he has told them that a loss would mean the election had been "rigged." They don't believe their country is that bad, yet.

We are rushed to the bus several minutes before the speech is over. There is a lot of ground to cover before we are back at the airport.

Trump wraps up with his signature line—"We will make America great again"—and once again there are fireworks above the rally.

Fireworks are expensive; I wonder whether there is so much campaign cash left that the campaign cannot possibly spend it all on advertising or get-out-the-vote efforts in the last days. Or maybe a really unique show is the best way to inspire voters.

I wonder what the man himself is thinking—whether he thinks he is going to lose, and is just savoring the glory of being the people's hero; or if he believes he is going to win, and is preparing himself for the day after, for the immortality that seems to surround presidents, for the heavy responsibilities that come with the office.

He promises the North Carolina crowd, "I will never let you down." How can they believe him? He cannot possibly do what he promises—can he?

The final few days are beginning to shape up, for both campaigns. Trump will return to North Carolina at least once before it is all over.

He is also planning to hit most of the other major swing states: Nevada, Colorado, and Pennsylvania. And vice presidential nominee Mike Pence will be filling in the gaps that remain.

Clinton has a slightly less grueling schedule—but more surrogates, including her husband and daughter, to help. It is all aimed at reaching local media. We count the time to the election in hours now.

One state remains more important than the rest, if the polls are to be believed: New Hampshire. It only has four electoral votes, but each of those is critical. And it is a small state, so every trip there could potentially swing the result.

Trump intends to return there twice in the next four days, including his last campaign stop before Election Day itself. But if John McCain, who loved New Hampshire, and Mitt Romney, who governed next door, could not win there, how can Trump?

November 4, 2016

The sun shines brightly on a New York morning for the first time in days. Today is the first day of a four-day marathon that will take Trump through at least eleven swing states, some of them twice.

The Pence plane is on a complementary journey, through many of the same places. The Clinton team is also fanning out, but the candidate herself will have a far more limited schedule. She will trust her turnout machine—which is vast, and includes the efforts of an array of non-profit organizations—to do its job.

We are heading back to New Hampshire. This time, the sunshine offers us a more flattering glimpse of the fall foliage, still spectacular in its late stages.

The circumstances of the race have changed fundamentally since the last New Hampshire rally, a week ago—even though some polling data suggest that the race had already begun to shift in his favor before the revelation about the FBI. Opinions differ as to when Trump's comeback began, and why, and if it matters.

Perhaps Trump had a better third debate than people realized at the time. Perhaps he did well enough to demonstrate his competence, and showed enough passion to mobilize his supporters while drawing reluctant Republicans to back the ticket. Or perhaps his message about a "rigged" election, while politically risky, resonated with voters. It transpires that even Bill Clinton thinks elections are rigged against the interests of working-class voters, to at least some extent.

Or perhaps the seeming likelihood of a Hillary Clinton presidency triggered a reaction. People—perhaps even Trump supporters—like the idea of opposing Trump's worst tendencies. But Hillary Clinton has flaws of her own. And suddenly voters are realizing what a Clinton presidency might mean. If there is probably more opposition to Clinton than there is strong support, that would explain the shift.

Another explanation comes from *Dilbert* cartoonist Scott Adams, whose keen insights have made the 2016 election more interesting and entertaining than it otherwise might have been. When the *Access Hollywood* video first came out, he said it marked the end of Trump's chances.[1] Now, however, he says that Clinton may have made a mistake by highlighting it. Her better argument was that Trump is a danger to national security. Trump's offensive remarks are sensational but not actually scary. Clinton is now the "scarier" candidate, because the legal troubles hanging over her head mean that her presidency could be a short one.[2] If she were somehow to be removed from office, she would be replaced by her running mate Senator Tim Kaine (D-VA)—who comes across as the ultimate beta male. Whenever they appear on stage together, she seems diminished by his presence. He has a high-pitched, nasal voice and seems overly excitable. He does not compensate for her flaws.

We ramble along a picturesque country road toward the Atkinson Country Club, where Trump will be speaking in a large basement hall. This is more of a traditional campaign setting than most of Trump's other events. The conventional political wisdom is: better to have a hall that is too small and crowded than one that is big and empty. The capacity of the room is about 1,000; the overflow, about 200, gather around speakers outside.

I note that the setup in the room allows me to move fairly close to the front, the better to shoot close-up photographs of Trump and the other speakers. I have made do, throughout this trip, with my cell phone camera, which is fuzzy at long range, but has the advantage of being less bulky, and also allows me to upload photos and video immediately. In the battle for scoops and narratives, timing is often of the essence, and it can make the difference in the broader debate.

This turns out to be a rare rally where the introductory speeches are at least as interesting as the main event. The first speaker is Kate Quigley, the sister of Glenn Doherty, one of the four men who were killed at Benghazi. Her speech causes the entire room to fall silent. There are audible gasps, and evident tears, in the audience as she tells the chilling story of how Hillary Clinton lied to her family about what had caused her brother's death.

Then there is John Sununu, again. He recalls his speech the week before, which was the last before the FBI news exploded. He says that while there may never be a "smoking gun" in the investigation, the revelation "ripped the scab" off the truth that "the Democratic Party has been infused with a culture of corruption for the last twenty-five years." He also urges the audience to reach out to supporters of Senator Bernie Sanders, who was a direct victim of the Clintons' dirty tricks.

Midway through Sununu's speech, a few people begin to chant: "Lock her up!" A heckler in the audience shouts: "Execute her!" Sunni interrupts his remarks to rebuke the man. The heckler tries to explain: "For treason." Sununu rejects that idea, and rebukes the man again.

He then continues his speech.

But evidently word spreads throughout the media that someone has suggested Clinton be killed. Indeed, within hours, Democrats are fundraising off the remark.

The crowd is patient as Trump takes his time. I chat with some of those around me. A middle-aged woman tells me that she loved Trump's pledge to pass term limits for Congress. "I want him to go in there and blow up all the corruption, not just on the Democratic side."

A man next to me tells me that his main issue is the VA (Veterans Affairs) hospitals, which President Obama promised to fix but instead allowed to fester. He likes Trump's plan to privatize the VA system.

Eventually, Trump takes the stage, to the usual wild cheers. He looks rested, and confident.

He delivers his stump speech—and interrupts himself to ad lib about New Hampshire's drug problems. He says that he was deeply affected by the stories that residents told him during the primary about their communities' struggles with heroin and other drugs. And that is one claim the traveling press can certify: he has mentioned New Hampshire, and its struggles with heroin, often in other states.

Trump touts his momentum in the state, and recalls how the media speculated in February that he was about to lose the primary, before he won it handily, in a "landslide." A good precedent for Tuesday. A heckler—perhaps the same man who shouted earlier, but it is impossible to be sure—interrupts Trump: "Save us!" he cries. Trump responds, "We're gonna save ourselves."

It is one of the more poignant moments of the campaign; I make it the headline for my coverage.

■　■　■

After the rally wraps, the traveling press corps bundles into the van and boards the plane for Ohio, where Trump will hold another rally in a hangar before heading to Florida. I hop off; this is my last stop of the week, before the Sabbath. Thanks to Secret Service precautions, however, I have to wait in a van on the tarmac until both planes take off. Trump's plane takes its time, and I worry about making my flight to New York. Finally, the cops let me out, and I race to the gate.

I make my flight—barely. Checking the news, I see that the media are reporting that someone yelled "Execute her!" during Trump's rally, some outlets without reporting Sununu's prompt response. One blogger, from the left-wing *ThinkProgress* blog, calls it the "ugliest" rally of the campaign, though he was obviously not there.

I am reminded that part of the value of being personally on the campaign trail is the ability to hold the media accountable. If I am not there, anything goes. There are no other conservative outlets represented in the traveling press corps.

A sunny Sabbath in Manhattan offers me one last chance to rest before the final push. There are two newsworthy events on Saturday. The first is the close of early voting in Nevada, and it does not look good for Trump and the Republicans. There is a surge in Latino turnout, with long lines outside a Mexican supermarket in Las Vegas. Veteran local political observer Jon Ralston crows, "Trump is dead." That message is a bit premature, but Democrats are very encouraged.

Republicans must brace for the worst. This is exactly what they feared—at least, if it holds in other states. Latinos are, or have been, among the lowest-propensity voters. But with Trump, they have a reason to turn out. His "wall" against illegal immigration; his clumsy remarks about Mexicans in his launch speech; his criticism of a Mexican-American judge presiding over the Trump University case in San Diego—all of those remarks have been fodder for months.

Still, it is not clear that any other Republican would do much better. Opinion polls suggest that Trump is running about even with Mitt Romney among Latinos, which itself was not terribly good. The generic Republican candidate will typically only receive about 30 percent of the Latino vote; the sole exception was George W. Bush in 2004, who received 44 percent. Bush speaks Spanish and promised immigration reform, and there was also the benefit of post-9/11 goodwill.

Republicans had the distinction of fielding the first major Latino candidates of any presidential primary, in Senators Marco Rubio and Ted Cruz. But neither did particularly well among Latino voters. Former Florida governor Jeb Bush speaks Spanish, has a Mexican-American wife, and promised a fairly liberal immigration reform policy. But he was rejected by primary voters, for a variety of reasons—not least of which was their desire to move past the Bush dynasty.

Democrats feared that Rubio might appeal to Latino voters. But they could have run against him by running against his party, which had rejected the "Gang of Eight" immigration reform effort of 2013 and resisted President Obama's "executive amnesty" policies.

The Democrats' Latino mobilization effort had long been in the works, and Trump's remarks were icing on the cake. In any case, the news from Nevada was not good for Trump.

And it was risky for the country. If Hillary Clinton eked out a narrow win thanks to the Latino vote, the entire election might be seen as illegitimate.

Already, many Republicans feared that illegal aliens were registering to vote.

The Democrats' message to Latino voters has focused on immigration reform and the promise of amnesty for illegal aliens. Democrats had used "undocumented" residents to register new voters and in even more senior campaign roles. Inevitably, the Democrats plan to renew their push for immigration reform after the election. If they do so after winning the election on the basis of the Latino vote, they may see it as poetic justice—as will Trump's many opponents in the Republican establishment, who have long tried to push their party toward amnesty, and who agonize about hostility to immigrants among Trump supporters.

But there is a risk that these changes in policy will be seen as having been achieved on behalf of, or even by, illegal aliens at the expense of citizens.

That would not necessarily make the election illegitimate—although many Americans might think it so—but it would raise legitimate questions of justice.

Is it right that those who have not obeyed the law should be able to change it? While citizens by birth, and those who have earned their right to vote by following the law, should be effectively overruled?

■ ■ ■

Another piece of news has happened during my flight to Denver, where I will rejoin the press after the Sabbath. A scuffle broke out on the floor of Trump's rally in Reno, Nevada, and the Secret Service rushed him offstage.

Evidently, some of the people near the man—who appeared to be a protester—saw him reach into his waistband, and someone shouted that he had a gun. As it turned out, he was unarmed, and Trump returned to the stage to thank the Secret Service and continue his speech.

Yet the event underlined the tensions behind the 2016 campaign, and the fears on both sides. Some of those fears were being deliberately stoked by the Clinton campaign and its supporters.

After the scare in Reno, for example, Daily Beast reporter Olivia Nuzzi tweets: "Remember: Trump helped foster a climate of violence at his rallies. In February, he promised to cover legal fees for his violent fans."[3] That continued a pattern of Trump being blamed for violence, no matter the source or the target.

In June, when anti-Trump protesters literally beat Trump supporters as they left a rally in San Jose—even chasing them several blocks through downtown streets, and attacking them in their cars—the mayor of the city blamed Trump for having incited the rioters against him. It was an alarming leap in moral reasoning: the perpetrators of violence had been exempted from any responsibility for their actions; the targets of violence, most of them innocent local citizens, were ignored.

Also ignored, by Nuzzi and others, is the proof that Democrat operatives working with the Clinton campaign and the Democratic National Committee had deliberately incited violence at Trump rallies and other Republican events for more than a year. Until it was exposed by James O'Keefe—with an assist from Breitbart—the tactic had worked quite effectively.

Trump's opponents—both on the Democratic side, and in the Republican Party—have also argued that he represents fascism, and that his rise through the Republican primary was the American version of the rise of Adolf Hitler.

That toxic idea could serve as an excuse for violence against Trump: after all, if he is a totalitarian bent on world war and mass extermination, wouldn't someone who assassinated him be a hero, not a murderer?

The Reno event is not the first time that Trump has required the immediate protection of the Secret Service. In March, a man in Ohio had rushed the stage at a Trump rally. He was tackled, but the incident highlighted the fact that the threat against the Republican nominee was real. On the Left, and among Trump's opponents, the incident served as a joke rather than as a signal to tone down some of their rhetoric, which could provide the grim pretext for a crazy person to act.

■　■　■

Tension, and uncertainty, with just seventy-two hours left before the result of the entire election will be known. Leading poll guru Nate Silver has given Hillary Clinton a 3-point lead in the final stretch.

If the polls are wrong, and if Trump is about to benefit from one of the most extraordinary late finishes in political history, there is little sign of it. Commentators on MSNBC, nervous though they are about Clinton's prospects, begin to speculate about how Trump might accept losing the election.

And yet Trump himself sounds confident and continues to fight. The election is, at least, closer than anyone expected just weeks before. His enduring strength is his stomach for a fight, his refusal to allow bad news, and bad polls, to slow him down. That resilience is, in itself, quintessentially American.

And if he fails—as he is likely to do, according to the odds, and all the experts—perhaps America will lose that swagger, never to recover it.

CHAPTER NINE

The Trump Revolution

Larry Schweikart

Joel's observations on the campaign trail in early November reflect his appreciation for the steadfastness of Donald Trump's supporters. Months earlier, when Trump was proving the naysayers wrong by winning the Republican nomination, and as he entered the general election phase— where, once again, no one gave him a chance—the perseverance of those Trump supporters would be crucial. They would prove willing to ignore purported gaffes and missteps that would have doomed any other candidate. Trump's candidacy represented a fundamental rejection of the accepted way of doing things in presidential campaigns, as both the Democrats and their allies in the media were astonished to discover that "scandals" that would have destroyed any other Republican candidate did not work against him.

After Cruz's ungraceful exit, the remaining states fell to Trump and he amassed far more than the number of delegates needed to secure the nomination.

Planning for the convention was, well, unconventional. Early on, Trump had flirted with the idea of giving the event more of an entertainment flair, suggesting he would bring "some showbiz" to the stage with sports figures and celebrities. (He called the 2012 GOP convention the most boring show he'd ever seen.)[1] And he had plenty of slots open for them: still intent on demonstrating their disgust with Trump, many Republican stalwarts, including all of the Bush family, John McCain, and Mitt Romney announced they would not attend the convention. Marco Rubio would make a video appearance only. Many other GOP stalwarts (most of them RINOs) announced they would not attend in a deliberate snub of Trump.

Normally, this would have been a serious blow to the nominee, but Trump was able to showcase his attractive family members and their accomplishments. His wife, Melania, and children Ivanka, Eric, and Donald Jr. brought out a softer side of Trump many had not seen. They "humanized" the billionaire in a way no traditional political speakers could have.

The convention's first-night focus on the families of the Benghazi casualties—though they were widely ignored by the drive-by press—was an important reminder of the stakes of the election.

Actor Antonio Sabato Jr. and Silicon Valley magnate Peter Thiel also spoke at the convention.

Candidates who had run against Trump and lost did speak, but the situation involving that of Ted Cruz was a bit delicate. After a meeting between Cruz, Trump, and GOP officials, it was agreed Cruz would be given a prime-time speaking spot. The assumption was that he would endorse Trump. When the time came, Cruz refrained from endorsing Trump and urged the delegates to "vote your conscience"—to a massive chorus of boos. Cruz's line would be used against Trump in a Clinton commercial, but at least in the short term the slight seemed to hurt Cruz more. His favorability ratings in Texas plunged; a poll for the 2018 senatorial election saw him losing to former Governor Rick Perry; and his biggest financial backer deserted him.[2]

Trump's own acceptance speech went too long. He delivered it from a teleprompter and probably yelled too much. It featured the memorable phrase "I am your voice"—which, oddly, the Trump team abandoned quickly after the convention. Nevertheless, the initial response to Trump's speech was incredibly positive—one Frank Luntz focus group gave it 70 percent approval, and an instant poll done the following day was over-whelmingly positive. Cruz's speech was hanging on like a bad aftertaste. Nevertheless, by the time the GOP convention ended, Trump led in the polls in several states—including battleground states—with margins as high as 5 percent in some.

It was all about to crash.

The Hildabeast

When the Democrats had their at-bat, it was inevitable that the Bernie Sanders supporters would be stymied, stifled, and crushed. That was obvious even before the WikiLeaks releases.

Julian Assange, the founder of WikiLeaks who was living under the protection of the Ecuadorian Embassy in London to avoid prosecution—he had been threatened with extradition to Sweden on an allegation of rape—had once released classified video and documents supplied by Bradley Manning supposedly showing American war crimes in Iraq and Afghanistan. Assange claimed that the attempt to extradite him was really a cover to transfer him to the United States for charges over WikiLeaks. On July 22, WikiLeaks released a series of documents from the Democratic National Committee (DNC) showing that the DNC under chairwoman Debbie Wasserman Schultz had schemed to rig the primary election against Bernie Sanders. The emails revealed that Schultz, the DNC, or both had been involved in staging questions with the media, suggesting questions for Sanders to reporters, and had indulged in a barrage of bigotry and name-calling. Schultz, along with several other DNC staffers, had to resign to protect Clinton, but it was pretty obvious who had directed the entire primary effort to crush Sanders. Schultz was merely the "fall girl."

The Clinton forces so thoroughly planned the convention with an eye toward minimizing all indications of Sanders's resistance that the issue was largely ignored by the media. (Later, WikiLeaks would reveal that the DNC had colluded with the Clinton campaign to ensure Sanders's destruction.) Hillary gave a measured, if uninspired speech, complete with dire warnings about a "President Trump." But the real fireworks involved another speaker: Khizr Khan, whose son, a captain in the U.S. Army, had been killed in Afghanistan in the line of duty. Brandishing a copy of the U.S. Constitution (while his head-scarf-covered wife dutifully stood by in silence), Khan claimed that Trump didn't know what was in the document.

Trump took the bait, responding to Khan on Twitter, where it appeared he was casting aspersions on the Khan who had given his life for his country (he was not). Gleeful media networks ran with the Khan dust-up for a week, and Trump's poll numbers began to fall. Trump had already drawn horrified media condemnations by saying he questioned whether he could receive a fair trial in the Trump University case because of a "Mexican judge," Gonzalo Curiel. Trump stated that "one's heritage makes them incapable of being impartial"—*precisely what the Left had argued for years in advocating minority judges over whites!*[3]

Yet, did these episodes really hurt Trump?

The polls said so, but now, more than in the primaries, the polls themselves seemed suspect.

Who You Gonna Believe?

Political observers insisted that Trump's campaign had suffered severe blows from the Khan and "Mexican judge" incidents, and to support their case, they pointed to...polls. But a quiet and sinister development had taken place within the world of polling itself. With little fanfare, pollsters began to jigger their sampling methods. Reuters, which had Trump up before the Democratic convention, was one of the few to make a public announcement: it was abruptly changing its methodology, immediately after—as Neil McCabe reported on Breitbart—"their tracking polls showed a 17-point swing in favor of the Republican nominee Donald J. Trump, exposing the 'Secret Trump Voters' Democrats fear."[4] In fact, polling methodology was being rejiggered across the board in less obvious ways. For example, other immediate post-convention polls sported such utterly unsupportable methodology as:

- Suffolk and *USAToday* polls asked for "youngest [voter] in the home" (thereby tilting the poll toward Clinton)[5]
- CNN/ORC sampled only 26 percent Republicans[6]
- Samples in a dozen polls were significantly weighted toward Democrats (including +6, +7, and even +9 samples)[7]
- Many polls oversampled women by anywhere from 2 to 4 points[8]

It was not surprising that Hillary suddenly took the lead—in some cases, a significant lead—in both state and national polls. That explains her post-convention "bump."

One of the most astounding (and unremarked—except by those in the know) incidents regarding polling in the 2016 election involved Google, which had been doing national polling. Baris actually got an email from a friend at the company saying that Google's state polling of Florida had Trump way up, and if Trump moved ahead of Clinton in their national poll, Google would stop polling entirely![9]

In the end state polling would prove to be off by horrendous margins, with national polling off by less. Only the USC Dornsife/*Los Angeles Times* poll and the People's Pundit Daily poll, run by my fellow "Deplorable" Richard Baris, would be even close. PPD had the final national margin at about .6 percent for Trump; although Trump lost the popular vote, that was still much closer than any other poll.[10] The USC/*LAT* poll, run by a former director of the RAND Corporation poll, was within about a point, although also off in Trump's favor nationally.[11] Almost no polls erred in Trump's favor in state races, however, which proved key.

Most of the major national polls were off by one to three points—and virtually *none* of them had Trump winning the electoral map.[12] RCP's "no toss up" electoral map had Clinton winning 272–266, and did not give Trump Pennsylvania, Michigan, or Wisconsin (yet did give him Nevada).[13] When it came to state polls, only PPD had Trump winning Wisconsin (by a tiny fraction), while only PPD and Trafalgar showed him ahead in Pennsylvania.[14] No major poll showed Trump winning Michigan, and none even had him remotely close in Minnesota.[15]

What happened? Without access to the corporate minutes of ABC, CNN, Fox, NBC, and other media outlets, it is difficult to know. Perhaps the pollsters and their corporate bosses were simply trying to get results that made sense to them, living in an elite establishment world where they never met a Trump voter. Or were they trying to ensure a Clinton victory by discouraging Trump voters? As it turned out, whatever their intentions, the pollsters likely hurt Clinton badly. According to one insider, Clinton's campaign didn't do much polling of its own and late in the campaign relied heavily on the outside "public" pollsters. Google CEO Eric Schmidt actually warned the Clinton campaign that the polls might not be so reliable—but everyone else, including the television pundits and reporters, was relying so heavily on them that Clinton's staff blew off Schmidt.[16] It was a case of the campaign literally believing its own side's mythology—although clearly some inside the campaign knew it was in trouble, as we will see.

New Generals

By late July, Trump had—according to the media—wasted several weeks in his battles with Khan and Judge Curiel. These analyses didn't take any notice of the ongoing, massive rallies that Trump had never stopped conducting. As would later be revealed, those rallies were advertising gold. Yet there was some truth to an oft-repeated claim by the drive-by media, that Trump's campaign was in "turmoil." Manfort, just like Lewandowski before him, had been the right man for the campaign at the right time. (After Manafort's hire, the two had butted heads and vied for power, and once Manafort established himself, Lewandowski was eventually let go, winding up as a commentator on CNN.) Manafort had successfully navigated the delegate fights, secured wavering delegates, and reinvigorated the campaign at state levels that Lewandowski could not have. But once the campaign moved into the general election against Hillary, Manafort seemed as out of his element as Lewandowski had in March.

Now, in early August, Manafort's position was on the line. Trump turned to a new pair of generals to lead his campaign. He elevated a political pollster, Kellyanne Conway to campaign manager and Breitbart News chief Steve Bannon to campaign CEO. (Later, he would bring on board a third well-known figure, Citizens United CEO David Bossie, as a campaign advisor.) For Conway, the unflappable GOP spokeswoman who regularly appeared on a number of television shows and who now became the first woman to run a Republican general election campaign, the opportunity was a dream. Now Trump's fate was in her hands. If Conway was steel, Bannon was the nitroglycerine, offering ground-breaking strategy advice and outside-of-the-box tactics. Trump still maintained a bare-bones staff, employing few pollsters or specialists—instead benefitting from the data, expertise, and analysis of a "crowdsource"-style army of volunteers (we Deplorables were among them) who collected facts on the ground, ran the numbers, and communicated our evidence and insights to Bannon and other campaign insiders.

While Trump was creating a dynamic and insightful campaign operation, Clinton's team was developing a so-called "data-driven campaign" that relied too heavily on algorithms. (Think of the scene in *Rocky IV* when Rocky is training in the snow of Siberia while Drago is in his sterilized chrome-and-glass room.) Clinton's data system, named "Ada" for a nineteenth-century female mathematician, used inputs of polling numbers and ground-level voter data, all churned into "400,000 simulations a day of what the race against Trump might look like." Clinton and her aides "were convinced their work, which was far more sophisticated than anything employed by President Obama or GOP nominee Mitt Romney in 2012, gave them a big strategic advantage."[17]

Convinced they were battling a Neanderthal—both in temperament and in technology of his campaign—Clinton became overconfident.

Her ads focused on Trump as a poor role model to children or little girls, or on his unpredictable and reckless nature. Since Clinton had nothing positive to say about her own tenure as secretary of State or her brief stint as a U.S. senator, all her ads could do was "go negative" on Trump.

Meanwhile Conway and Bannon had fixed Trump's "messaging problem." They had their candidate back on track with a series of policy speeches on veterans, the economy, and national defense. Trump now eschewed "Jerry Springer"-style ad libbing for the more controlled and focused teleprompter speech. This not only allowed him to make his points in reserved—even presidential—tones, but also kept him from drifting into unscripted comments that the press could make into one more scandal that might possibly, finally "implode" his campaign. As Trump's speeches showed that he had a grasp on the details of the issues, the media—surprise!—immediately ceased all discussion of policy details and returned to Trump's personality, but it was too late. The Donald was on a roll.

September Collapse

On the weekend of September 9–11, Clinton's aura of "inevitability" evaporated. There were two different incidents that were critical. First, at a New York City fundraiser on September 9, Clinton said half of Trump's supporters were "racist, sexist, homophobic, xenophobic [and] Islamophobic" and belonged in a "basket of deplorables."[18] While it was no worse than many things Clinton (and half the GOPe) had already said about Trump's supporters, the "deplorables" comment seemed to be particularly offensive. It got some attention even in the mainstream press, and Trump supporters embraced it. On Twitter, Trump voters began to label themselves with "Deplorable" in front of their name—"Deplorable Pam," "Deplorable Joe," and so forth. Clinton was forced to retreat in the face of the firestorm, but while the "deplorables" story was still brewing, another incident suddenly changed the dynamics of the race.

Since the primary campaign, Hillary Clinton had been given to extremely long and unpredictable coughing spells. On one occasion, when Clinton was interrupted by a heckler in the audience, she froze. Secret Service agents surrounded her as if she had been shot at, and one of them—or perhaps a political handler—kept repeating to the rigid Clinton, "Just keep talking." Finally she resumed. It all seemed very odd.

Rumors circulated that Clinton had any number of diseases—the most popular theory being Parkinson's. Then at a September 11 memorial ceremony in New York, Clinton nearly collapsed and had to be held up, then pushed into a van ("like a side of beef").[19] The video was chilling. Clinton was literally out cold on her feet. Suddenly pundits began to review the bizarre head nod that Clinton had given to a reporter earlier in the campaign and her strange reaction to the balloon drop at the Democratic National Convention. She was "diagnosed" by would-be doctors on the web as having Parkinson's Disease.

The contrast between Clinton's weak and sickly appearance and Trump's nonstop energy was hurting Clinton's campaign, as was her seeming inability to attract a crowd. Speculation was rife that her health was the reason she couldn't appear in public more. Meanwhile, Trump's ability to generate massive crowds at the rallies was beyond dispute. Pundits claimed that Mitt Romney had drawn 30,000 to a rally in Florida in 2012, and Walter Mondale in 1984 had a rally with 100,000 in attendance. But Romney and Mondale had managed such feats once, while Trump did it three or four times a week—and in the last week of the campaign would have two to three rallies *a day*, or more. Sheer attendance, however, was only part of the value of those events. Unnoticed was the massive media attention from local outlets. As we have seen, that local coverage allowed Trump to broadcast his unfettered message to entire communities—amounting to tens of millions of dollars in free advertising. And it permitted him to get his message out unfiltered because of the nature of local news, which did not have the biased expert talking heads explaining to viewers what they had just seen. Asked about the impact of the rallies, Trump campaign CEO Steve Bannon texted me: "huge."

Still, the media discounted the rallies as merely the reaction of a minority of rabid voters. They didn't see the attendees as a cross-section of the electorate—or the rallies themselves as an effective marketing device. They also missed the fact that the rallies enhanced the Republican ground game. That was one area where the media was still sure that Hillary had a massive advantage. But rally attendees were more likely to volunteer, staff phone banks, tell neighbors, and so forth. In short, *no one* in the drive-by media ever came close to understanding the real value and purpose of the rallies—they simply dismissed them as mere preaching to the choir, underestimating Trump as a sort of traveling tent evangelist. How would he break through to the "undecided," the independent, and the non-partisan voters, the media kept asking?

Easily, it seemed. With only a month left in the campaign, Trump appeared to be surging. Even several of the apparently biased polls had him leading Clinton. Internally, things looked even better for Trump.

Having known Steve Bannon for years in a number of different relationships—as a subject in some of the videos he directed for Citizens United, as a fellow speaker at Young America's Foundation events, and as a friend—I had been helping the campaign through memos sent to Bannon for months, mostly with data analysis of Ohio and Florida. The news from Ohio was particularly telling.

Back in 2012, Deplorable Dave, I, and a few others who had been watching the absentee voting in Ohio concluded that Republican turnout was substantially up, while Obama's Democrat turnout was off compared to 2008. That led us to conclude that Mitt Romney had a very good chance of winning Ohio.

But there was a serious flaw in our analysis in that election: under Ohio law, any voter who does not vote in the presidential primary is designated an "unaffiliated" voter, even if still registered as a Democrat or Republican. As the absentee numbers came in, I was not paying attention to the "U" voters, on the assumption that they were indeed, well… genuinely unaffiliated voters. In fact, they were Democrats who had not voted in the 2012 primary because Obama had no primary opposition.

The result was that we underestimated the number of Democrat voters, and Obama won Ohio by over 160,000 votes.

But in 2016 we had a secret weapon. Deplorable Don Culp devised a brilliant way to track the "U" voters. He looked at every household in Montgomery Co., Ohio (Dayton and its suburbs)—a county that Obama had won by 20,000 votes and which no Republican had won since George H. W. Bush. It was a typical "blue" county in Ohio where, if the vote was close, a Republican could win with very strong turnout. Culp, examining the voting records for every "U" household in the county in 2000, 2004, 2008, and 2012, was able to correctly label each "U" household as "D," "R," or genuinely unaffiliated. With this new lens, Culp concluded that Republicans were hanging very tough with Democrats in absentee ballots (while in 2012 they had lost them by 12,000). In fact, the numbers said the Democrats were in real trouble. And it was even worse for them elsewhere. And, if we knew this, someone in the Clinton campaign almost assuredly knew it as well.

Analyses of Cuyahoga County—home of Cleveland—showed that the combined impact of GOP registration increases and Democrat registration losses totaled over 97,000. And when the infamous "U" voters were accounted for? Democrats could be down as much as 140,000 going into Election Day. A rule of thumb in Ohio politics is that a Democrat needs to come out of Cuyahoga County with an advantage of 125,000 to 150,000 to win the state. With the collapse of Democrat registrations there, that was now an utter impossibility. In addition, through selected information we were able to garner about absentee ballots, it was clear the Republican voters were energized and the Democrats were not. Of course, we couldn't count actual votes—only "Ds" and "Rs"—but Culp and I knew that the Democrats could not win Ohio, and Trump's victory there wouldn't be close. And we knew this by October 1.

If we knew it, we thought, surely Clinton's team knew it. But were Clinton herself and John Podesta getting that info?

Richard Baris was seeing the same trends nationwide. By early October, Trump was surging across the board.

And there was still more. For weeks over the summer, posters "Ravi" and "SpeedyinTexas" at the website FreeRepublic had been meticulously tracking registration changes in key Florida counties, as well as in Pennsylvania and North Carolina. These "Freepers" had clear evidence that the North Carolina vote would not be as close as 2012—Trump would certainly win there, while Pennsylvania was definitely and genuinely "in play." Pennsylvania was hard to track because ballots in that state were not marked "R" or "D." (The same was true in Virginia, where there was no early voting.) Asked how Pennsylvania looked, Steve Bannon texted me, "No one seems to have a handle on it." Thus despite the work of "Ravi," "SpeedyinTexas," and others showing Pennsylvania was "gettable," the Trump campaign remained cautious, thinking that Michigan was an easier state to win. (We later learned that some of Hillary's team were already urging her to make a desperate move to hold Michigan, but her headquarters refused to act on the information—indicating turmoil and widely different views within the Clinton camp as to how well they were doing.)[20] I kept thinking, *Either the Trump staffers really are unsure—but they can't be with these statistics—or they are sandbagging. They want Clinton to think Pennsylvania is safe so she won't move more resources in, thinking it's safe for her.*

Either way, there were strong indicators that Trump was already winning Ohio, North Carolina—and was poised to win Michigan, and probably Pennsylvania.

But there was even more.

The same "Freepers" had been tracking the Florida absentee ballots, as had a key operative inside the Trump campaign. Almost daily, we would discuss our separate analyses. The upshot was usually the same: Republicans were performing better than in 2012, and could be expected to take Florida easily, possibly by 250,000 votes. Deplorable Drew, a Trump operative working independently in Florida, had the margin at 3–4 percent, based on a formula allocating undecideds at a rate of about 5 percent net gain for Trump. While I thought it could possibly be higher, I shied away from any predictions about how "undecideds" would vote, still burned by that bad call in Ohio in 2012. I preferred to just count "Rs" and "Ds"—and those numbers looked very good.

And there was one more state we knew Trump had: Iowa. Democrat absentees were well below 2012 levels there—at times some 40,000 lower. We all compared notes and knew that, regardless of what the polls said, Trump would carry Iowa easily. Later it was revealed that the Clinton camp *knew* they had lost Iowa. Her allies there, the Service Employees International Union, strongly recommended the Democratic campaign pull out of Iowa and go to Michigan, which they had heard Clinton was losing. ("Everybody could see Hillary Clinton was cooked in Iowa.")[21]

Armed with these numbers, I was making daily reports to Team Trump. Unknown to me at the time, so was Deplorable Drew—and our reports were remarkably the same. And unknown to both of us, Deplorable Greg had his own spreadsheet…. with the same results. (None of us was seriously thinking Wisconsin would fall to Trump, yet, although we did have some indicators.)

If I knew Trump was winning Iowa, Florida, North Carolina, and Ohio in the first week of October, and if we all suspected that Michigan and Pennsylvania were likely to fall, then the Clinton campaign had to know it as well.

There were other good signs for Trump in that first week in. We received an internal polling memo showing that Trump was down only 3 points in Oregon, only 1 in Minnesota and Michigan, and only a couple of points in such states as Connecticut and Rhode Island. The same memo showed Trump up in Virginia, Florida, New Hampshire, Ohio (big, as we knew), and Pennsylvania. To be honest, the numbers seemed too good to be true, even given the (exclusive) numbers that we had. I contacted Team Trump at the highest level and asked, state by state for most (not all) of the states on the list, "Are these numbers correct?"

"Yes," came the reply.

In short, by the first week in October, Trump was poised for a massive victory, possibly of 350–360 electoral votes, with a 4 percent popular vote lead. Baris's polling showed a similar surge, especially among Americans who had not voted in a long time. Clinton was winning only single digits of these low-participation voters. If they went to the polls in large numbers, Trump would win in a landslide. And *someone* in the Clinton campaign had to be getting this information as well. The question was, *Who was Hillary listening to?* The public pollsters who were saying she was a shoo-in, or some brave soul who dared broach the truth?

It turns out that brave soul—the "someone" in the Clinton campaign that we Deplorables figured must have figured out what we could see—was Jake Sullivan, Clinton's policy director, who actually said she would lose. And she *wasn't* listening to him. According to Glenn Thrush, Sullivan continually told the Clinton team they were in trouble, but no one listened.[22] Part of the deafness came from Clinton's attachment to the Obama 2012 playbook. But in retrospect, Obama won that election very narrowly, taking five key states that gave him the victory with fewer than 500,000 votes. (Trump would win by an even smaller margin of votes, but was within 750,000 votes of taking an *additional* seven states with 73 electoral votes. Even landslide elections in the Electoral College can be won by such narrow margins.)

Clinton's dedication to the Obama model meant overreliance on data and on a computer program built by an acquaintance of her campaign manager, Robby Mook. Elan Kriegel, whom Mook had hired to help Terry McAuliffe win the 2014 Virginia governor's race, had concocted an intricate algorithm (named "Ada") that ran unceasing simulations based on mind-boggling data inputs. These computer results were used to "steer ad spending, the candidate's travel schedule, even the celebrities Clinton would invite to rallies."[23] *Politico* reporter Glenn Thrush wrote that Mook was obsessively protective of the Ada data, in part out of concern for job security. But it turned out to be as flawed as Mitt Romney's infamous "ORCA" program in 2012.

It remains murky to what degree Clinton was relying on the faulty public polls, and to what degree her own polling and data were just as bad. But one thing is clear: Sullivan was telling Clinton the polls were wrong. On daily conference calls he urged the campaign to spend more time in Michigan, Pennsylvania, and Wisconsin (which Clinton didn't visit *one time*). But she wasn't listening to him. And no wonder. Her "polling team"—whether from internal polls or from aggregating the public polling data—was giving her more pleasant news. According to Thrush, on Monday November 7, "Clinton's polling team assured the candidate she would win."[24] One caveat about Thrush's reporting: it is *not* correct that "most of Trump's own data" showed he would lose. Quite the contrary, everything our group sent Trump showed he would win, and probably by a substantial margin in the Electoral College.[25]

Indeed, our Basket of Deplorables was increasingly confident about a Trump victory. Four weeks out from the election, we didn't see how Clinton and her allies in the press could change the dynamic of the race. Internal polling by Trump at that point showed him within 2 percentage points in Minnesota, up in Florida and North Carolina, tied in Pennsylvania, up 1 point in Michigan, and down only 3 in Oregon. If anything, it seemed to us that he was verging on blowing out Clinton. And it seemed that the media had been launching everything it had at Trump for over a year, to no effect. They were out of ammunition.

Or so we thought.

Sex Bomb #2

Just before the Sunday, October 9, debate, the "October Surprise" that many thought Trump had dodged suddenly hit. Late Saturday night, a tape from *Access Hollywood* surfaced in which Trump excused boorish behavior toward women. As a "star," he claimed, "you can do anything" to women—"you can grab them by the pussy."[26] The tape also had Trump saying he had pursued a married woman. Predictably, the GOPe distanced itself immediately, with Paul Ryan claiming he was "sickened" by the remarks and rescinding Trump's invitation to a scheduled "unity" rally in Wisconsin. Reince Priebus piled on, as did Representative Jason Chaffetz of Utah, who said, "I'm out." Senator Mike Lee even said Trump should step down as the nominee.

Trump quickly issued a statement expressing his "regret." "I said it, I was wrong, I apologize." But then Trump pivoted to talking about Bill Clinton, who hadn't just spoken of groping women, but actually done so, and to Hillary, who had excused and empowered his predatory behavior for years.

Trump quickly disabused anyone of the notion he would be stepping down. Quite the contrary, Trump characteristically went on offense. As buzz built about what might happen in the debate that evening, Trump called a press conference where he stunned the media: Clinton accusers Juanita Broaddrick, Paula Jones, and Kathleen Willey were at the table with him. Broaddrick had said Clinton raped her, Jones had filed a sexual discrimination suit against Clinton that was settled out of court, and Willey had alleged Clinton groped her in the Oval Office. A fourth woman at the table, Kathy Shelton, had been twelve years old when Hillary Clinton defended her accused rapist in court.

The flabbergasted media, stung that they had been fooled, railed about Trump's audacity. But he just kept up the pressure. He invited the women to the debate, where a shocking photo of Bill Clinton looking at them epitomized Hillary's problem: she could not attack Trump for saying things that her own husband was credibly accused of doing. Once again, the media's kill shot misfired. And once again, Trump critics found the tables turned on them—Trump had punked them yet again. Many of the Republicans who had leaped to denounce Trump quietly crawled back to him, including Priebus.

Then WikiLeaks struck again, this time revealing collusion between the Clinton campaign and the debate moderators: Hillary received some of the primary debate questions in advance. Once again, the facade of an "objective press" was blown up, although the Wiki revelations did not make it far beyond the internet and the radio talk shows.

Sex Bomb #2 did have an effect, however. Bannon admitted in a text to me that "it's killing us with women" in New Hampshire. Absentee counts would reveal that immediately after the tape came out there was a spike in voting for Libertarian candidate Gary Johnson by Republicans. The tape almost certainly was a factor in the closeness of Florida, and likely cost Trump New Hampshire (by a razor thin margin). Baris's polls reflected the drop. Still, after a week, the damage seemed to be controlled, and Trump was on offense yet again.

We don't know the details of the decision to drop the *Access Hollywood* tape on October 7. But TMZ reported that NBC had held the tape for "maximum impact" on the election.[27] Maybe, despite the dishonesty of the mainstream polls and the Clinton campaign's reliance on them, the Democrat camp and their allies in the media had divined the Trump landslide that was in the making. And they did save themselves from a blowout landslide by releasing the tape early. Had they waited until the last weekend of the campaign— the traditional time for releasing such damaging oppo research, and likely the original plan—it's unlikely the impact would have cost Trump nearly as many votes.

That's what Baris's polling showed—though the rest of us Deplorables didn't see it at the time, as he only shared specific data when we asked for it. After all, he had a business to run, and this *was* proprietary information. Nonetheless, Baris's polling had identified a group he called the "wanna-be elites"—mostly white voters in places such as Charlotte, North Carolina, or Loudon County, Virginia—were particularly offended by the *Access Hollywood* tape. Baris was convinced that this was what ultimately happened to the "monster vote"—that Trump had 64–68 million lined up to vote for him before the tape, but the "wanna-be elites" dropped him, even as the low-propensity voters stood their ground. Though I didn't see this analysis by Baris until later, it supports my suspicion at the time that Trump had Clinton on the ropes and was poised for a landslide before the tape.

Energy, Stamina, Persuasion

Clinton seemed to have recovered from her September collapse, and the impression was fading from voters' minds. She seemed healthy enough in the debates and a growing number of public venues. But her relative lack of energy still made a poor contrast with Trump's ebullience in the rallies during the final days. In essence, both candidates had rebounded from nearly fatal episodes (Trump's tape, Hillary's "seizure") to regain their previous footing. In the final week of the campaign, there would be no more distractions.

Joel was a firsthand witness as they each bombarded Florida, North Carolina, Iowa, and Ohio with personal visits, but increasingly Trump added appearances in Michigan and Pennsylvania, and Clinton had to respond, though late in the game. But she could call on Obama to show the flag for her, while Trump had no one to match his own star power, although vice presidential candidate Mike Pence had steadily grown in popularity and crowd-generating ability. (Clinton's veep candidate, Tim Kaine, was incapable of drawing flies: his appearances often saw crowds of fewer than thirty people.) Only in the final week, with large concerts featuring Beyoncé, Bruce Springsteen, Katy Perry, and other rock stars, did really large crowds show up for Clinton. (Trump quipped that he didn't need rock stars to pack a house.) Most of the time her appearances were in front of a few hundred people (and no one knew how many of them were staffers or paid union members), while Trump continued to draw tens of thousands.

An early observer of Trump's speaking techniques, *Dilbert* creator Scott Adams had predicted in 2015 that Trump would win, based on Trump's "persuasion methods."[28] While Adams hedged his bets slightly from time to time, he always maintained that Trump's persuasion techniques, especially his ability to identify an opponent with a single phrase ("Lyin' Ted," "Low Energy Jeb") were wildly effective.

All the indicators of political victory—the rallies, his internet and social media dominance, the enthusiasm of his supporters—were on the side of Donald Trump. All indicators save one: the polls. And the media were clinging to the polls for dear life. Aboard the press plane, Joel was inundated with negativity as the media refused to even entertain the notion that Trump might win.

Fox News, in particular, had a penchant for selecting the most negative poll for Trump on any given day and ignoring polls that had him doing better. Occasionally, Fox would even tout a poll from another source when one of their own Fox polls had Trump doing slightly better.

Still, with only two weeks out, while Trump had regained some momentum and the damage of the sex tape had washed through, in most polls of key battleground states he led only in Iowa, Ohio, and North Carolina, while Florida remained a virtual tie. Hillary remained up in Colorado, Virginia, Pennsylvania, New Hampshire, Wisconsin (big), Michigan, and Minnesota. And increasingly—whether from the Clinton campaign or from polling—the media buzz was that the formerly solidly red Arizona and Georgia were "in play." (For the record, this is a common mantra in the media prior to a general election; in fact neither state is ever "in play" for Democrats.)

My contacts in the Trump campaign told me they were feeling even better about Michigan, though they seemed unwilling to commit to Pennsylvania. "Our people on the ground tell us we can win Pennsylvania and Virginia," Bannon texted me, seemingly without conviction. But he was more confident about Michigan. "We're up one there."

Indeed, the situation in Michigan was almost too good to believe. Pollster-strategist Jamie Coe, an independent outsider, not one of our "Deplorables," told me Macomb County was going very strong for Trump. One poll had Trump up double-digits in this traditionally blue, union county. After a Trump rally there, Coe said, "I've never seen so many blue collar people at a Republican rally in my life." Oakland County was still the key: Trump could lose there, but not by double digits. One week out, Coe's sources told him Trump was only down single digits in Oakland. That meant the rest of red-county Michigan stood a chance of overcoming the overwhelmingly Democrat Wayne County, home to Detroit. *Bannon is right about Michigan*, I thought, *but he's wrong about Pennsylvania. Trump will win there.*

Early Onslaught

In Michigan, much of the optimism came from absentee ballots where, as in Ohio, Republicans were showing up very strong. Ballots from Democrat strongholds were down between 15 and 18 percent, while red county absentee votes were coming in ahead of schedule.

Florida, however, began to tell a more worrisome story. There, Republicans had maintained a very healthy lead over their 2012 pace, when Republicans won the absentee battle by 79,000. At one point, the margins were so great it looked as though Trump could blast through Florida with a popular vote margin of over a half million. The voting was slowed by Hurricane Matthew in the first week of October, which did not make landfall in Florida but nevertheless disrupted postal service and diverted people from politics as they repaired houses and cleared trees. After Matthew passed, Democrat absentees in Florida picked up and what had looked like an easy Trump win turned into a potential dogfight.

At first our estimates continued to show Trump would win by 3 percent or more, but then numbers began to look more disconcerting. With the election only a week away, it began to seem as though Trump could possibly even lose the absentee battle—and Florida.

Then, miraculously, the Republican absentee ballots flooded in, restoring Trump's edge. (While the final absentee totals did not quite match Romney's in 2012, the shortfall was made up elsewhere—in "early ballot" shortfalls by the Democrats.) Since 2012, Florida had strongly emphasized "early voting" not just absentee but in person (Florida's secretary of State site even changed the nomenclature on its website from "absentee" to "early voting by mail" in mid-campaign.) Deplorable Drew, a Republican strategist working on Trump's campaign in Florida, said to me, "Florida has gone nuts pushing early voting. You see ads all the time." In 2012, early voting was bad news for Romney. He had won the absentee ballot by 79,000, and won the vote on Election Day itself, but lost the state by a total margin of 74,000 votes because he was trounced in the early in-person voting. After that, Republicans naturally looked on early voting with trepidation. But as with everything else about the 2016 election, what had happened before didn't matter.

Early voting in Florida's blue counties was solid, but not off the charts, while early voting in red counties was quite strong. Moreover, election websites such as Michael MacDonald's U.S. Elections Project, which collected detailed demographic data, began showing severe shortfalls, compared to 2012, in the black and youth vote. African American early voting in Florida was down between 3 and 4 percent, while in North Carolina the daily shortfall in early voting was averaging almost 8 percent.[29] Yet despite these obvious problems in mobilizing the Democrat base, experts such as Mac-Donald and Democrat consultant Steve Schale, who regularly touted Clinton's strength, continued to insist that the Democrats were *winning* the early voting.[30] Richard Baris wrote an article on Florida warning Democrats that Trump was "in far better shape" than Romney before election day, that the Hispanic "surge" Schale and others were touting would do no more than bring Democrats closer to their 2012 levels (which they had trailed up to that point), and that independents were breaking for Trump.[31] It was true that in sheer numbers Democrats were "winning" in Florida, Iowa, Ohio, and North Carolina early voting (as determined by "Republican" vs. "Democrat" ballots). But they *always* won the early voting. The significant question was how their margin compared to the margin in the past. You needed that piece of information to tell whether their advantage in the early voting would be strong enough to swamp the Republicans' advantage on Election Day. In Iowa, for example, the Democrat absentee voting was down by almost 40,000 from 2012 and right on track with the trajectory in 2014, when Jodi Ernst had won her senatorial race by an 8 percent margin. (In fact, Trump would go on to win Iowa by 9.6 percent.) In both Florida and North Carolina, voting by 18–30-year-olds was down about 3 percent.

So while the Democrats "led," they were leading by margins well below their 2012 levels—and they had lost North Carolina by 2 percent and barely won Florida in that election. After early voting in Florida (which supposedly showed Clinton doing well), she still trailed the 2012 early voting numbers for Obama by over 140,000![32] These were not favorable trends for Clinton, no matter how much Democrat consultants and analysts claimed otherwise.[33] McDonald still had Clinton winning Iowa on election eve![34] But with only a week remaining, MacDonald and some other experts began changing their tune and glumly admitting that Clinton was trailing Obama's 2012 performance and that the general election did not look good.[35]

Deplorable Pollster Richard Baris of People's Pundit Daily was told that the Clinton team had all but pulled out of North Carolina. Similar stories about Ohio abounded, although Clinton did stage a last-minute celebrity-filled concert event in Cleveland. None of this changed the math, which we thought her team had to know—North Carolina, Iowa, and Ohio were already gone, and she would need a miracle to win Florida. Indeed, on December 7, Baris published statistics showing that Clinton "lost Florida before election day"—something we "Deplorables" and Deplorable Drew had been telling Team Trump.[36]

A Florida Miracle?

Why did Hillary's team ignore such obvious signs that her campaign was in trouble? In part, Clinton had subscribed to the theory that "people of color," millennials, and unmarried women would outvote the white middle class. Pollsters such as Stanley Greenberg and Celida Lake agreed with the theory, and indeed it seemed that Obama had succeeded with this coalition in 2012, virtually writing off white voters (who nevertheless voted for him in large numbers anyway). Thus last-minute reports of a "surge" in Hispanic voters seemed like the Florida miracle Hillary needed—they might save the state for her after all. On November 6, the *Miami Herald* gleefully reported that a "record number" of Hispanic voters in Florida was "boosting" Clinton. Florida political science professor Dan Smith claimed that 565,000 Hispanics had voted early in-person (a 100 percent increase over 2012) and that of the total 900,000 Hispanics who had voted in the state, a third of them had never voted before. But other early voting analysis showed that these were not younger voters (who were more likely to back Clinton); their numbers were actually down. In fact there was no real evidence that these Hispanics were Hillary voters. Of course, the *Miami Herald* was able to find anti-Trump Hispanics to quote, but post-election analysis would show that Trump carried sizeable minorities of the Hispanic vote in Florida. In other words, while the news wasn't necessarily bad for Clinton, it was far from the Florida miracle that the press was touting.[37]

Something more surprising was happening—though the media chose to ignore it: white voters were showing up in greatly increased numbers.

The white vote was up by more than 3 percent in Florida, and by a similar percentage in North Carolina, too. In fact, across the country, whites were voting in high numbers. After Trump's victory, leftist commentator Van Jones would complain of a "whitelash," and he wasn't entirely wrong: for more than twenty years whites had been disparaged, criticized, and blamed for all the ills of the world. Universities and the media had championed identity politics for every group—except whites. Without appealing to whites on racial grounds, Trump tapped into this dynamic. And whites are four times more numerous than Hispanics in Florida, so that even if there was in fact a 100 percent increase in Hispanic voters—*and even if every single one of them voted for Clinton* (and they did not)—that advantage could be offset by a much smaller increase in the percentage of whites coming out to vote for Trump. When combined with the decreased black and under-thirty vote, and the percentage of Hispanics (especially Cubans) voting for Trump, even a massive increase in Hispanics might not have sufficed to win Florida or North Carolina for Clinton.

The white vote was especially important not only in Florida and North Carolina but also in the tier of blue union states in the Midwest—Wisconsin, Michigan, Ohio, and Pennsylvania. There, disenfranchised voters who had been unemployed by Obama's energy and trade policies had voted for Trump in the primaries and were willing to give him a chance in the Oval Office. By small but consistent margins these white voters would make the difference in the election.

As the final weekend of the campaign unfolded, Trump supporters held their breath awaiting one more "dirty trick" as promised by #NeverTrump GOP consultants Rick Wilson and Liz Mair. Wild rumors swirled: there was supposed to be a tape about a twenty-year-old rape accusation, or Trump had used a racial slur on the set of *The Apprentice*, it was said. But on Friday, November 4, Mair said that she had nothing, and Wilson's frenzied Tweeting turned up no new revelations. One source told me that an acquaintance who edited tapes at NBC was continually approached by all the major "news" outlets for a comment—they wanted her just to *say* NBC still had more offensive tapes. The drive-by media were calling "several times a day" just trying to get *anything* that they could use as an excuse to launch another smear campaign. The tape editor—a Clinton voter—finally stopped taking their calls because NBC had nothing else. Trump was home free. Now all he had to do was win the election when almost every pollster (save two, Deplorable Richard Baris's People's Pundit Daily and USC/*LAT*) claimed he was behind.

The final "No Toss Up States" map at RealClearPolitics showed Clinton winning 272–266. But they were being cautious; on their final general election polling page, the numbers looked completely hopeless for Trump.[38] RCP did include the accurate USC poll in their final average, but they refused to acknowledge Baris's PPD and did not include Rasmussen, either. (Rasmussen had Trump +2 in its national poll, while IBD had the popular vote close, at a one-point advantage for Clinton.) What all the pollsters except Baris seemed to be missing was that Trump was not campaigning for the popular vote lead, but for specific victories in the battleground Electoral College states.

Otherwise the polls were a disaster, given that the final was Clinton +1.3 in the popular vote and a big Electoral College loss. The RCP average was Clinton +3.2—off by 1.9 points. But many of the polls were off by three or four points, and Monmouth (the worst), missed the final result by 4.7 percentage points:

- Bloomberg: Clinton +3
- *Economist*/Yougov: Clinton +4
- ABC/*Washington Post*: Clinton +3
- NBC/*Wall Street Journal* Clinton +5
- CBS: Clinton +4
- Reuters/Ipsos: Clinton +5
- Monmouth: Clinton +6
- Fox: Clinton +4

The huge gaps between the polling and the actual election results demonstrate just how biased the pollsters were, but Clinton's eventual popular vote margin—largely from California where, according to one study, the vote is heavily weighted by illegals—obscured the state-by-state errors in polling that caused Electoral College predictions to be so far off.[39] A look at the state polling shows even wider misses by the pollsters than in the national polls.

The RCP national final state averages had Clinton winning Florida by 3.2 percent, New Hampshire by the same margin, Pennsylvania by 1.9 percent, Michigan by a whopping 3.4 percent, and Wisconsin by 6.5 percent. In reality, Trump won all those states except for New Hampshire. Of the last four Florida polls, only Trafalgar group had Trump up—by 4 percentage points—while Quinnipiac, Gravis, and Opinion Savvy had Clinton up by 1, 1, and 2 percent respectively. Both Quinnipiac and Gravis had Clinton up in North Carolina, which Trump also won. A Christopher Newport University poll of Virginia, the last state poll done, had Clinton up there by 6 percent (she won by 4.9). Emerson, the last poll taken in Ohio, had Trump up 7 percent and was considered an outlier: the RCP average without Emerson was Trump +2.3 percent. In fact, Trump won Ohio by 8.6 percent. Trump won Michigan by .3 percent, but the final RCP average was Clinton ahead by 3.4 percent, and except for a Trafalgar poll (also considered an outlier), the RCP average would have been Clinton +4.75! In Pennsylvania, again excluding Trafalgar (which got it dead on), Clinton was leading by 2.4 percent, but lost by 1.2 (an error of 3.6 percentage points).

How did the "outlier" Trafalgar poll come so much closer than the others? By designing a question that flushed out the "secret Trump voters." Trafalgar asked, "How do you think your neighbor will vote?" That allowed people who weren't willing to admit to voting for Trump to project their own vote on their neighbors. This was the infamous "shy Trump" voter in action. But the badly skewed averages swamped Trafalgar. The worst polling came in Wisconsin, where Trump won by 1 percent but the RCP average was Clinton +6.5 and the last Remington Research poll there had her up 9 percent—a whopping 10 percentage point error!

Were the pollsters completely blinded by their own bias? Or were they hoping to dampen turnout for Trump and make a Clinton victory a self-fulfilling prophecy? Either way, they not only misinformed the public; they misinformed *the Clinton campaign*. Thus the biased polls set Clinton herself up for the biggest fall of the night! They were only setting up their own side for a crushing disappointment—and an insane reaction to the election results.

Richard Baris was one of only two pollsters close to the actual election numbers. His People's Pundit Daily was showing sharp leaps in Trump support in both Pennsylvania and Michigan. As he told me after the election, "We really didn't have Florida all that close." Key to his findings were the "disenfranchised voters" who hadn't voted in several cycles. They were overwhelmingly for Trump, to the point that "Clinton never got close to 7 percent with these voters."[40]

A Long Night

In the days leading up to November 8, I predicted on Twitter and Facebook that if Trump was in fact ahead or tied in key states such as New Hampshire, Pennsylvania, Florida, and Virginia it would be immediately obvious because of the "no calls." That is, the networks would immediately call *any* Clinton state they could on the smallest of margins but would hesitate to call a Trump state even when victory was obvious. That had occurred in 2000, when, as Bill Sammon showed in his book *At Any Cost*, the networks withheld their calls of states such as Georgia, where George W. Bush had a 5-point lead, for over an hour, while calling states for Al Gore with less than a 1 point lead in half that time.[41]

It seemed like the mainstream media would do everything in their power to keep from giving Trump any momentum. But the polls closed late in a lot of important, big, elector-rich states that were firmly in Clinton's column: Illinois was in the Central Time Zone, New Mexico and Colorado on Mountain Time, and California, Washington, and Oregon in the Pacific Zone (with Hawaii even further behind them). In short, almost one hundred electoral votes for Clinton would not come in until late. Once the election moved beyond the Northeast, Trump could be piling up electoral votes for a couple of hours.

Clinton supporters, including those in the GOP who were still burning over Trump, insisted it would be a short night. Mike Murphy, a #NeverTrump Republican political consultant, insisted, "My big prediction: I think she'll win FL quickly; will be clear in early numbers. Then cable news will do a huge 180 on 'long night.'"[42] GOP consultants had insisted *throughout* the campaign that Trump was losing college-educated voters—despite the fact that in poll after poll, primary after primary he won that group. He lost *post-graduate* voters, but not by much and almost always only to Marco Rubio. Yet GOP pollster and #NeverTrumper Stuart Stevens tweeted, "As new NBC/WSJ poll shows, Trump is on track to be the first Republican to lose college educated whites since FDR era." It simply wasn't true. Trump finished the election with an advantage with…college-educated whites. Stevens would later again insist, wrongly, that Trump was losing "every demographic in (the) country that is growing. From college educated whites to Hispanics."[43] In fact Trump won college-educated whites and did far better with Hispanics than Mitt Romney. But the facts seemed lost on the NeverTrumpers.

My prediction proved accurate. As polls closed in New Hampshire, Virginia, and Pennsylvania…there were no calls. The message was obvious to those who knew how the media plays the game: Trump was very much in the race in all these states, and most likely leading.

An Election for All Time

Trump wrapped up his campaign in Raleigh, North Carolina, then joined Mike Pence and his family in Manchester, New Hampshire. "Tomorrow the American working class will strike back," he announced. "My only interest is you," he said, pointing to the crowd. "When we win tomorrow, we are going to drain the swamp.... I will be a champion for all Americans against this corrupt and unfair system.... We will be a rich nation again."[44] He staged one last rally, improbably after midnight in Grand Rapids, Michigan. He then returned to New York and would spend the following evening at his campaign headquarters with his staff to watch the returns as supporters filled the Hilton ballroom.

Pence had proven to be a brilliant choice. Thoroughly loyal, Mike Pence was far more combative on the campaign trail than he appeared to be as Indiana governor, but in a "nice" way. He was a hard man to hate, and when he stated "Trump Truths," they often came off as less threatening. Of course, GOPe types claimed Pence should have been at the top of the ticket—but Pence's fire was largely stoked by the man at the top. Like many of Lincoln's Civil War generals, Pence was a superb division commander, not general of the Armies. That was Trump, who set the tone, direction, and vision for everything.

On Election Night, all the major staff was at work at Trump Tower, with Trump on one floor and everyone else, including Bannon, Conway, and the seventy- to hundred-member campaign staff in the "war room" on a different floor. Early on they seemed baffled and, yes, panicked by early returns in Florida and Ohio. I got a call from Deplorable Drew, who had flown to New York to be on hand with Team Trump wondering what was going on. "We're collapsing across the board," he fretted.

"No, you aren't," I replied. "You're just seeing the early and absentee votes that we have been tracking for the past three months actually be posted. And as you know, these *always* favor the Democrats. Relax." I knew our absentee and early-voting numbers had the Democrats in a massive shortfall compared to 2012, as did Baris. But there was tremendous anxiety on the other end of the phone. "What do your own numbers say?" I asked to reassure him.

"They say we'll win Florida by 3 points."

"Trust your numbers," I replied.

By that time, I had shut off almost all media and was tracking the actual numbers. We "Basket of Deplorables" had set up in a virtual war room of our own—a Twitter chat room called "Trump Gurus Unite." In that electronic bunker I was joined by pollster "Deplorable Greg" Den Haese with his unmatched information about southern Florida voting; "the Naked Archaeologist," an anonymous archaeologist-historian whose Twitter handle is Maximus Paulus; and Grammy-nominated musician Chris Bowen, with the five of us hurling statistics at each other.

Greg was tracking the numbers—especially in the Florida red counties, where the GOP was stacking up votes well beyond its 2012 numbers—by the minute. When combined with the early voting shortfall of Democrats, we all were confident Trump was in terrific shape.

I called Deplorable Drew back in New York: "You're crushing it in the red counties. Don't worry about the early vote stuff. It's behind 2012 and will soon be washed out."

But Team Trump remained concerned about Broward County, which seemed to be manufacturing votes out of thin air. Even Greg was concerned. "How many more votes are there in Broward?" I asked. Baris and Greg did some quick math. "Not enough for Hillary, and the Panhandle is just now coming in.

"But," Baris added, "it's going to be close."

"I don't think so," I told him. "Just keep watching the red counties."

By that point (perhaps 4:00 p.m. in Arizona, where I was two hours behind Greg and Richard, not to mention Team Trump), I was convinced Trump had won Florida. I ate dinner at 5:00—and was still avoiding the drive-by television media, so I had heard nothing from the mainstream talking heads—and took our dogs out for a walk, peaceful and completely confident Florida was ours. Ten minutes into the walk, Deplorable Drew called me: "Larry, we're only 10,000 down in Florida."

"Told ya so."

Now he had another worry, though: "But we're crashing in Ohio."

"HUH?" I knew this was silly, if not impossible. I knew we would win Ohio by at least four (and my estimate was low, as it turned out—Trump won by 8.6 percent).

"My Ohio guys are saying that it's terrible there. We have two of them—they know Ohio—and they are walking around with their heads down, like a relative just died."

"Well," I countered, "You've got the wrong Ohio advisors. You're seeing the same thing that you saw in Florida: early votes and absentees being racked up first. When the real votes come in, it won't be close." We didn't speak again about Ohio, because within an hour it was obvious: Ohio wasn't even close, with the final margin close to nine points.

By that time Baris, Deplorable Greg, and I were wrapping up Florida. "She doesn't have any more votes in Broward," said Greg. "It's over, barring massive fraud."

"I'm calling Florida," said Baris at 9:20—an hour and a half before Fox made the same call.

Then the real stunner hit. At 11:30 Fox News called Wisconsin for Trump and Megyn Kelly sternly announced that Trump had "pierced the Blue Wall." At Trump HQ, chants of "Lock Her Up" erupted. Indefatigable naysayer Nate Cohn Tweeted, "Fox News Calls Wisconsin for Trump. That's it."

At Clinton HQ a shocked hush fell over the crowd. Consultant Mike Murphy tweeted, "I've believed in data for 30 years in politics and data died tonight. I could not have been more wrong about this election."[45] But the data is *never wrong*—if you're actually willing to look at it. Baris saw it. Deplorable Drew saw it, Deplorable Greg saw it, and I saw it. The problem was that the establishment pollsters, consultants, and media just didn't want to believe the data.

As the *New York Times* began to shift its prediction board on Pennsylvania, Baris spoke with the Clinton campaign and reported, "They aren't happy.... They appear to be expecting the loss in PA. They say there is another county out and they believe it will go Trump." Baris called Pennsylvania for Trump, spoke to the Clinton campaign again, and told us, "They're crying at Clinton HQ. They hung up on me...but they know they lost."

When Did They Know?

The signs that Clinton was losing were everywhere, long before Election Night.

Did she *know* she was going to lose?

I had long suspected that someone in the Clinton camp must be seeing what we could see. It seems highly unlikely that Jake Sullivan's accurate warnings that Hillary was losing Michigan and possibly Pennsylvania were not being taken seriously by some higher-ups in Clinton's campaign. Baris and I separately got reports at various times that, for all intents and purposes, Clinton's team had pulled out of North Carolina and Ohio—though she did have a last-minute rally in Cleveland. Personally I think some in the Clinton camp, probably campaign chairman John Podesta, knew *as early as Thursday, November 3*, that they would likely lose

My reason for believing they knew this is that the campaign canceled its gigantic New York fireworks display. As the *Washington Examiner* reported, "The first public sign that Hillary Clinton's campaign was unsure of victory was when they canceled the fireworks" that had been scheduled for election night—something they did on the Thursday *five days* before the election.[46] We Deplorables had learned about the cancellation on Friday, though it wouldn't be reported by TMZ until Monday, the last day of the campaign. Such a response would only have been rational if in fact someone in the Clinton camp was seeing the early voting and absentee numbers that showed Ohio clearly out of reach for Hillary, Iowa safe for Trump, and Florida and North Carolina as likely losses for the Democrats.

This was exactly the opposite of what the drive-by media were reporting—that Trump had to "run the table" on Tuesday night. Quite the contrary. It was Clinton who had to draw the inside straight. She was still campaigning in Iowa, ostensibly just to keep Trump there, yet was down badly in the final *Des Moines Register* poll. She had to hold every single remaining competitive state: New Hampshire, Virginia, Wisconsin, New Mexico, Maine, Pennsylvania, Colorado, Nevada, Oregon, and Michigan. While some of these seemed safe—the final polls had her seemingly secure in Oregon and Maine—she was actually trailing the polls in Nevada and was barely ahead or tied in most of the others. (Ironically Nevada was one of the *most* reliable states for Clinton that night, meaning once again the polls had been wrong. Hillary had put resources into the wrong place because she was getting bad information from the "lyin' pollsters," as Donald Trump might call them.)

It wasn't just the cancelled fireworks that make me think the Clinton camp must know more than they let on. There was also John Podesta's utter lack of confidence on Episode 26 (the final episode) of *The Circus*, HBO's documentary series on the 2016 election. When *Politico* reporters asked if Clinton would win, he dodged and stammered.

These little warning signs suggest that some in Clinton's camp knew deep down that they were in serious trouble. The as-yet unanswered questions are, "Who? And did they tell Hillary?" Sullivan had warned the campaign repeatedly that the polls were wrong, and based on Podesta's November 7 response to the *Politico* reporters in *The Circus*, it appears he believed Sullivan. But it would appear that he never informed Clinton herself that she was losing—until the networks called Wisconsin.

Did campaign manager Robby Mook know? Possibly, but it's likely that he believed his "Ada" computer model more than he believed Sullivan's warnings—and had convinced Clinton of its inerrancy. Since the public polls seemed to support Ada, Mook had the better case than Sullivan. My guess—but only a guess—is that Podesta really believed Sullivan, but kept hoping that Ada was right.

At any rate, the "we're gonna win easy" cohort of the Clinton campaign had reserved the glass tomb known as the Javits Center for the coronation event. The symbolism of the Javits Center was obvious: Hillary would break what the *New York Times* called the "highest, hardest glass ceiling" and become president.

But whatever some in Clinton's inside circle knew, her supporters were utterly unprepared for defeat. As Myra Adams, a Republican reporter writing for the *Washington Examiner* in attendance at the Clinton victory party, wrote, "the word 'arrogance' [was] swirling in my brain."[47] According to Adams, the "buzz in the air" at the Javits Center was that victory was certain, and defeat not even a remote possibility. GOPe bloggers and consultants took the same attitude as the Democrats. But in fact Clinton had already lost North Carolina, Florida, Iowa, and Ohio before the networks even got serious about calling states.

What Adams was seeing was, in fact, the story of the entire campaign. Clinton had been propped up by phony polls, inside "yes men," blathering talking heads, and dubious "analysis" by traitorous GOPe consultants all spouting the same absurdities despite the realities of the data. The detachment from reality was on display again on Election Night, when, as Adams noted, "the large screens throughout Javits and in the media filing room kept cutting away from the harsh reality of actual voting results to play Clinton's...propaganda videos."[48] By then the failing Clinton strategy was exposed. It seems that her team had hoped to somehow build an aura of inevitability to depress Trump's base, and especially the "secret Trump voters." So for Clinton to win, everyone had to pretend she had no problems at all. Maybe that strategy discouraged attempts to inform the candidate herself of unpleasant realities. Everyone played their role, including the pollsters, the media talking heads, the drive-by columnists.

The Trump campaign, on the other hand, thanks to us Deplorable gurus and a host of other volunteer analysts, was armed with the real numbers. And those numbers were unbelievably positive for their candidate. I blame the last-minute case of the jitters—in some cases, the Trump people simply weren't believing their own ground reports—on the "experts" that Trump had brought in over the previous two months, who were still evaluating the race as a typical campaign. When they finally saw the light and agreed that the numbers we "Gurus" were sending them were correct, they breathed a sigh of relief. Even when Trump arrived in the war room around 8:30 p.m., several staffers were still spooked by the posting of the early voting and absentee numbers. "The early results were in and looked terrible," Deplorable Drew told me later when we discussed the evening. But just as Trump reached his campaign's war room, the Florida results began to turn in his favor.

We have seen how we Deplorable "Gurus," hunkered down in our own virtual war room, knew Trump had won Florida long before the media announced it. I texted that and other reassuring news from our analysis to Bannon all night.

But the Trump supporters starting the Trump victory party at the Hilton—they had already been drinking for hours—didn't know about Baris's call. It wasn't until Fox announced Florida, then Wisconsin, that the room erupted. Karl Rove had been pontificating as usual, saying nothing, but hinting that Trump would lose when, at 10:59 p.m., Bret

Baier, announced that Donald Trump had won Florida, on top of Ohio
and North Carolina. Megyn Kelly somberly said "if you need the inside
straight, he is well on his way."

By 11:30, when Kelly announced that Trump had "pierced Hillary
Clinton's blue wall" to win Wisconsin, it was clear that Trump would
win at least 269 electoral votes, though until and unless the Maine Second Congressional District was called for him, the election might still
end up a tie and go to the House of Representatives. Still, Trump was
waiting for calls of further states, especially Pennsylvania, that would
put the decision beyond challenge. Once again, we Deplorable gurus were
way ahead of the drive-bys. Baris spoke with the head of the Luzerne
County, Pennsylvania, GOP, who told him at midnight Eastern Time
that it was over. "I know my state," he told Baris. There were not enough
remaining votes for Clinton to win—Philly was all voted out. Baris called
the keystone state at 12:05 a.m., November 9.

Fox did not call Pennsylvania until two hours later—1:57 a.m. with
Bret Baier labeling 2016 the most "unreal, surreal election we have ever
seen." With Pennsylvania in hand, Fox was calling the presidency for
Trump, but it wasn't until about 3:00 a.m. that Trump and his team
began to move over to the Hilton. Megyn Kelly recalled a conversation
related to her by Trump's wife, Melania, when pondering a presidential
run. Reportedly, Melania said to Donald, "Don't do it. You'll win." And
now he had.

Merely moving the campaign staffers down the elevators in Trump
Tower from the war room took shifts, shuttling people to the lobby. Most
then walked over to the Hilton, about half a mile away, while Trump
and Pence rode in secure vehicles.

When Deplorable Drew got to the Hilton, he noticed that the normal open bars were doing a land office business. "One guy was dead
drunk on a window sill and I had to rescue him," and he had to drag
another guy out of a closing elevator door. In another corner, there were
two other guys—looking like Mr. Smith from *The Matrix*—passed out.
In front of both Trump Tower and the Hilton there were protesters and
oodles of security. There were dump trucks filled with dirt to stop

vehicles, as well as the concrete anti-vehicle barriers and the standard wooden barriers. SWAT and other police were swarming, and the protesters were "burning flags and all that shit," according to Drew, as we reminisced about the evening a few days after the election.

And on the networks, talking heads were predicting the end of the world, with mumbled inanities about horrible things that would happen to women and minorities.

Then next day, November 9, Deplorable Drew looked down from a balcony at Trump Tower, where he saw crowds of protesters that looked like the "bug scenes from *Starship Troopers*." The noise, he recalled, was overwhelming, and the opposition frightening.

But Trump had won. He won big.

Although Michigan wouldn't be called until Thanksgiving, Trump won that state and the other late-called state of Arizona for a total of 306 Electoral Votes. The popular vote is still being counted as of this writing, but Clinton will walk away with a large popular vote margin—virtually all of it attributable to piling up votes in California. Trump won far more states, far more counties, and far more battleground states. Hillary ran up the "yardage," so to speak, in California, New York, and Illinois. There is no doubt Trump's victories in the "blue" states he took were close: the difference in Michigan was about 10,000 votes; Wisconsin, 37,000; and Pennsylvania, 57,000. My prediction that the election wouldn't be close, but that it would be determined by a number of close votes in key states, proved correct.

But other states could easily have swung Trump's way. New Hampshire went to Hillary by just over 1,700 votes. She won Maine by only 20,000 votes. And she took Minnesota by a final margin of just over 45,000 votes, virtually all of them "early"—on Election Day, Trump carried Minnesota by nearly 2 to 1 outside Hennipen County. In sum, Trump lost seven states—with more than 70 electoral votes—by under 750,000 votes. A shift of those 750,000 votes would have given Trump a landslide victory of about 380 electoral votes. Moreover, if you examine the "flip factor"—the question of how many voters would need to flip to make each state competitive—an "out of reach" state like Oregon would have flipped with a mere 65,000 voters switching their votes. And third party candidates Stein and Johnson accounted for more than 131,000 votes, or almost 7 percent of the total there. Gary Johnson, with his 73,000 votes in New Mexico, likely handed that state to Clinton, and most likely Nevada as well, where he won 37,000 votes and the final margin was a mere 26,000. A Trump reelection campaign minus Gary Johnson could easily carry New Mexico, Nevada, and Minnesota.

Trump shocked the experts on many counts. He won Laredo, the most Hispanic city in America, with 35 percent of the Latino vote. His 8 percent of the black vote, while not as large as many expected, perfectly matched that of Mitt Romney and doubled that of John McCain. And his 28 percent of the Hispanic vote nationally exceeded that of any recent Republican candidate. Trump carried whites, including the college educated, and won white females. Trump did much better with union households than any Republican, losing to Clinton by only 8 points nationally with those homes, cutting Obama's 2012 margin in half.[49]

There are strange accounts about how Clinton took her loss. Around midnight of Election Night, Todd Kincannon claimed on Twitter he was told by an unnamed CNN reporter that Clinton melted down and "became physically violent toward Robby Mook [her campaign manager] and John Podesta" and "had to be briefly restrained."[50] According to Kincannon, CNN had blocked the story: "CNN has banned all 'Hillary in the bunker' stories."[51] Ed Klein, *New York* magazine editor in chief, reported that an "old friend" of Clinton's had said the morning after the election that she was "weeping," and "crying inconsolably, she couldn't stop crying." She was "blaming James Comey" and even Obama for her loss. "It's never her fault," Klein said.[52] Another blogger reported that Clinton was "in a psychotic, drunken rage" on Election Night, "straight-up Hitler-in-the-bunker shit…even included psychotic screaming about 'the Russians.'" An unnamed CNN reporter said Hillary had received sedatives that night, then "needed so many amphetamines Wed morning she had unexpected nosebleeds all day."[53] "Federal Spy Guy" claimed on Twitter that, according to a Secret Service source, when Podesta told Hillary she needed to make a statement to her followers at Javits Center admitting she lost, Clinton said "fuck them—you do it." Whatever the truth of the matter, she either could not or would not address her supporters.

Podesta finally marched out around 2:00 a.m. and told the crowd to "head home" because the election was "too close to call." (In fact everyone could see Hillary had lost Wisconsin, Ohio, Florida, Iowa, and North Carolina.[54] The only thing that remained to be determined was how big her electoral loss was.) It was just one more untruth from a campaign built on lies. Obama called Hillary at 1:30 a.m. on Election Night, urging her to concede, but she did not take his advice. Some of her aides thought Obama's request was a betrayal, and that Clinton needed to wait longer.[55] Finally, late in the morning on November 9, the day after the election, Clinton made a statement conceding to Donald Trump and vowing to work with him to make his presidency a success.

Shortly thereafter, she would join recount efforts by Jill Stein to overturn the election results in Michigan, Pennsylvania, and Wisconsin.

Edison research found that of those who said they did not particularly like either candidate, Trump won by significant percentages, especially in the battleground states. For example, Trump won 22 percent of the "neithers" in Wisconsin, 17 percent in Pennsylvania, and 20 percent in Michigan. These were people who perhaps had not decided *for* Trump, but who clearly opposed handing Hillary the presidency. The Edison numbers also cast doubt on Obama's presidential approval ratings, suggesting that people may have not been honest about their feelings when asked. Those results underlined the ulterior motives that people often have for answering polls the way they do—and once again proved the horrid state of polling.[56] Hillary led Trump in the popular vote in the United States by almost two million. That would prove the largest popular vote deficit ever, of all the numerous times that a candidate had won the popular vote yet lost the election, including 1824, 1860, 1876, 1888, and of course 2000.

And even after conceding and declaring Trump the winner, Clinton would not go away. She resurfaced two weeks later to join in when Green Party candidate Jill Stein contested the vote in Wisconsin and demanded a recount. Stein was funded with suspicious money pouring in over the web (her entire campaign had raised just over $3 million, yet in less than a week she raised over $5 million for a recount). But there was no chance of overturning anything with the recounts. The margin was sufficiently large for Trump in Wisconsin (and one county's recount only added to Trump's total) that nothing would come of it. As Bannon told me, "Wisconsin is locked!" Stein missed the deadline for a Pennsylvania recount, attempted to "contest" the election, and was blocked by a judge from doing so. Michigan's recount was also shut down by the courts. The Wisconsin recount was completed—actually giving Trump a net gain of a few votes. But the recount circus only reminded Americans why there needed to be change in the system. For the second time in twenty years, the party that was the clear loser was refusing to accept the result of a free and fair election.

Victory Dance

Even as the last minute recount shenanigans petered out, the tough part for Trump was only beginning: forming a government and governing. But what he had already accomplished already was unprecedented. Here was a non-political figure, largely self-funded, not only lacking the support of his own party but facing its active opposition; a person opposed by not one or two but *sixteen* primary candidates, all of whom were expected to do better; a candidate who ran against not one but *four* major general election contenders (Jill Stein, Gary Johnson, Evan McMullin, and Hillary Clinton); and a candidate who defeated all of these *and* the deliberate, determined, and unanimous opposition of the American "drive-by" media—to still win.

In 2012, Barack Obama won twenty-seven states—but Trump won thirty in 2016. Of the states Obama won, his average margin of victory was 17.5 percent, while Trump's average was 18.8 percent. Trump's winning vote margin was double that of Mitt Romney in states they both carried. Clinton, on the other hand, seriously underperformed Obama in key areas, especially North Carolina, Michigan, and Pennsylvania (particularly in the cities). Astoundingly, Hillary exceeded Obama's vote totals in Broward County, Florida—perhaps another reason to suspect vote fraud there. While Jill Stein and Clinton would drag out the recounts, nothing would change the fact that President Trump would take the oath of office in January 2017.

Trump's election was a testimony to the brilliance of the Founders and the Electoral College and a statement about the independence of the American voter. In the end, all the predictions, experts, polling, and browbeating by the elites could not prevent Donald Trump from speaking to the American people.

And on November 8, 2016, the American people answered. You could almost hear them roar, "Make America Great Again."

CHAPTER TEN

On the Campaign Trail:
From Seven-State Sunday to Election Day

Joel Pollak

November 6, 2016

Acool, bright morning in Denver, the starting point for Trump's seven-state swing. Starting in Colorado, he will visit several swing states where he has battled closely with Hillary Clinton— and a few that he hopes to shift over from the "blue" column.

He will hold rallies in Iowa, Minnesota, Michigan, Pennsylvania, and Virginia before arriving in Florida to begin the final day of campaigning on Monday. His hope is to win enough swing states, and steal a blue state or two, to secure victory.

The blue state gamble is not a new idea, but one that Trump is uniquely positioned to achieve. In 2008, John McCain briefly considered campaigning in Michigan, but called off plans to contest the state, much to the chagrin of his running mate, Alaska Governor Sarah Palin, who took the title of her subsequent memoir, *Going Rogue*, from her desire to defy the advice of the campaign professionals and hit Michigan anyway.

In 2012, Mitt Romney hoped to break through the Democrats' wall of blue states by choosing Representative Paul Ryan as his running mate. Ryan was a rising star from Wisconsin, where state Republicans had withstood a brutal national onslaught by Democrats in an effort to reverse Governor Scott Walker's public sector union reforms. Romney had hoped Ryan could win his home state, and campaigned there. But that effort also failed.

Trump was always a risky candidate because his ideas, and his rhetoric, stood a good chance of repulsing the moderate voters that Republicans need in order to win swing states.

But his unorthodox positions on trade and immigration have connected directly with voters in the Midwest—including Democrats. For the first time since Ronald Reagan a Republican nominee is appealing directly to the concerns and interests of the working class.

It is a huge gamble, but a rational one, given Republicans' disappointments running moderate candidates in the previous two presidential races, and their frustration with some of the conservative leadership in Congress.

If the battle could be won, it would be by taking big risks only Trump would take.

Seven-state Sunday is that gamble.

■   ■   ■

We arrive in Sioux City, South Dakota, and board a large bus—the press corps has grown again—to drive across the border into Sioux City, Iowa. The line outside the convention center is enormous—so large it draws whistles from the journalists as we arrived.

I speak to a woman in line who tells me she is sure that Trump will win Iowa, because no one she knows is voting for Hillary Clinton. She also says she hoped to see a more "presidential" Trump onstage.

And "presidential" he is—more disciplined and on-message than I have seen him yet. However, he starts about twenty minutes late—to the titters of the Iowa crowd, who evidently are used to more exacting punctuality.

He wins them over with his messages about Obamacare and corruption, presenting the 2016 election as a choice between being governed "by the people," or by the "corrupt political class." The crowd is less rowdy than elsewhere; the people stand in rapt attention.

There are many families, and a special section for seniors. Many of those at the rally are farmers. One woman from a farming family tells me that her Obamacare premiums have risen by $4,000 in one year alone. She does not know where they are supposed to find the money.

Her sister, standing nearby, says that America should one day have a female president—just not this one. When Trump first began running, she recalls, everything he said he stood for was a policy she agreed with.

Out of the convention center and back on the press bus, our driver struggles to negotiate a narrow left turn as he strives to keep up with the motorcade. He sideswipes a Chevy Impala whose owner has simply been waiting—perhaps a little too close to the intersection—outside the convention center.

No one is injured, through the incident can hardly have helped the frosty relations between locals and the national press. Not only are we "the most dishonest people in the world," but we also wreck things, then leave.

■   ■   ■

The next rally is in Minneapolis, perhaps the least likely of all Trump's campaign stops. The true-blue state of Minnesota was the only state to vote for Walter Mondale over President Ronald Reagan in the 1984 election. It is reliably "progressive" ever since, with a few interruptions.

Yet some polls have shown a close race there, including a Breitbart News/Gravis poll in late September—prior to the first presidential debate, and Trump's woman problems—that showed a 43–43 tie.

The Minnesota event is a classic airplane hangar rally, with the crowd waiting for Trump to land, the mogul-cum-candidate taxiing to the front in his private plane and descending the staircase to applause. The spectacle never fails to disappoint.

The afternoon sun sparkles in the balmy weather, with temperatures of 70 degrees on the tarmac. The enormous crowd swings into view as the press plane taxis to a halt.

Police on the ground tell me that 5,000 people were inside the hangar before the doors were closed. A total of 17,000 had registered for the event, and there are thousands gathered along the perimeter fence of the airport—including some standing and watching the proceedings from a "dirt hill" outside the airport—on the far side of the airport, across an ocean of asphalt.

This is a massive rally, among the largest, and the noise inside the hangar is deafening.

While we are still waiting for the Trump plane's door to open, I speak to some of the people waiting excitedly to see him.

Two middle-aged women near the media tent are quietly hopeful about his chances in the state. "I want to do my part—being here, being aware, praying, and voting. I believe Mr. Trump is the man we need to support and to pray for," one tells me. She adds that she hopes others were also becoming "aware."

The woman next to her tells me she supports Trump because she is pro-life. She then adds an observation that puts a lump in my throat: "The opposite of control is freedom. Trump is going to return control to the people, and give us freedom again, so we can flourish."

I look around the room, and think of that simple impulse, amidst the din of the hangar and the rumbling of flights taking off on the runway. The fight to be free continues long after freedom is won.

The traveling press is rushed out of the rally early, to be ready to take off again for the next stop. But on the way out, I happen to be following a prominent TV journalist with a camera crew and producer in tow. He stops to ask a woman a question that I cannot quite hear. A journalist behind me tells me to keep moving; I explain that there is nowhere to go, in the scrum.

Finally, once outside the hangar, the journalist and crew approach some of the people by the airport fence—who have been waiting hours outside. It is impossible to hear the question, or anything else, above the noise—so I ask the man to whom he had been speaking what the journalist had wanted to know.

It turns out that the TV journalist is asking him, and others, about the newly-released letter by FBI director James Comey indicating that the agency has reviewed the 650,000 emails found on Anthony Weiner's computer and sees no reason to revisit its July decision not to prosecute Hillary Clinton for mishandling classified information.

Obviously, the TV journalist can barely contain his excitement. But there is literally no point to these interviews. Trump's supporters are not at the rally because of James Comey. And after waiting for hours at the event they have no reason—and possibly no way—to know what had just happened in the news. (The internet reception, at least inside the hangar itself, is shockingly, prohibitively bad.)

Yet here comes the mainstream media, ambushing people to feed a preconceived narrative that has nothing to do with Minnesota.

It rankles me as I board the flight. But I am too busy to ask about it; I have my own stories to file. We have mere minutes, if that, before we have to stow our laptops and take off for Michigan.

■　■　■

We are headed to Sterling Heights, Michigan, and the Freedom Hill Amphitheater. Though there are just hours left in the campaign, this is to be the first of two remaining stops in Michigan, in a crucial last-ditch effort to pry the state from Democratic hands.

We arrive after sunset, and late. Even with a police motorcade, it is nearly an hour to the arena. A friend of mine who lives in the area sends me snapshots from inside the venue. It is packed to capacity, with thousands more having been turned away.

Controversial rock 'n' roll musician Ted Nugent entertains the crowd, and speaks to the "Michiganiacs" in the audience, whom he hopes will go home and "fix" anyone they knew who needed to be "fixed" on the subject of Trump.

We finally arrive, and the joint is jumpin', as they say. Not only is it full, but it is boisterous. This is a younger crowd than we are used to seeing. There are plenty of older folks, but the young people are much more visible than at other rallies.

There is a group of young men with red caps and a Detroit Redwings t-shirt or two right behind the media pen. There are two gorgeous young women, beaming at the stage. There are children on shoulders, some holding signs.

Trump finally has a full response to Comey's letter. His answer: "Hillary's guilty. She knows it. The FBI knows it. The people know it. And it's up to the American people to deliver justice on November 8th."

It is a defiant statement—but also, in the circumstances, an appropriate one. Regardless of what Comey did or did not say or do, the election will resolve whether she will be prosecuted, or if the American people are content to let a woman who was willing to be criminally careless with the nation's secrets in order to protect her political ambitions become president of the United States.

Trump launches broadsides at NAFTA, at Obamacare, at the Syrian refugee program—his usual routine. But he hits the NAFTA point harder than usual, and he reaches out explicitly to union members and to Democrats who may be in the audience. Cheers go up when he does.

The past three presidential campaigns have been about turning out the base, and this one is no exception. The difference is, Trump understands, as too few in his party do, that some of his natural base are also Democrats.

The young people in the audience are remarkable. They tell me that they trust Trump to fix the country's problems. Two young women tell me about his successful business career, that Trump is doing this because he loves them, that he is giving up a life of comfort to put the country back on track. Whatever he said about women, whatever he may have done to women, is of no real concern to them. They are fully behind him. Call it celebrity; call it charisma; either way, it is real.

A Trump staffer smiles at me and pumps his fist. He's right; the mood is electric. Nothing I have seen in previous campaigns compares to this. Even when huge crowds greeted Sarah Palin in 2008, there was an edge of sadness to every event. Her supporters hoped and prayed, but they knew it was over. Mitt Romney drew crowds but coasted into Election Day, protecting a lead that simply did not exist, and may never have existed, as a hurricane blew into New York.,

■　■　■

We are now extremely late. We have two rallies left in the day, and the second was supposed to have started already. There are reports that the second venue, in Loudon, Virginia, is already full—and we will not be there for hours. On Twitter, clever analysis projects a red-and-blue map showing Clinton winning narrowly while still losing Ohio and Florida. The map presumes Clinton holds Michigan, Pennsylvania, and Virginia—the very three states we are targeting tonight.

This is a hangar rally—perhaps the last. And, if Trump loses, perhaps the last time we will see this kind of spectacle.

We rush down the jetway and onto the tarmac. The air outside is cold—so the hangar is closed, to keep the heat in.

Trump's plane lands behinds ours with a whistling sound, then taxis toward the hangar. Inside, lights flash and float across the room, while the theme song for the opening of the Chicago Bulls blares over the speakers.

Soon, the theatrical music begins. The entrance is a dramatic reveal, but with a difference: given that the door of the hangar is closed, instead of the plane pulling up to it, the large doors of the hangar slide open slowly to reveal the plane as Trump appears at the top of the stairway. He climbs the stage, then waves a Terrible Towel, beloved symbol of the Pittsburg Steelers. He predicts a win in Pennsylvania, then adds that Election Day will be a big surprise, a "Brexit-plus-plus-plus," he tells the crowd.

He delivers an abbreviated version of his speech, hitting key points on Obamacare, Hillary Clinton's corruption problems, the Syrian refugees, and immigration. The children in the crowd atop their fathers' shoulders have stayed up well past their bedtime, and we still have one more stop to make.

A retiree in the crowd, near the media pen, tells me, "I can't stand the Clintons, going back to the 60s. This guy's got flaws, but if he'd campaigned like this for the last eight or nine months, he'd be far ahead today."

■ ■ ■

And we are off again, racing toward Virginia, hoping to be there before midnight. We feel the engines kick in at cruising altitude; the pilots seem to be pushing it. The landing gear slides out at 11:35 p.m.

We land as the crescent moon sets. We file onto the buses and head out into the dead of the night. It is impossible to imagine that anyone will still be at the Loudon Fairgrounds, still waiting for Trump. Three hours? After midnight? On Sunday, with school and work Monday?

After a bus ride of about twenty minutes, during which most of the press corps tries to catch some rest, we arrive after midnight—and are shocked to see an overflow crowd, at least hundreds of people strong, outside a barn. Inside, there are thousands of people who have been waiting for the better part of the day to see Trump. Children rest on their parents' shoulders, some long since asleep, others fighting to stay awake. Real people—working people—listen intently as Trump begins.

His speech is his essential stump speech, and his closing argument. He is going to repeal and replace Obamacare; he is going to preserve the Supreme Court; he is going to fight corruption and "drain the swamp" of American politics.

And yet the setting is unique, among thousands of people who have stayed awake so late. He is impressed; he dubs the speech the "Midnight Special," from the stage.

And as I speak to parents who have stuck it out, and hear why they came, I am on the verge of tears, moved by their passionate concern for their country.

I have never seen or heard anything like it. "We are going to win," I text my wife. "We"—we conservatives, we who have endured the past eight years, fighting every day to defend our core values against an unrelenting onslaught.

Of course, I cannot know that, really. And when we return to the bus in a few hurried moments, I see stories about how Senator Harry Reid, on his long-overdue way out as the Senate Minority Leader, has used his political machine to help boost Latino turnout in his home state, making it virtually impossible for Trump to take Nevada.

But this night almost feels like a turning point, like a moment I will look back upon and know that this is when things changed.

November 7, 2016

On November 7 we wake, improbably, in humid Florida, to begin the final sprint in the 2016 campaign.

It is impossible to know what this final day of the campaign will bring, much less Election Day tomorrow. The major mainstream media polls show that Clinton should defeat Trump by a modest but solid margin.

But here are two national polls that show Trump ahead. And his chances in battleground states are better than anyone expected. He may win Florida and Ohio. The question is what else he can win.

We roll into the Sarasota Fairgrounds. At the fence, a group of young women holding "Fuck Trump" signs greet us. Even after so many months of acrimonious debate, protest, and fighting, it shocks me that people would do that—especially because it is likely to make Trump fans seem more sympathetic than Clinton supporters.

As the rest of the press corps files into the arena, I take a detour out to the fence to interview the protesters. I am not disappointed; they are the epitome of leftist intolerance.

One woman holding a "Fuck Trump" sign tells me that she has no interest in changing the minds of Trump supporters. She just wants them to know that Hillary Clinton supporters are there.

A young woman standing nearby is waving a Mexican flag—which also strikes me as a bizarrely counter-productive way to make her point. She tells me she is a U.S. citizen. Why the Mexican flag, I ask? Because, she says, she is representing "my country" and those who cannot vote.

As I am speaking to her, a scuffle breaks out behind me. It is a full-on catfight—shoving, hair-pulling, and everything—between some of the protesters and a female Trump supporter who evidently took offense.

Police have to break up the fight, but no arrests are made. One protester sits tearfully on the ground and is comforted by others, as a kind woman hands them pamphlets, which they accept gratefully—until they turn out to be about salvation through Jesus Christ.

Inside the rally, Trump is beginning his first speech of the last day of the presidential campaign. He is buoyant, optimistic, telling the crowd that they can win if they go out and vote—he did the hard work already, he jokes.

They cheer him when he cites polls that show him winning in various states—and perhaps he is, but there are other polls, too. One wonders if people will feel deflated, or even cheated, if the world after tomorrow turns out to be other than advertised.

The mood in the arena is somewhat subdued, despite the excitement. Most believe Trump can win Florida, but they are not sure, and some have prayer on their mind.

A woman tells me that only God can make America great again, even if Trump is His instrument. Another man, a local retiree, says that whether he wins or loses, "at least Trump exposed the politicians for what they really are." That is true. But I am not sure it is adequate consolation if those politicians are left in office.

We clamber out of the arena into the sunshine, board the bus, and join the motorcade to the airport. The mood is bittersweet. In the arena, during the event, journalists were already saying their good-byes. Two years on the road together—often without their families—had built close friendships.

The world beyond the campaign begins to loom larger—a world outside a press bus, a campaign plane, a media pen. A world of spouses and kids and bills and exercise and new things that lie ahead.

■ ■ ■

After a long, merry flight, we descend to Raleigh once more. The late afternoon sun warms our faces as the wind whips our jackets and scarves on the tarmac, while we stand patiently in line to be "wanded" by the Secret Service.

Soon we arrive at the J. S. Dorton Arena, which looks like a giant hollow saddle made of glass, steel, and concrete. This is the first rally since Toledo, two weeks ago, where the room is not full, with some space on the floor and empty seats in the back.

Still, it is an impressive crowd by any measure. A woman, noticing that I am a journalist, taps me on the back and asks if I go to all the rallies. "Are they all as big as this?," she wants to know.

If there are a few empty chairs, the rally more than makes up for the gap in the sheer number and diversity of signs. I jot down every variety of sign that I see—almost all of them homemade: Latinos for Trump, Gays for Trump, Moms for Trump, High Schoolers for Trump, and more.

I run into Frank Luntz, the Republican pollster, who had tweeted the day before about the need for reconciliation. I had responded on Twitter that it should start with him and me. I have never, personally, had any kind of real argument with Luntz, even if Breitbart has been rough. I convince him to pose for a selfie, then ask him if Trump has a chance. Yes, he says—if he can win Florida, North Carolina, Nevada, and New Hampshire.

I feel confident in three out of the four—but Nevada may turn out to be difficult. Is it possible, I ask, for Trump to take one or more of the blue states, to compensate? No, Luntz says, looking at me as if I fell off the moon.

He may be wrong—and wouldn't it be sweet if he were, I think. That's the essence of the Trump gamble—to upend the conventional wisdom.

Later, Fox News has the same projection: a map moving in Trump's direction, but with Clinton maintaining a narrow edge, and winning all of the Midwestern states Trump has been targeting, including Michigan. Well, we shall see.

Trump starts his speech early—five minutes before advertised, which he occasionally does. It is standard fare, and if he is disappointed by the less-than-packed crowd, he doesn't show it. In fact, he goes out of his way to praise the size of the crowd, and then talks about the huge crowd he drew in Michigan the night before. The crowd in Selma, North Carolina, was even larger, but he may be trying to kill two birds with one stone, mentioning two states in one speech. Michigan, he reminds the audience, is in play.

There is something remarkable at the close of Trump's speech, and it is not something I have heard before, or at least not something to which I have listened very closely. He says: "We're fighting to bring us all together.... Just imagine if we started working together, under one God, saluting one American flag."

Clinton is running on unity—indeed, the word "together" is part of her campaign slogan—and Trump is trying to deny her that claim, as well as to finish his own campaign on a high, positive note.

I wonder if he thinks, at all, that he may lose. If he does, he is very good at hiding it, but there are signs that he has at least considered the possibility. At this rally, as at many before, Trump invites his audience to consider what losing would mean, not just for the country, but also for the effort itself—a "waste," in his words. They may say good things about us after we lose, he tells the audience, but there's no real consolation in that. His supporters have to go out, he tells them. They have to vote.

■   ■   ■

Next stop: Scranton, Pennsylvania, a place I have not been for some twenty years or so, since I went to a Jewish youth group summer program nearby and we volunteered in Scranton for a day of community service. I watch the sun set out the window—setting on the campaign. As we land, I decide: I am tired of being nervous.

But this is how I would have wanted this to end: a close fight to the finish, on Midwestern home turf. Like the Cubs, you have to be in *position* to win, then *decide* to win.

The Scranton event is everything the Donald Trump campaign has been: loud, exciting, and nearly impossible to manage.

The hall inside the Lackawanna College Student Union seats 4,200 and can fit an additional 300 on the floor, and the fire marshal tells me that it is completely packed. The crowd inside stomps and roars. The warm-up speech, by former New York mayor Rudy Giuliani, lights a fire under the crowd— but he reminds them that voting is better than yelling.

Trump emerges soon after. Amidst the noise, it is difficult to conduct interviews, because no one can hear anyone else even at close range.

Photography is also a challenge in the low light.

Some Trump supporters have put together an amazing display: "DRAIN THE SWAMP," in six-foot-high green letters, across several rows of the rear upper deck. It is nearly impossible, however, to make the letters out in the relative darkness. There are other homemade signs among a sea of official Trump campaign signs.

There are people of all ages, from the youngest to the oldest. Three-month-old Jameson observes the proceedings from a stroller, dressed in a red shirt: "adorable deplorable." Despite the chaos, there is no violence or fear whatsoever in the hall.

The only scuffle erupts inside the media pen itself, where two journalists jostle over camera space on the riser in back. Trump is in his element. If he wins, it will be because of these people—the hard-edged, forgotten Americans.

What amazes me, as I speak to them, is their absolute faith that Trump will win. In the media, we scrutinize poll numbers and imagine best-case scenarios. For them, the desire is the proof.

"God's behind him," a black man tells me. "You don't have a name like 'Trump' and come out losing. There's too much poetry in this country for that."

Jameson's father tells me he is sure Trump can win Pennsylvania, and the election. He points to his son: "It's about this guy."

Lots of politicians like to claim places like Scranton as their own—places they are from, before they went to more interesting, cosmopolitan places. Vice President Joe Biden claims roots in the town, as does Hillary Clinton herself.

But the people of Scranton have nothing to gain from Biden or Clinton or their party. They have run out of options and run out of patience. They are eager for the change Donald Trump is promising them. And they are dead certain it will come.

■ ■ ■

We race down the highway to the Wilkes-Barre airport and speed away to New Hampshire for a final rally, featuring Trump's running mate, Mike Pence.

There is a humorous moment on the way to the arena, just outside the airport. As we are enduring the routine search by the Secret Service, on a back road outside a large building, Trump's motorcade approaches. We have to move quickly. The Secret Service orders the press corps to stand "up against the wall." "I guess that means Trump's already won," one wag comments, to laughter.

And so for the third time in two weeks, I find myself in the Granite State, where Trump hopes to do what neither John McCain nor Mitt Romney—both of whom felt they had an edge in New Hampshire—could accomplish.

As we enter the arena in Manchester, I am beginning to understand why Trump is here, and why his campaign is optimistic.

A full capacity crowd of 11,700 stands on its feet and cheers the warm-up speaker, who in this case happens to be Giuliani. Brightly colored beams of light sweep the arena; the scoreboard reads "PRESI-DENT 45 TRUMP 45"; the floor is packed.

It's not a political rally, it's a rock 'n' roll concert, or a Stanley Cup final. It's thrilling, and while the journalists put on their poker faces, I am certain that they are impressed. This is the kind of stunt only Donald Trump could pull off.

After Pence re-appears on stage to introduce Trump, the nominee emerges—with his family in tow, the delightfully congenial, well dressed and photogenic bunch. Ivanka draws the loudest cheers from the crowd, and compliments her father on his campaign, adding that the real work begins after tomorrow.

If the past several months—to say nothing of the last month itself—have taken a toll on them, they do not show it. They remain his best, and still underused, asset.

This is a special occasion, and Trump has a few twists in store. The first is a personal one: he reveals that New England Patriots quarterback Tom Brady has voted for him, and that coach Bill Belichick has written him a letter of support. The crowd goes wild, and Trump reads Belichick's letter aloud, in which the coach praises Trump's campaign effusively. The media, whom Belichick criticizes directly, will spend the rest of the evening debating the authenticity of the Belichick letter.

The next surprise is a tagline: "Tomorrow, the American working class will strike back."

Here is the billionaire nominee of the Republican Party, the party of the rich, declaring himself to be the champion of the working class, and directing them to the barricades.

It is ironic. It is the essence of Bernie Sanders's tragicomic campaign, and it is the same sentiment that Hillary Clinton and her party vainly strive to emulate in every election.

And, however flawed the messenger, however problematic the policy prescriptions that Trump might propose to address it, that message sums up how Americans of many different classes and walks of life feel about our government.

Strip away the words "working class"—are we a society of classes?—
and keep the core: strike back.

That is the cause to which Donald Trump lent his name and his
legacy. It is the essence of opposition, fighting for power.

■ ■ ■

On the flight to Grand Rapids there is a curious dichotomy of moods.
The campaign staff seem quietly assured of Trump's victory. The media
are quietly confident about his defeat.

Perhaps this is always the way it will be, even when a Republican
wins a decisive victory, as long as the media are as liberal as they are,
and as long as the culture of most of the big states—California, New
York, Illinois—continues to shift left-ward.

We descend into chilly Grand Rapids, landing at midnight. The countdown clock at the front of the press plane has hit zeros. Election Day.

I snap a shot of the plane and post it on Facebook, along with a
prayer: "May God grant us the wisdom to choose the best candidate,
and the grace to survive the worst." I'm in an ecumenical mood.

And I'm feeling, despite all the evidence in the polls, that Trump actually has a chance to win, and that it's the best that our side can expect.

We enter the convention hall where the final rally is to be held. It is
a huge cavernous but well-lit space, where thousands of people have just
heard Mike Pence speak, and have waited for hours to hear Trump
himself.

I wonder if Trump is savoring the moment, if he feels like this may
be his last time in the spotlight. If he loses, he will have his concession
speech, and then he will be unceremoniously booted from public life.
This campaign will have consumed him, totally.

Whatever his private thoughts, onstage Trump sticks to the script,
and the message, which I take as a sign that he still expects to win. He
has been undisciplined enough that if he was certain he would lose, he
might seize the opportunity to improvise an attack on his various enemies, or a last-minute statement from the heart.

He reminds the audience that Ford, and other companies, are abandoning Michigan—and he promises to stop the exodus of jobs.

There are families with small children in the bleachers, fathers and mothers with kids on their shoulders. Some head home after they have watched him for a few minutes, but most stay through until the end.

Four young women at the edge hold hands and shout "Hillary! Hillary!" until they are escorted out of the rally. A final Trump event would be incomplete without at least some trouble from the Left.

Trump's voice echoes off the walls, making the hall feel emptier than it really is. Finally, for the last time on the campaign trail, he concludes with "We will make America great again."

The press piles onto the bus, and then up the stairs to the plane. I reflect on the event. Going to Michigan was the right thing to do, but could it backfire? After New Hampshire just two hours before, the new rally felt somewhat anti-climactic. But rallies don't vote, for good or ill.

And after a long flight and short rest, it will be time for the judgment of the people.

November 8, 2016

I wake in New York to a bright Manhattan sky, after a mere two hours of sleep. It's Election Day. I get up, after several attempts, and the first thought on my mind is that Trump is going to lose.

It just seems inevitable.

I search myself for the source of the feeling—why does it seem so real to me today? Perhaps because that last rally, in Grand Rapids after midnight, was not so energetic?

Perhaps the arrival of Election Day means there is no more time for Trump to make the case, and he has not yet closed the deal? Or maybe I am just exhausted?

I decide that the best thing is to move through my morning routine. The cartoonist-turned-pundit Scott Adams, whose political musings I have followed throughout the election, wrote a business advice book, *How to Fail at Almost Everything and Still Win Big*.[1] One of the most important points he makes is that goals are for losers, and "systems"—routines, or ways of doing things—are for winners. I decide to be a winner, even if my side loses the election.

It occurs to me that there are two elections, and two Americas, at stake.

In the minds of the media, collectively, is the standard model of how an election happens. Each side secures its base's support, and then spends the rest of the campaign trying to reach voters in the middle. According to that view, Trump is losing, because he has done things to alienate voters in the middle, and he has even suffered attrition among his own Republican base—with the defection of the conservative #NeverTrump faction.

The America to which that view corresponds is one in which the media play a crucial role, because journalists see themselves as the conduit to that elusive middle ground. It is for them to interpret the candidates and their merits (or lack thereof) for the marginal voter.

The media define what the "middle" is to begin with, by framing the debate so as to exclude certain ideas from the mainstream. Thus the media has considered Trump's loss a foregone conclusion—long before Tuesday.

The other America, the other election, is one in which the outsiders set themselves against the insiders who hold power in America. Who is an outsider is not necessarily obvious: they may not be the poor, and they may not even be the unemployed. More likely, they are the alienated—those who are denied the fruits of their labor, those whose votes are taken for granted, those who are shut out of public life because their experiences are inconvenient and their ideas too challenging.

To reach that America, Trump had to use the media—but also to challenge it, to defy it, to evade it, to circumvent it. And instead of appealing to the political middle, or even to his own political base, he had to reach across to the political base of the other side, and build a new coalition of voters, even from within the core of the Democratic Party. He had to find those who were not well-served by the existing system, whose aspirations were not contained in its bounds.

It was still unclear, on Election Day, which America would turn up at the polls—which America we had, indeed, become. The conventional wisdom at the end of the election was still what it had been at the beginning. Trump couldn't win without securing the Republican base and winning the moderate middle. Instead, he had done virtually everything he could to offend and alienate those moderates—and the media had taken every opportunity to amplify the offense and the alienation. In any case, in times of economic growth, no matter how modest, it is unusual for the incumbent political party to lose a major election. (The great Alexis de Tocqueville believed otherwise—that rebellions are most likely in times of rising expectations.) Regardless of the fact that the Obama economy was largely inflated by printing money, it was still growing somewhat—pointing to a Clinton victory.

The only way Trump would win was if he pointed to precisely those aspects of the existing system that were obnoxious to the country, and which would not be cured by continued anemic economic growth and by the retention of the stable political status quo. Clinton's flaws would have been exploited by almost any Republican, but only Donald Trump could have posed a distinct alternative that had any chance of challenging her—potentially the first female president—at the ballot box.

■　■　■

At midday, I leave the gleaming towers of Manhattan behind and take an Uber to the far side of Queens, to visit the Ohel, the resting place of the Seventh Lubavitcher Rebbe, Menachem Mendel Schneerson.

His grave is considered holy by many people—not only Jews—and was most famously visited by Victor Espinoza, the jockey who rode American Pharaoh to the victory in the 2015 Belmont Stakes the next day, winning racing's first Triple Crown since 1978.

The "Rebbe," as he is known to his admirers, continues to inspire, even two decades after his death. His positive moral example and his teachings are described by Joseph Telushkin in *Rebbe: The Life and Teachings of Menachem Mendel Schneerson*.[2]

One of his teachings, for example, is the importance of doing good as soon as the opportunity arises. Another is the importance of being able to disagree—but without ruining relationships over disagreement.

For that reason, I have had occasion to think of him often during the course of the election.

And others did, too, evidently: Ivanka Trump and her husband, Jared Kushner, had prayed at the Rebbe's Ohel on Saturday night. Their visit was seen as a way to entreat God's assistance at the polls on Tuesday, or perhaps to shore up Jewish support. In social media, some credited their prayers at the Rebbe's Ohel for saving Trump from the "assassination attempt" in Reno.

I have never been here before—though my wife has—and I enjoy the opportunity to reflect on the past year and a half, as well as—cautiously—to imagine the future.

I write a note of prayer, and as I place it on the wall by the Rebbe's gravesite, a wind picks up the piece of paper and gently carries it down to the grave itself, where it joins thousands of other petitions and prayers that people have written, folding their notes in half or ripping them before spreading them below.

On my way out, I chance to run into a cousin of mine, a religious man who has just moved to Israel and is in New York for the funeral of his wife's grandfather.

After our happy reunion, he offers me a ride into the city. I politely decline, since I am in a rush, and I call an Uber to take me back to Manhattan, where I hope to work in the afternoon before joining the Breitbart crew at the Trump "victory party"—win or lose—to follow.

The car arrives, and then takes a detour to pick up another passenger.

In my haste to make the arrangement, I had ignored the fact that I had selected Uber's "pool" service. Now I am stuck on a massive side journey through Queens, where I have never spent time and from which I have no idea how to extricate myself.

I am growing more and more stressed as I look at my watch, wondering how I am ever going to make it back to Manhattan in time. I imagine being stuck in traffic gridlock after dark, far from the victory party.

And then I look out the window, and notice what we are passing. This is Queens—the neighborhood where Donald Trump grew up in the 1940s and 1950s. From poor to rich, from battered bungalow homes with peeling paint to stately brick mansions, from leafy streets to jam-packed highways.

This was the journey Donald Trump had taken from Queens to the top of towers in Manhattan, skyscrapers not yet built or imagined.

Rough, down-to-earth Queens is still part of the man today.

I reach the city just before sunset. I meet my friend in Union Square. We eat sandwiches and walk around, enjoying the mild air, talking about everything but the election. I watch the children in the playground and think of my own. I feel exhausted.

■   ■   ■

At my friend's apartment, I lie down for a nap for exactly 15 minutes. I wake to the news that pollster Frank Luntz, citing some new numbers, has projected Hillary Clinton to be the next president of the United States. People are still voting, but the election seems over.

I dress for the evening and head uptown, in a state of resignation. I spend the subway ride pondering different options for drowning my sorrows. I conclude that none of them is any good, and I may as well just do my work.

I find my way to the hotel, past a few Trump supporters. The street in front of the New York Midtown Hilton is still largely empty.

Walking into the building feels like going to a funeral, as people prepare to console one another.

I pick up my media pass and find my Breitbart News colleagues. Florida results are not looking good.

"Hi," says our political editor, Matthew Boyle. He looks ashen, and his handshake is weak. "He's going to lose," Matt says, taking a gulp of beer.

I hug Breitbart's London editor, Raheem Kassam, who not only covered the historic Brexit vote, but as a key player in the UK Independence Party helped bring it about. He agrees with Matt: Florida is the end.

I am bracing myself for the worst. And then it emerges somehow that the panhandle counties are still voting. They are?

Wait—Pensacola and the "redneck Riviera"? This thing is not over.

And sure enough, within about half an hour, Trump takes the lead in Florida. Matt's mood changes completely. "He's going to win," he says to me. I don't know—I still expect a Clinton victory. Hadn't Frank Luntz said so? What numbers had he seen? What about Nevada?

But then Ohio numbers start coming in, and they are looking good. Very good. We are still in it. The liberal Northeastern states are all lining up behind Clinton, as expected. But Trump—perhaps somewhat unexpectedly—is delivering the conservative states in the South and the Mountain West.

Nothing yet on Michigan, or Pennsylvania. That, I realized, is where the election will be decided. The Upper Midwest. Trump's huge gamble.

This is Game 7, all right. Now, somehow, I find myself calming down. I am in Cubs mode.

Instead of watching the television—which I could do anywhere—I decide to work, to write about the mood swings and the tension in the air. And as I do so, I feel just a little glimmer of that familiar feeling, that sense I had in the Armory Ballroom in New Hampshire, the feeling that Trump is going to win. I quickly suppress the thought. He is still likely to lose. It would be nice, looking back, to have believed in a win, this late in the game. But it seems impossible.

Yet now more results are coming in, and the margins are looking solid in Florida. Senator Marco Rubio, who had run such a brutal campaign against Trump in the closing days of the primaries, easily wins reelection to his seat. Ironically, Trump will have him to thank, in part, for driving turnout.

North Carolina is looking promising, Ohio even better. And now the reporting is starting to change. The *New York Times*, which had barely given Trump a 20 percent chance earlier in the evening, upgrades the race to a 50–50 tossup.

The mood in the unabashedly conservative and pro-Trump Breitbart camp is still quite nervous—but, as a colleague says, a "good kind of nervous." The financial markets are beginning to panic. Is that a story? No—if Clinton were to pick up a couple of major states, the markets will swing the other way.

Underneath my dress shirt, I am wearing a t-shirt bearing the face of Andrew Breitbart. I am not going to reveal it unless Trump is winning decisively. I begin to think about when: Wisconsin, or Michigan.

I send some encouraging text messages to my wife. I watch the monitors, which are tuned to Fox News. The conservative network is showing the tense, bewildered scene at the Clinton party at the Jacob K. Javits Center.

I keep ignoring those who say Trump is going to win—including the *Times*, which is now putting the probability of a Trump victory above 90 percent.

Then, suddenly, Wisconsin is called. "It's over," I tell the people near me, as I remove my tie, and bare my Breitbart t-shirt to the world.

■ ■ ■

The Upper Midwest. Trump's gamble paid off. All of those families with children waiting well into the night, all those teenagers in Sterling Heights, that unbelievable half-mile-long line in Eau Claire—all of those people pushed him into office.

Even the people in that barn in Virginia, where Clinton eked out a narrow win—they were part of Trump's march to victory. The people at the airport in North Carolina, the moms in Orlando. They needed him. They believed in him.

Just moments ago, when I had thought Trump was on the verge of defeat, I imagined that if he should, by some "miracle"—we were using that word—actually win, I would jump up and down for joy, break down in tears, tear through the streets in delight.

Instead, I settle down to work—just as I would have done if he had lost. I interview the delightful Indian man from the Republican Hindu Coalition, who claims that his organization swung 25,000 key votes.

I take photographs of the people celebrating. I walk upstairs and set myself up in the special media balcony with a view of the party below, where red "Make America Great Again" hats are being passed out and happy people are hugging and smiling. They won.

I tell my Breitbart News colleagues that we will remember this night for the rest of our lives. I arrange for two friends, one of whom has been a devout Trump supporter from the beginning, to join the Trump victory party—at this moment in history, the hottest ticket in the world.

If he had lost narrowly, Trump would still have achieved a respectable result. He would have put the fear of God—and the electorate—into Washington. But at some point being in the World Series just isn't enough—as the Cubs decided in Game 7. It was time to win this thing.

Trump has 254 electoral votes to Clinton's 212. We ready ourselves for the call that will seal it—Michigan, or Pennsylvania, or some combination of other states. It is just a matter of time.

And then, surprisingly, nothing happens, for at least an hour. The Associated Press has called Pennsylvania—Pennsylvania!—for Trump. But Fox News will not, yet.

At 2:00 a.m., Clinton campaign chair John Podesta appears onstage at the Javits Center—walking across a map of the United States to reach the podium—and declares that Clinton would not be conceding, that every vote must be counted, and that everyone should go home and "get some sleep."

Clinton will not even be coming to her own party.

It is an extraordinarily cynical gesture. And after the Clinton campaign has raised alarms about Trump's suggestion that he might not accept the election results if he lost, it is amazingly hypocritical. If that was a threat to "democracy," what is this?

But the Trump supporters will not go home. And toward 3:00 a.m., Fox News finally calls the election for Trump, and Clinton calls him to concede. Cheers, mayhem; President Trump!

Mike Pence appears at the podium to introduce Trump, who walks onstage with his happy, well-dressed family, to the *Air Force One* theme, which had greeted the plane in hangar rallies.

Trump's speech is magnanimous; he reaches out to his opponents; he thanks his staff. And then he walks on, into history.

Former New York mayor Rudy Giuliani compares it to Andrew Jackson's win in 1828. Knowing Steve Bannon, I am sure he has precisely the same thought at that moment.

The faces in the press gallery in the balcony are stoic, even grim. The print journalists and networks seem to slink away; only the photographers seem engaged in the moment. I exchange glances with two ashen-faced journalists on their way out; they look completely disoriented. They know the way to the exit, and not much more.

I exchange hugs with friends and colleagues. I meet my friends and we walk out into the night. We have just seen one of the most amazing events in American political history.

Back home, in the East Village, we toast the victory on a balcony overlooking Third Avenue, just before 5:00 a.m. I look toward Freedom Tower and think about what we have just seen, what has been achieved tonight.

The enormity of Trump's victory has not yet sunk in. But perhaps it is beginning to.

What the Election of Donald Trump Means

When I began this campaign diary, I believed that while Donald Trump had a chance to win, he would lose. He was far behind in the polls, and although he was starting to recover, defeat was the safer bet.

Though details of everyday life on the campaign trail would obviously reveal themselves, I sketched a rough idea of the theme for the project in advance. That theme was the tragic hubris of Trump's effort. I saw a "yuge" man about to fall, and I wanted to explain that fall, but also to cushion it somehow, to leave hope for the future.

And yet on some level I always knew that Trump had a chance. The fact that the media were so overly keen to declare it "over" was a sign that it wasn't. I had even predicted—perhaps after a glass of wine or two—as early as the summer of 2015 that Trump was going to be

president. (The wine may explain why my friends remember the prediction, but I do not.)

Certainly, by late 2015, I knew that no other Republican could beat
Hillary Clinton—but Trump had a slim chance.

I never really considered the implications of a Trump victory, though.
Perhaps because the loss seemed so much more real, and so much more
frightening.

So before I even hit the trail, I composed a concluding chapter for
this book, about what a Trump loss would mean. Suffice it to say that a
Trump loss would have meant that Obama would never be held accountable for abusing his power, nor Clinton for her malfeasance.

I was also deeply concerned about the rifts in the conservative movement and the Republican Party, which had become very personal.

There were open threats of retribution against those who had supported Trump, once Hillary Clinton had secured her victory.

Those who backed Trump, on the other hand, were saying that they
would blame the #NeverTrump faction for refusing to rally behind the
party's nominee. If the GOP was destroyed by civil war, that would mean
the end of effective political opposition to the Left.

It was almost impossibly daring to imagine a Trump victory—and
even more difficult to imagine one in which he won while Republicans
retained control of both houses of Congress.

Yet that is exactly what happened. Voters fed up by eight years of
Barack Obama's "progressive" governance gave Republicans full control
of the executive, both houses of the legislature, and the judiciary, with a
key Supreme Court vacancy to fill and more to come.

And so now I can afford to think through the consequences of
Trump's victory. The first is that Trump has saved the Supreme Court.
The seat vacated by the death of Antonin Scalia will no longer be filled
by the qualified but liberal Merrick Garland. It will be filled by a conservative, restoring the court's prior 5–4 balance. And with several
conservative justices nearing retirement, and liberal Ruth Bader Ginsburg
aging, Trump may be able to bolster or even increase that edge.

The second consequence is that Obamacare is dead. Already reeling from staggering premium increases and the withdrawal of insurance companies from several states, the massive program that Obama and the Democrats had rammed through Congress on party lines was imploding. Hillary Clinton's solution would have been to extend the power of the state. Republicans have wanted to repeal and replace the program for years. And now they will.

The third consequence of a Trump victory is that Speaker Paul Ryan will be able to pass his tax reforms and budgets. Ryan has developed several innovative ideas to tackle the national debt, the entitlement crisis, and the tax code. For several years, these were merely academic, as he had been forced to compromise with Democrats or face government shutdown. Now, despite a rocky relationship with Trump, he could fulfill his ideas and his leadership potential.

■　　■　　■

If that was all that a Trump presidency could achieve—saving the Supreme Court, repealing Obamacare, and passing Paul Ryan's budgets—it would deserve to be judged a success. Yet Trump has promised more. Many of those core promises from the campaign trail will be harder to implement in the short term—but not impossible, given the window of opportunity voters have given Trump and the GOP, and presuming that Trump will be willing to deal with the Democrats.

On immigration policy, Trump's presidency represents the best possible chance to reach a grand bargain, in Nixon-to-China fashion: a wall on the southern border, the deportation of criminals, and an end to sanctuary cities in exchange for allowing many of those already illegally in the United States to achieve legal status, and even citizenship, at a later time. Republicans would accept it—because no one had been tougher on the issue than Trump.

On foreign policy, Trump's election represents a step toward restoring America's global deterrent. The very fact that foreign nations see him as unpredictable is, itself, a great asset, one that no other candidate could have brought to the office. Trump also brings a simple, and effective, approach to diplomacy that he had perfected in the world of real estate, where he was kind to friends and devastating to enemies.

Obama's hapless policy has often seemed just the opposite.

And on corruption, Trump has promised to "drain the swamp." That will never be easy, as long as he has to rely on the cooperation of Congress to do it. Senate Majority Leader Mitch McConnell has already—on the day of Trump's election—said that term limits are not on his agenda. And so Trump will have to maneuver, as presidents before him have done, within his executive ambit to find ways of undoing incentives for corruption and influence-peddling.

If there is any reason to believe that Trump will be more successful than his predecessors who made similar promises, it is that Trump owes very few favors to anyone. He self-funded his campaign through the primary, and he is certainly wealthy enough not to need to find ways to further enrich himself while in office. His best way of draining the swamp may be simply to shrink it—to limit government to living within its means.

In fact he may have to, because the consequences of printing money to keep the economy afloat—and incurring $20 trillion in national debt—could soon come home to roost.

Indeed, if there is any reason to doubt that a Trump presidency can succeed, it is the fact that so many of the country's problems have simply been deferred during the Obama administration, or hidden by a media that could never quite bring themselves to hold Obama to a universal standard.

So many of these problems were created by Democrats—the national debt, for example, had doubled under Obama—and it would have been politically easier for Democrats to be the ones to clean up their own messes. A Democrat trying to balance the budget, for example, might face internal opposition but would have unusual credibility with the public, and would likely face minimum media resistance, despite the pain of whatever cuts he or she sought to make.

So Trump faces unprecedented crises. And the questions that Hillary Clinton raised about his temperament are legitimate. Any person might struggle to face up to the challenges of the presidency, but with Trump America has chosen a political outsider who had run a privately held company and does not have an exceptionally reassuring record of working with other people. He has also flip-flopped on several critical issues, and might, perhaps, do so again.

■   ■   ■

Still, it is going to be far easier to heal the divisions among conservatives in victory than in defeat. Now it is the Democrats who are facing their own internal reckoning.

The Clintons led them to defeat; the infrastructure the Clintons commanded ran the entire party and its satellites. The fact that the only real challenger to Hillary Clinton was an aging socialist who threw away his best chance at victory revealed how moribund the Democrats' internal political culture has become under Obama.

The core of the Obama revolution remains the far Left, which is dealing with electoral defeat not by turning against its political leaders, but against the rest of society. As Donald Trump's victory was announced, left-wing protesters in cities on the West Coast staged riots in city centers and on college campuses. The protests and violence grew much worse the following evening, nationwide.

Before the voting, the media and the Hillary Clinton campaign had stoked alarm over the idea the Trump might not accept the results of the election if he lost (conveniently forgetting that he had pledged in the first presidential debate, to support Clinton if she won).

They warned darkly of riots, and public disorder. And now here they were, rioting and fomenting violence, repeating the same hysterical claims that Trump was coming for blacks, Muslims, gays, and Latinos.

But the media are the biggest losers of all. During the election they dropped all pretense of objectivity in their coverage, doing whatever they could to persuade Americans to vote against Trump.

They ignored the story of Trump's outreach to the Democratic base—something that no Republican since Ronald Reagan had done—in their fixation on the minutiae of every Trump "scandal," to which they attributed inordinate importance. The public had seen through them—and beaten them.

That is not to say that the media will simply recede, and give up resisting Trump. They will return, with a vengeance. And it will be good for the country that they do so, because the media will be a critical part of the political opposition to Trump. Under President Trump, the media will finally do the job that they have refused to do under the Obama administration, holding the president accountable to the Constitution and to his own campaign promises.

But perhaps—one can always hope—the media that comes back will be wiser, and a tad humbler. In the 2016 campaign, journalists pushed aside even their own commercial interests in service of a political cause that tacitly united them all. The traveling press corps, which shared the belief that Trump could never win, completely missed the opportunity to tell a story about America on the verge of a potential political watershed. Maybe now they'll be a little slower to throw the next big story away.

Meanwhile, there will be two other sources of political opposition to a Trump administration. One is the remnant of Bernie Sanders's "political revolution" and the far Left in general, led by Senator Elizabeth Warren of Massachusetts. What they lack in political achievement, they make up for in ideological coherence. They oppose Trump's offensive rhetoric, seeing it as symbolic of all that they despise—but more than that, they continue to believe in radical, redistributive policies.

The other source of opposition will be the #NeverTrump faction within the conservative movement, which opposed Trump out of a sense of ideological pique. They will likely have good reason to oppose some of what Trump may seek to do with his powers. They will hold him accountable for his promises on the Supreme Court and other issues. And they will seek to prevent him from reaching deals on terms too favorable to big government or the Democrats.

■   ■   ■

All of that lies in the future—and all of it is to the good. One reason a Trump presidency need not be feared—or at least not panicked about, in the dramatic fashion of many of Trump's critics—is that he will face stiff opposition on nearly every side.

True, he has shown that he can overcome such opposition, but that was when he was running for office and could appeal directly to the voters. Once in office, facing the task of governing, he will have to make compromises.

He seems to understand that. Indeed, one of the most encouraging signs is that Trump's victory speech showed a great magnanimity. He said: "I pledge to every citizen of our land that I will be President for all Americans, and this is so important to me. For those who have chosen not to support me in the past, of which there were a few people [laughter], I'm reaching out to you for your guidance and your help so that we can work together and unify our great country."[3]

Hillary Clinton did not give a concession speech that night. But she did so the following morning. "I know how disappointed you feel because I feel it too.... We have seen that our nation is more deeply divided than we thought. But I still believe in America and I always will. And if you do, then we must accept this result and then look to the future. Donald Trump is going to be our president. We owe him an open mind and the chance to lead," she said, steady and dignified.[4]

After such a bruising election, it was encouraging to see that these candidates—who could barely stand to shake hands with each other—were willing to lay the foundation, at least in words, for the country to come back together.

Trump's fans might gloat, but he would not. He knew how close he had come to defeat, and how much he owed to the few allies who came to his aid when he was fighting a lonely, losing battle—especially the voters, who lifted him up.

It was those voters—and especially the people of Michigan, Pennsylvania, Wisconsin, Iowa, Minnesota, Virginia, and Ohio—those people in the Upper Midwest and Appalachia and the Great Plains who never stopped believing in him, who told me in the waning hours of the campaign that the reason they had come to see their candidate was that they wanted to be a part of history.

They were certain that he would win, when the polls and pundits said otherwise.

I heard one other statement, over and over again, in those last days. It was that his voters felt a debt of gratitude toward him, that he did not have to be running for president and putting his life on the line and his family through hell. They were convinced he was doing it because he cared about them.

Trump's energetic, non-stop campaign, which at times took him across more than half a dozen states in a single day, convinced them that he wanted to be with them, and to lead them.

And it was his resilience that impressed even his critics—like the comedian Dave Chappelle, who voted for Clinton in Ohio and then joked that Trump was the most "gangsta" candidate in history, because he simply kept fighting no matter what happened.

The *Access Hollywood* tape, the lawsuits, the unforced errors—he looked past them all and kept moving toward victory. In an America that had forgotten how to succeed, Donald Trump showed us how to persevere.

I began this project thinking I was watching a tower collapse, a mighty man falling. Instead I find myself, improbably, writing the story of a man who descended from his tower and built the people up. I thought he would be humbled by defeat. Instead, I saw him humbled in victory— by the electoral process, by the people, and by the great trust placed in him.

He helped America renew itself. He is already making America great again—because Americans have willed it so.

Epilogue

Joel Pollak and Larry Schweikart

I n the weeks that followed the election, the Left, and the media, struggled to reconcile themselves to the result. Those who had warned that Donald Trump could win—such as left-wing filmmaker Michael Moore tried to explain that Trump voters in the Upper Midwest were not racist, but merely fed up with the political system and disenchanted by the Democratic presidential nominee.[1] A few liberal intellectuals, such as Thomas Frank, noted that the media had failed by siding openly with Hillary Clinton, setting themselves up as part of the establishment the public detested:

> With the same arguments repeated over and over, two or three times a day, with nuance and contrary views all deleted, the act of opening the newspaper started to feel like tuning in to a Cold War propaganda station. Here's what it consisted of:

- Hillary was virtually without flaws. She was a peerless leader clad in saintly white, a super-lawyer, a caring benefactor of women and children, a warrior for social justice.
- Her scandals weren't real.
- The economy was doing well / America was already great.
- Working-class people weren't supporting Trump.
- And if they were, it was only because they were botched humans.
- Racism was the only conceivable reason for lining up with the Republican candidate.

How did the journalists' crusade fail? The fourth estate came together in an unprecedented professional consensus. They chose insulting the other side over trying to understand what motivated them. They transformed opinion writing into a vehicle for high moral boasting. What could possibly have gone wrong with such an approach?[2]

But the introspection was short-lived. It was quickly replaced by denial. Green Party candidate Jill Stein initiated recounts in several Upper Midwest states—and the Clinton campaign, after initially urging the voters to accept the result of the election, threw its support behind the effort. In the end, the recount changed nothing.

So the Left looked for scapegoats. When Trump named Joel's former boss, Breitbart News Executive Chairman Stephen K. Bannon—who had helped turn the campaign around—as his incoming chief strategist and senior counselor, the media revived earlier false charges of anti-Semitism that had greeted Bannon when he was initially appointed CEO of the campaign. Hysterical diatribes by Democrats transformed Breitbart News from a merely objectionable conservative outlet into something to the right of *Der Stürmer*. On the very same day that CNN's Brian Stelter called for the media to examine its own biases, he labeled

Breitbart a "white nationalist" website. The Anti-Defamation League gave weight to the lies, and fueled the frenzy, by accusing Breitbart of being the "premier" website of the alt-right—a charge it was later forced to withdraw, after it admitted that there was no record of Bannon actually saying anything anti-Semitic.

The next scapegoat was "fake news"—a proliferation of false news stories, shared widely on social media, which allegedly swung the election to Trump. There was certainly plenty of "fake news," much of it from the Left: when National Public Radio traced some of the fake news to its origins, it found a left-wing activist based in Los Angeles who had created false stories to mock conservatives for believing in them.[3] But the "fake news" label was soon applied to any news of which the Left disapproved, including legitimate conservative outlets like Breitbart. This was more than a semantic squabble: Facebook came under pressure to eliminate "fake news" sites from its news feed, and Google promised to block "fake news" sites from hosting its advertising. There was no real evidence that "fake news" had affected the election result in any way, but the hue and cry about it allowed the Left to advance its effort to shut down opposing viewpoints and put conservative outlets out of business.

Finally, there was the Russian hacking conspiracy theory. A leaked CIA report suggested that hackers affiliated with the Russian government had been responsible for breaching, and exposing, emails of the Democratic National Committee (DNC) and Clinton campaign chair John Podesta. For months, Clinton had accused Trump of colluding with the Russians—a charge with no evidentiary basis whatsoever. Now President Barack Obama himself called for a full investigation—though Obama had to admit that there was no proof the voting itself had been affected by hackers. Democrats convinced themselves that their election loss had been the result of intervention by a foreign power. GOP pollster Frank Luntz—who had prematurely declared Clinton the next president of the United States on Election Day—poured cold water on the Democrats' fever dream: "Did Russia also hack Hillary's campaign calendar and delete all her stops in rural Wisconsin, Penn., and Michigan?" he tweeted.[4] Ironically, the Democrats' sudden concern about hacked emails underlined Republican concerns about Hillary Clinton's illicit private server, which had not housed mere political information but national security secrets and classified information, with few protections whatsoever.

The Republicans had finally fulfilled the early promise of the Tea Party movement by holding the Obama administration—including Hillary Clinton, its chosen successor—accountable for its policy failures and its abuses of its constitutional powers. A loss would have crushed the Republican Party, perhaps forever. But victory produced new unity among conservatives, with most of the #NeverTrump faction laying down its rhetorical arms, at least for a while.

Meanwhile, House Democrats reelected Representative Nancy Pelosi as Minority Leader, despite her continued failure to lead the party out of the electoral trough she had dug in the 2010 election. And Senate Democrats elevated New York's Chuck Schumer to lead their caucus. With liberals from San Francisco and New York atop the party, the Democrats then set about looking for a new DNC chair, and the leading candidate was Representative Keith Ellison of Minnesota, who had once been a member of the Nation of Islam and an apologist for the anti-Semitic Louis Farrakhan. The party of Thomas Jefferson and Andrew Jackson was now essentially a municipal "archipelago"[5] of leftist radicals and urban elites.

When the smoke dissipates Clinton will have set a record for most votes by a losing candidate, highest percentage advantage in votes by a losing candidate, and—arguably—stupidest campaign ever run. On the other hand, Clinton could have run a near-perfect campaign and still not won. She was just that unpopular. To paraphrase the movie title, "We Just Weren't That Into Her."

Do not misunderstand: Donald Trump was the only Republican candidate who could have beaten Clinton. Larry argued early in 2015 that any Republican not named "Bush" could beat her, but in retrospect both of us see that that simply was not the case. Trump showed that he had the ability to sustain attacks that would have completely ended the candidacies of Marco Rubio, Ted Cruz, or any of the other Republican hopefuls. One might say, "Oh, but they wouldn't have had the baggage Trump had." The truth is, if it didn't exist in the real world, the Clinton campaign and its allies in the press easily would have manufactured it. For example, had Cruz somehow beaten Trump, the *National Enquirer* story would have come back with a vengeance and dozens of "former mistresses" would have come out of the woodwork. The difference would have been that Cruz would not have been able to withstand such ginned up charges, as Trump was.

That said, it's worth noting that Trump did not do better than Mitt Romney except in a few key states.[6] In Iowa, for example, Trump barely exceeded Romney's total by 70,000, but won by almost 10 points. He actually received 2,682 *fewer* votes in Wisconsin than Romney—while winning the state! And in Virginia, Trump had 53,000 fewer votes and lost by almost two points more than Romney.

But in some key states, Trump's numbers were stunning. In Ohio, he beat Romney's 2012 total by almost 180,000 votes—a number that would have beaten Obama in 2012! Likewise, in Florida Trump would have crushed Obama by 350,000 votes. In Michigan Trump blew past Romney's totals by 164,000 votes, and in Pennsylvania Trump surpassed Romney by almost 300,000 votes.

It was the perfect storm. Trump's stunning, come-from-nowhere campaign was *the* political story of the century and Hillary Clinton was possibly the worst Democratic candidate since Michael Dukakis. She pulled 75,000 fewer votes than Obama in Pennsylvania; 168,800 fewer votes than Obama in Iowa; 238,000 fewer in Wisconsin; 295,700 fewer in Michigan, and a whopping 433,545 fewer votes than Obama in Ohio. In five key Midwestern, largely blue battleground states, Clinton came up *1.2 million* votes short of Obama's 2012 total. The Electoral College was completely flipped by Trump's victories in Ohio, Florida, Iowa, Wisconsin, Michigan, and Pennsylvania. He could have even lost North Carolina and Arizona and still won. And it must be repeated: Trump was well under one million votes from sweeping seven other states totaling more than 70 electoral votes, meaning he was remarkably close to a 400 electoral vote blowout of Reaganesque proportions.

Liberals still whined that Clinton had received more popular votes than Trump—as of this writing, about 65.8 million to Trump's 62.9 million (remarkably almost the exact number Larry predicted he would win). But given that the U.S. population increased by over 3 percent since 2012, Clinton should have had closer to 68 million to equal Obama's percentage of the electorate. Trump, on the other hand, exceeded Romney's 2012 total by 2 million, and virtually *all* of Clinton's popular vote advantage came from one state: California.

What this all means is that Trump was the best candidate possible for the times, while Clinton was possibly the worst. (Still, notions that Bernie Sanders would have done better are perhaps fantasy. His radical views would have lost him Colorado, Nevada, New Hampshire, and several other states.) The weak Democrat field produced one of the weakest candidates in history. Hillary won fewer electoral votes than Barack Obama, John Kerry, Al Gore, or Bill Clinton. It had to be grating on Clinton that she performed worse than two other losing Democrat candidates.

But her loss was only the tip of the iceberg. Republicans held onto Congress, losing only two seats in the Senate and six seats in the House. And the GOP also won control of five state House chambers and two state Senate chambers, winning several dozen new legislative seats nationwide.[7] Republicans held a "trifecta"—control of both state houses and the governor's mansion—in 25 states, while Democrats had that power in only 5.

Meanwhile, Trump set about choosing his cabinet and administration, assembling an impressive array of seasoned leaders from business, politics, and the military. The picks were overwhelmingly conservative, with a few choice positions also going to Republican moderates. The Left complained bitterly that Trump's Cabinet lacked diversity—though as even the *New York Times* public editor had to admit, "Only two of the 20-plus reporters who covered the presidential campaign for The New York Times were black. None were Latino or Asian. That's less diversity than you'll find in Donald Trump's cabinet thus far. Of the *Times*' newly named White House team, all six are white, as is most everyone in the Washington bureau."[8]

Trump's approval ratings improved steadily during the course of the presidential transition. By the time of the Army-Navy game in December, people wondered if he had effectively taken over the role of president already.

Expectations are high, and the challenges facing the new administration are great. Trump will not have much of a honeymoon. As Luke 12:48 says: "For unto whomsoever much is given, of him shall much be required; and to whom men have committed much, of him they will ask the more." His opponents on the Democratic side are deeply divided, but he will face resistance from Congress and the media nonetheless. Perhaps Trump's greatest challenge will be to fulfill his own promises. One of the last things George Orwell wrote was, "For a left-wing party in power, its most serious antagonist is always its own past propaganda."[9] That applies all the more to Trump, who has not won the popular vote, and faces protests virtually every day before and immediately after the inauguration.

Yet if there is anyone who can overcome such resistance, and succeed, it is Trump. In the 2016 presidential election, he proved that for him—and for America—anything is possible.

Acknowledgments

This book would not have been possible without the patience of my wife, Julia, and our children, Maya and Alexander, who endured my absences and tolerated my occasional seclusions. This book would not have been possible without the patience of my wife, Julia, and our children, Maya and Alexander, who endured my absences and tolerated my occasional seclusions. Thanks to my agents at Javelin, Matthew Latimer and Keith Urbahn, as well as to the whole Regnery team, especially Harry Crocker. Special thanks are also due to the Breitbart News team: Steve Bannon, Ana Barrera, Matt Boyle, Wendy Colbert, Brandon Darby, Ezra Dulis, Noah Dulis, Wynton Hall, Jon Kahn, Rebecca Mansour, Alex Marlow, Frances Martel, Michelle Moons, Adelle Nazarian, Larry Solov, and many more. Thanks also to my parents, siblings, and relatives, most of whom are still speaking to me. Thanks to Rabbi Boruch Rabinowitz and Dovid Tenenbaum of the Living Torah Center, and the whole congregation.

And thanks to the countless interlocutors on social media, whose sparring kept me in fighting shape throughout.

—Joel Pollak

Thanks to the "Deplorable Gurus," pollster Richard Baris, "Deplorable" Don Culp, "Deplorable" Greg Den Haese, the anonymous "Deplorable Dave" in Ohio, the "Naked Archaeologist Maximus Paulus" on Twitter, "Deplorable" Drew, and Chris Bowen. Also thanks to Steve Bannon. Roger Williams, my agent, was relentless in putting this together, and Elizabeth Kantor, our editor, did an astounding job of ensuring that this got out in a timely manner.

—Larry Schweikart

Notes

Cold Open

1. Hillary Clinton, quoted by Domenic Mantanaro in "Hillary Clinton's 'Basket of Deplorables,' In Full Context of This Ugly Campaign," National Public Radio, September 10, 2016, http://www.npr.org/2016/09/10/493427601/hillary-clintons-basket-of-deplorables-in-full-context-of-this-ugly-campaign.

2. Barack Obama, quoted by Mayhill Fowler, in "Obama: No Surprise That Hard-Pressed Pennsylvanians Turn Bitter," Huffington Post, updated November 17, 2008, http://www.huffingtonpost.com/mayhill-fowler/obama-no-surprise-that-ha_b_96188.html.

3. David Brooks, "A Return to National Greatness," *Weekly Standard*, March 3, 1997, http://www.weeklystandard.com/a-return-to-nationalgreatness/article/9480.

4.   Michelle Moons, "Donald Trump Meets with Families of Americans Killed by Illegal Aliens,"Breitbart News, July 11, 2015, http://www.breitbart.com/california/2015/07/11/donald-trump-meets-with-families-of-americans-killed-by-illegal-aliens/.

Chapter One: The Most Astounding Election in American History

1.   Jerome Hudson, "32 Times Establishment Media and Pollsters Assured the People of Donald Trump's Defeat," Breitbart News, November 23, 2016, http://www.breitbart.com/2016-presidential-race/2016/11/23/32-times-establishment-media-pollsters.

2.   See note 4 below.

3.   See, for example, Harry Enten and Nate Silver, "Will Trump Clinch the GOP Nomination before the Convention?" *FiveThirtyEight*, March 21, 2016, http://fivethirtyeight.com/features/will-donald-trump-clinch-the-republican-nomination-before-the-convention/; Harry Enten, "It's Still Not Clear that Donald Trump Will Get a Majority of Delegates," *FiveThirtyEight*, March 16, 2016, http://fivethirtyeight.com/features/its-still-not-clear-that-donald-trump-will-get-a-majority-of-delegates/; and Harry Enten, "Wisconsin Could Be Trouble for Trump," *FiveThirtyEight*, March 31, 2016, http://fivethirtyeight.com/features/wisconsin-could-be-trouble-for-trump/.

4.   On August 19, 2015, I replied to @Milo_Gibaldi on Twitter: "Trump will be pres. I'm more convinced than ever. Maybe Fiorina as veep" and on November 20, 2015, to "Steve": "In 8 **Trump will win** a bunch of blue states—IA, PA, MI, maybe NJ." Wow. Three out of four blue states ain't bad. Three days later I explained at FreeRepublic how Trump would win the nomination.Larry Schweikart, post 25, FreeRepublic, August 22, 2015, http://www.freerepublic.com/focus/f-news/3327057/posts, in response to "Quinnipiac Swing State Poll (FL, OH, PA) Trump Leads GOP in FL, PA," referring to "August 20, 2015—Biden Tops Trump In Florida, Ohio, Pennsylvania, Quinnipiac University Swing State Poll Finds," Quinnipiac University Poll, August 20, 2015, https://poll.

qu.edu/2016-presidential-swing-state-polls/release-detail?ReleaseID=2271. See also Larry Schweikart, "FOX POLL: Trump Beats Clinton 45–40, Eclipsing Bush," FreeRepublic, October 15, 2015, http://www.freerepublic.com/focus/news/3348924/posts?page=1, and Schweikart, "The Ongoing Trump Genius," Free Republic, December 8, 2015, http://www.freerepublic.com/focus/f-news/3370006/posts, where I wrote, "Trump is the likely nominee until proved otherwise." See also Schweikart, post 19, FreeRepublic, March 2, 2016, http://www.freerepublic.com/focus/f-news/3404375/posts, responding to John Sexton, "Democratic Strategist: Trump Could Beat Clinton 'Like a Tied Up Billy Goat,'" Hot Air, http://hotair.com/archives/2016/03/02/democratic-strategist-trump-could-beat-clinton-like-a-tied-up-billy-goat/: "by the time it's done, they will be comparing the electoral map more to that of 1984 and 1988 than any other year."

5. See Larry Schweikart, post 36, FreeRepublic, March 2016, http://www.freerepublic.com/focus/f-news/3411782/posts, in response to Harry Enten and Nate Silver, "Will Trump Clinch the GOP Nomination before the Convention?" *FiveThirtyEight*, March 21, 2016, http://fivethirtyeight.com/features/will-donald-trump-clinch-the-republican-nomination-before-the-convention/.

6. Schweikart, "Two Days Out: Final Impressions," FreeRepublic, November 6, 2016, http://www.freerepublic.com/focus/f-news/3489994/posts. I did err "bigly" in the popular vote, expecting Trump to win by 4 percent. See also Schweikart, post 26, on FreeRepublic, September 29, 2016, http://www.freerepublic.com/focus/f-chat/3475076/posts?page=26#26 in which I predicted, "By the time it's done, Trump wins easily...." in response to David K. Li and Bob Fredericks, "Clinton Is Now Beating Trump in 5 Must-Win Battleground States, *New York Post*, September 29, 2016, : http://nypost.com/2016/09/29/clinton-is-now-beating-trump-in-5-must-win-battleground-states/.

7. Interview of Richard Baris by Larry Schweikart, November 26, 2016.

8.   Larry Schweikart and Dave Dougherty, *A Patriot's History of the Modern World, Vol. 1* (New York: Sentinel, 2012).

9.   Interview of Baris by Larry Schweikart, November 26, 2016.

Chapter Two: On the Campaign Trail: Washington to North Carolina to New York

1.   Joel Pollak, "Exclusive: O'Keefe Video Sting Exposes 'Bird-Dogging'—Democrats' Effort to Incite Violence at Trump Rallies," Breitbart News, October 17, 2016, http://www.breitbart.com/big-government/2016/10/17/exclusive-okeefe-video-sting-exposes-bird-dogging-democrats-effort-to-incite-violence-attrump-rallies/.

2.   Joel Pollak, "New O'Keefe Video: Hillary Clinton Approved Robert Creamer Plan Directly," Breitbart News, October 24, 2016, http://www.breitbart.com/2016-presidential-race/2016/10/24/new-okeefe-video-hillary-clinton-approved-robert-creamer-plan-directly/.

3.   Joel Pollak, "NBC's Chuck Todd: 'The Presidential Race Is Over," Breitbart News, October 8, 2016, http://www.breitbart.com/bigjournalism/2016/10/08/chuck-todd-nbc-news-the-presidential-race-is-over/.

4.   Jesse Byrnes, "Van Jones: I wish Priebus was DNC chair," *The Hill*, May 18, 2016, http://thehill.com/blogs/blog-briefing-room/news/280410-vanjones-i-wish-priebus-was-dnc-chair-over-wasserman-schultz.

5.   NBC, "Weekend Update: Drunk Uncle on Donald Trump," *Saturday Night Live*, November 7, 2015, https://www.nbc.com/saturday-nightlive/video/weekend-update-drunk-uncle-on-donald-trump/2933539.

6.   Bill Clinton, quoted by Pam Key in "Bill Clinton Mocks Supporters as 'Your Standard Redneck,'" Breitbart News, October 12, 2016, http://www.breitbart.com/video/2016/10/12/bill-clinton-mocks-trump-supporters-standard-redneck/.

7. Bernie Sanders, quoted by Joel Pollak in "Bernie Sanders Is Running a Fraudulent Campaign," Breitbart News, October 15, 2015, http://www.breitbart.com/big-government/2015/10/15/bernie-sanders-is-running-a-fraudulent-campaign/.

Chapter Three: How We "Renegade Deplorables" Saw Trump Could Win—Back in the Summer of 2015

1. Trump claimed 15,000 attended, though official "clickers" of people in the building put the number closer to 4,900. But Jeff Dover used his experience in commercial real estate to estimate the square footage, the amount of footage average individuals had, and how much space was filled and concluded that the crowd numbered 13,440. See Jeff Dover, "Report on Trump's July 11 Speech in Phoenix," *Free Republic*, July 13, 2015, http://www.freerepublic.com/focus/chat/3311443/posts.

2. Dave Urbanski, "'The Silent Majority is Back!' Donald Trump criticizes border policy in fiery speeches," The Blaze, July 11, 2015, http://www.theblaze.com/stories/2015/07/11/watch-live-donald-trump-speaks-in-phoenix-about-illegal-immigration/.

3. "Donald Trump Full Speech in Phoenix, Arizona July 11, 2015-2016 Presidential Campaign Rally," YouTube, posted July 11, 2015, https://www.youtube.com/watch?v=r0UMsNUEZuI. An excellent video history of Trump's two-decade long path to the White House is "Donald J. Trump: The Long Road to the White House (1980–2015)," YouTube, posted by Chris Emerson, March 15, 2016, https://www.youtube.com/watch?v=mxf1XmVZ9qY#t=37.

4. Urbanski, "The Silent Majority Is Back!"

5. M. J. Lee and Pat St. Claire, "Trump Draws Thousands in Phoenix, Continues Immigration Theme," CNN Politics, July 12, 2015, http://www.cnn.com/2015/07/11/politics/donald-trump-phoenix-rally/.

6. Jeremy Diamond, "Donald Trump Jumps In: The Donald's Latest White House Run is Officially On," CNN Politics, June 17, 2015, http://www.cnn.com/2015/06/16/politics/donald-trump-2016-announcement-elections/.

7. In Rasmussen's June 14 poll, for example, 65 percent of Americans said the country was on the wrong track; see "Right Direction or Wrong Track?" Rasmussen Reports, http://www.rasmussenreports.com/public_content/politics/mood_of_america/right_direction_or_wrong_track). An August 2014 *Wall Street Journal* Poll showed that an astounding 76 percent said they did not have confidence that their children's generation "will be better than it has been for us;" see Patrick O'Connor, "Poll Finds Widespread Economic Anxiety," *Wall Street Journal*, August 5, 2014, http://www.wsj.com/articles/wsj-nbc-poll-finds-widespread-economic-anxiety-1407277801. A Rasmussen poll in July 2015 showed that 56 percent thought Congress was doing a "poor" job; see "Congressional Performance," Rasmussen Reports, http://www.rasmussenreports.com/public_content/politics/mood_of_america/congressional_performance. And a Pew poll said that only 23 percent of congressional Republicans had kept the promises they made in 2014. The same poll found that an astounding 75 percent thought that their party's leaders should be doing more to stop Obama (see the falsely-headlined poll "Negative Views of New Congress Cross Party Lines," with the inference being that people disliked Congress because it wasn't "getting things done," rather than out of conservative dissatisfaction with the failure of the GOP in Washington to stop Obama's agenda; Pew Research Center, May 21, 2015, http://www.people-press.org/2015/05/21/negative-views-of-new-congress-cross-party-lines/P).

8. Pam Key, "Perino: On What Planet are Trump's 'Absurd' Claims Actually True?" Breitbart News, June 16, 2015, http://www.breitbart.com/video/2015/06/16/perino-on-what-planet-are-trumps-absurd-claims-actually-true/.

9. Nick Gass, "John McCain: Trump 'Fired Up the Crazies,'" *Politico*, July 16, 2015, http://www.politico.com/story/2015/07/john-mccain-donald-trump-immigration-phoenix-120216.html.

10. Jason Noble, "Trump Comments on McCain War Record Spark Outrage," *USA Today*, July 18, 2015, which claimed the comments drew "sharp and immediate condemnation."

11. William A. Jacobson, "Did Donald Trump Just Strangle Himself with McCain 'War Hero' Comment?" *Legal Insurrection*, July 18, 2015, http://legalinsurrection. com/2015/07/did-donald-trump-just-strangle-himself-with-mccain-war-hero-comment/.

12. Jazz Shaw, "Trump Crosses One Red Line Too Many, Declares John McCain 'Not a War Hero,'" Hot Air, July 18, 2015, http:// hotair.com/archives/2015/07/18/trump-crosses-one-red-line-too-many-declares-john-mccain-not-a-war-hero/.

13. Eric Bradner, "Rubio: Trump's McCain Attack is a 'Disqualifier,' CNN Politics, July 19, 2015, http://www.cnn.com/2015/07/19/ politics/marco-rubio-donald-trump-john-mccain-disqualifier/.

14. Michael Dorstewitz, "Trump Twist: Chris Rock Said Almost Exact Same Thing about McCain in 2008 Stand-Up Joke," BPR/Bizpac Review, July 19, 2015, http://www.bizpacreview. com/2015/07/19/trump-twist-chris-rock-said-almost-exact-same-thing-about-mccain-in-2008-stand-up-joke-226659.

15. Jennifer Agiesta, "CNN/ORC Poll: Trump Elbows His Way to the Top," CNN, July 26, 2015, http://www.cnn.com/2015/07/26/ politics/cnn-poll-presidential-race/.

16. Steve Almasy, Pamela Brown, and Augie Martin, "Suspect in Killing of San Francisco Woman had been Deported Five Times," CNN News, July 4, 2015, http://www.cnn.com/2015/07/03/us/ san-francisco-killing-suspect-immigrant-deported/.

17. Eugene Scott, "Trump Defends Inflammatory Comments, asks "Who is doing the raping?'" CNN Politics, July 2, 2015, http:// www.cnn.com/2015/07/01/politics/donald-trump-immigrants-raping-comments/.

18. Dan Balz and Peyton M. Craighill, "Poll: Trump Surges to big Lead in GOP Presidential Race," *Washington Post*, July 20, 2015, http://www.washingtonpost.com/politics/poll-trump-surges-to-big-lead-in-gop-presidential-race/2015/07/20/ efd2e0d0-2ef8-11e5-8f36-18d1d501920d_story.html.

19. Jonathan Bernstein, "No, Trump Can't Win. Yes, Clinton Can,"
     Bloomberg View, July 20, 2015, http://www.bloombergview.
     com/articles/2015-07-30/no-trump-can-t-win-yes-clinton-can-.

20. Jack Shafer, "The Candidates Who Can't," *Politico Magazine*,
     July 7, 2015, http://www.politico.com/magazine/story/2015/07/
     the-trumpets-of-donald-trump-and-bernie-sanders-119818.
     html#.VcynUvkeq-0.

21. Andrew Prokop, "Donald Trump is Surging in the Polls. Here's
     Why He Won't Win," *Vox*, July 2, 2015, http://www.vox.
     com/2015/7/2/8881175/donald-trump-president.

22. John Sides and Lynn Vavreck, *The Gamble: Choice and Chance
     in the 2012 Presidential Election* (Princeton: Princeton University
     Press, 2013).

23. Prokop, "Donald Trump is Surging in the Polls."

24. Scott Eric Kaufman, "Donald Trump May be Losing the War—
     But He's Winning all the Battles," *Salon*, July 6, 2015, http://
     www.salon.com/2015/07/06/donald_trump_may_be_losing_
     the_war_but_hes_winning_the_battles/.

25. Cathy Burke, "Karl Rove: Populists Like Trump, Sanders Can't
     Win Major Party Nod," Newsmax, July 8, 2015, http://www.
     newsmax.com/Politics/karl-rove-populists-donald-trump-bernie-
     sanders/2015/07/08/id/654131/.

26. Quoted in Kaufman, "Donald Trump May be Losing the War."

27. Rush Limbaugh, "Putting the Debate Day Pieces Together: Giant
     Psyops Underway Against Trump," August 6, 2015, Rush
     Limbaugh Show, http://www.rushlimbaugh.com/daily/2015/08/06/
     putting_the_debate_day_pieces_together_giant_psyops_underway_
     against_trump; "Big Donors Warn Candidates on Eve of Debate:
     'Take Trump Out'," DC Whispers, August 5, 2015, http://
     dcwhispers.com/big-donors-warn-candidates-on-eve-of-debate-
     take-trump-out/.

28. Limbaugh, "Putting the Debate Day Pieces Together."

29. Jessica Taylor, "In 'Happy Hour Debate,' Candidates Struggle to
     Break Through," NPR, August 6, 2015, http://www.npr.org/

sections/itsallpolitics/2015/08/06/430077174/republicans-face-off-in-happy-hour-consolation-debate.

30. Ben Brody, "Carly Fiorina Knocks Donald Trump: 'I Didn't Get a Phone Call from Bill Clinton,'" Bloomberg Politics, http://www.bloomberg.com/politics/articles/2015-08-06/carly-fiorina-knocks-donald-trump-i-didn-t-get-a-phone-call-from-bill-clinton-?.

31. Kaitlyn Schallhorn, "Megyn Kelly Says Fox News Hosts Have Secret 'Plan' if Donald Trump Doesn't Play by Debate Rules," The Blaze, August 5, 2015, http://www.theblaze.com/stories/2015/08/05/megyn-kelly-says-fox-news-hosts-have-secret-plan-if-donald-trump-doesnt-play-by-debate-rules/.

32. Associated Press, "Seven Ways Donald Trump Hogs the Presidential Campaign Conversation," *Washington Post*, reprinted in the Readingeagle.com, August 15, 2015, http://readingeagle.com/ap/article/seven-ways-donald-trump-hogs-the-presidential-campaign-conversation. One has to wonder about the *Washington Post*'s choice of the word "hogs." If it were Hillary Clinton, the word would almost certainly have been "dominates."

33. AP, "Seven Ways Donald Trump Hogs the Presidential Campaign Conversation."

34. Kyle Olson, "Fox Gives Trump, Er Fox, Most Speaking Time During First Debate," *American Mirror*, August 7, 2015, http://www.theamericanmirror.com/fox-gives-trump-most-speaking-time-during-first-debate/.

35. "Erick Erickson's Tone-Deaf Mea Culpa," *Salon*, March 29, 2010, http://www.salon.com/2010/03/29/erick_erickson_howard_kurtz/.

36. Jack Mirkinson, "The Week Fox News Got Trumped: Roger Ailes Sold Out, Megyn Kelly Took Off & the Donald Won Very, Very Big," *Salon*, August 15, 2015, http://www.salon.com/2015/08/15/the_week_fox_news_got_trumped_roger_ailes_sold_out_megyn_kelly_took_off_the_donald_won_very_very_big/.

37. Rich Lowry, "The Phenomenal Incoherence of Donald Trump," *Politico*, August 12, 2015, http://www.politico.com/magazine/story/2015/08/the-phenomenal-incoherence-of-donald-trump-121309.html#.VczDAPkeq-0.

38. Schallborn, "Megyn Kelly Says Fox News Hosts Have Secret 'Plan.'"

39. Fredric U. Dicker, "GOP Chair: Trump Won't Be the Party's Nominee," *New York Post*, August 9, 2015, http://nypost.com/2015/08/09/gop-chair-doesnt-think-trump-will-be-the-partys-nominee/.

40. Angelo Codevilla, "America's Ruling Class—and the Perils of Revolution," *The American Spectator*, July 2010, http://spectator.org/articles/39326/americas-ruling-class-and-perils-revolution.

41. Codevilla, "America's Ruling Class."

42. Charles Murray, *Coming Apart: The State of White America, 1960–2010* (New York: Crown Forum, 2012), 78–90. Murray calculated the sum of standardized scores for a zip code's percentage of adults with a college education combined with its median family income, weighted by population.

43. Murray, *Coming Apart*, 90.

44. Ohio redistricted to place Turner in the 10th Congressional District, but he was originally elected to represent the 3rd Congressional District.

45. List of Members of the United States Congress by Longevity of Service, Wikipedia, https://en.wikipedia.org/wiki/List_of_members_of_the_United_States_Congress_by_longevity_of_service.

46. Codevilla, "America's Ruling Class."

47. Charles Prysby and Carmine Scavo, *Voting Behavior: The 1992 Election* (Washington, D.C.: American Political Science Association, 1993), 9–10.

48. Stanley Renshon, *The Clinton Campaign* (Boulder, CO: Westview Press, 1995), 53; Pat Benjamin, *The Perot Legacy: A New Political Path* (New York: Morgan James Publishing, 2013).

49. Benjamin, *The Perot Legacy*, 13. An independent study by Gordon Black, asking if voters had thought "Perot had a chance of winning, would he have gotten their vote" concluded Perot could have won if, in fact, voters *thought* he had a chance of winning.

50. Peter Goldman and Thomas M. DeFrank, *Quest for the Presidency 1992* (College Station, TX: Texas A&M University Press, 1994), 253.

51. Larry Schweikart and Michael Allen, *A Patriot's History of the United States* (New York: Sentinel, 2014), 816–818.

52. Karl Rove, *Courage and Consequence*: *My Life as a Conservative in the Fight* (New York: Threshold, 2010), 342.

53. Bernard Goldberg, *A Slobbering Love Affair*; *The True (And Pathetic) Story of the Torrid Romance Between Barack Obama and the Mainstream Media* (Washington, D.C.: Regnery, 2008).

54. "Flashback Video: The Day Trump Worked Jobs in His Hotel," 2011, http://ilovemyfreedom.org/flashback-video-day-trump-worked-jobs-hotel/.

Chapter Four: On the Campaign Trail: Ohio, New Hampshire, Nevada, Colorado, and New Mexico

1. Joel Pollak, "NYTimes Declares Ohio No Longer 'Bellwether' as Trump Pulls Ahead," Breitbart News, September 30, 2016, http://www.breitbart.com/bigjournalism/2016/09/30/ohio-new-york-times-declare-no-longer-bellwether-trump-pulls-ahead/.

2. Byron York, "Donald Trump's Great Big, Beautiful Missed Opportunity," *Washington Examiner*, October 26, 2016, http://www.washingtonexaminer.com/byron-york-donald-trumps-great-big-beautiful-missed-opportunity/article/2605690?platform=hootsuite.

3. Joel Pollak, "Mitt Romney: 'A Time for Choosing'…Someone. Not Trump," Breitbart News, March 3, 2016, http://www.breitbart.com/biggovernment/2016/03/03/mitt-romney-a-time-for-choosing-someone-not-trump/.

4.　M. L. Nestel and Jackie Kucinich, "Huma Abedin Swore Under Oath She Gave Up 'All the Devices' With State Dept. Emails," *Daily Beast*, October 29, 2016, http://www.thedailybeast.com/articles/2016/10/29/huma-abedin-swore-under-oath-she-gave-up-all-the-devices-containing-state-departmentemails.html.

5.　Phil Mattingly, CNN, October 28, 2016, 1:55 p.m. EDT; Tim Hains, "CNN Reporter on Clinton's Plane: She Learned About FBI Reopening Case at the Same Time Media Did," RealClearPolitics, October 28, 2016, http://www.realclearpolitics.com/video/2016/10/28/cnn_reporter_on_clintons_plane_she_learned_about_fbi_reopening_case_at_the_same_time_you_did.html.

6.　Charlie Spiering, "Clinton Spokesman: 'Boggles the Mind' Why F.B.I. Reviewing Email Investigation," Breitbart News, October 28, 2016, http://www.breitbart.com/2016-presidential-race/2016/10/28/clinton-spokesman-boggles-the-mind-why-f-b-i-reviewing-email-investigation/.

7.　Jane Mayer, "James Comey Broke with Loretta Lynch and Justice Department Tradition," *New Yorker*, October 29, 2016, http://www.newyorker.com/news/news-desk/james-comey-broke-with-loretta-lynch-and-justice-department-tradition.

8.　Charlie Spiering, "Hillary Clinton Supporters Boo James Comey at Campaign Rally," Breitbart News, October 29, 2016, http://www.breitbart.com/2016-presidential-race/2016/10/29/hillary-clinton-supporters-boo-james-comey-campaign-rally/.

9.　Rich Lowry, "This is Not Normal," *National Review*, October 28, 2016, http://www.nationalreview.com/corner/441574/fbi-re-opens-clinton-probe.

10.　James Comey, quoted in Rich Lowry, "Comey's Letter to FBI Employees," *National Review*, October 28, 2016, http://www.nationalreview.com/corner/441575/comeys-letter-fbi-employees.

11.　Michael James, "Obama: Hillary Will 'Say Anything and Change Nothing,'" ABC News, 25 January 25, 2008, http://blogs.abcnews.com/politicalpunch/2008/01/obama-hillary-w.html.

Chapter Five: The Wild Ride: Primary Season 2015

1.   The RealClearPolitics average, for example, had Carson at six on July 30, but double that by September; Cruz gained a point; and Fiorina shot up to six after the debate, while Bush, who had been at seventeen in July, dropped to half that in early September. "Fox News Poll: Sanders Gains on Clinton," August 14, 2015, http://www.foxnews.com/politics/interactive/2015/08/14/fox-news-poll-sanders-gains-on-clinton/.

2.   "Immigration Reform That Will Make America Great Again," August 16, 2015, https://www.donaldjtrump.com/positions/immigration-reform.

3.   "Immigration," https://www.donaldjtrump.com/positions/immigration-reform.

4.   David Harsanyi, Twitter, August 19, 2015, https://twitter.com/davidharsanyi?lang=en.

5.   "Voters Want to Build a Wall, Deport Felon Illegal Immigrants," Rasmussen Reports, http://www.rasmussenreports.com/public_content/politics/current_events/immigration/august_2015/voters_want_to_build_a_wall_deport_felon_illegal_immigrants.

6.   "Halperin: Trump Reached 'Turning Point,' 'Most' Estab Cands Think He Can Win Nomination," Breitbart, August 17, 2015, http://www.breitbart.com/video/2015/08/17/halperin-trump-reached-turning-point-most-estab-cands-think-he-can-win-nomination/.

7.   Henry J. Gomez, "Donald Trump Proves Us Wrong: Republican Presidential Power Rankings," Cleveland.com, August 17, 2015, http://www.cleveland.com/open/index.ssf/2015/08/donald_trump_proves_us_wrong_r.html.

8.   "CNN/ORC Poll: Donald Trump Now Competitive in General Election," CNN Politics, August 19, 2015, http://www.cnn.com/2015/08/19/politics/2016-poll-hillary-clinton-joe-biden-bernie-sanders/index.html.

9.   Jason Mattera, *Obama Zombies: How the Liberal Machine Brainwashed My Generation* (New York: Threshold Books, 2010); Vidya Rao, "Oprah Effect: Can Celebs Sway Voters?" MSNBC, October 25, 2008, http://www.today.com/id/27227264/ns/today-today_on_the_trail/t/oprah-effect-can-celebs-sway-voters/#.VdOK85ceq-0. Also see Larry Schweikart and David Dougherty, *A Patriot's History of the Modern World, Vol. 2: From the Cold War to the Age of Entitlement* (New York: Sentinel, 2013), 552–53.

10.   See the chart posted by "SamAdams76" on FreeRepublic under the thread "Overwhelming Majority of Trump's Online Following is Ineligible to Vote," http://www.freerepublic.com/perl/pings?more=385466368, reply 78.

11.   "Hillary Clinton Buying Twitter Followers? Audit Says 'Yes,' and Facebook Fans, Too," INQUISITR, April 14, 2015, http://www.inquisitr.com/2010037/hillary-clinton-buying-twitter-followers-audit-says-yes-and-facebook-fans-too/; David Martasko, "More than 2 Million of Hillary Clinton's Twitter Followers are Fake or Never Tweet—and She's Already Under Fire for 'Buying' Fake Facebook Fans," *UK Daily Mail*, April 14, 2015, http://www.dailymail.co.uk/news/article-3038621/More-2-MILLION-Hillary-Clinton-s-Twitter-followers-fake-never-tweet.html.

12.   Gabby Morrongiello, "Overwhelming Majority of Trump's Online Following is Ineligible to Vote," *Washington Examiner*, August 14, 2015, http://www.washingtonexaminer.com/vast-majority-of-trumps-online-followers-cant-vote/article/2570234.

13.   Robert Costa and David Weigel, "Trump's Audacious Southern Spectacle is Part of His Strategy," *Washington Post*, August 22, 2015, http://www.washingtonpost.com/politics/trumps-audacious-southern-spectacle-is-part-of-his-strategy/2015/08/21/31da2a88-4812-11e5-846d-02792f854297_story.html.

14.   "George Will: Guardian of the GOP Establishment," in RinoTracker, August 23, 2015, http://www.rinotracker.us/george-will-guardian-of-the-gop-establishment/.

15. Ibid.

16. Philip Bump, "Donald Trump's Immigration Comments Don't Seem to be Hurting Republicans—Yet," *Washington Post*, August 23, 2015, http://www.washingtonpost.com/news/the-fix/wp/2015/08/23/donald-trumps-immigration-comments-dont-seem-to-be-hurting-republicans-yet/.

17. Jeffrey Lord, "Jorge Ramos Gets Trumped," *American Spectator*, August 27, 2015, http://spectator.org/articles/63899/jorge-ramos-gets-trumped.

18. "2016 Republican Presidential Nomination," RealClearPolitics, http://www.realclearpolitics.com/epolls/2016/president/us/2016_republican_presidential_nomination-3823.html.

19. Monmouth University, "Latest Poll Results," September 3, 2015, http://www.monmouth.edu/university/monmouth-university-polling-institute.aspx.

20. Zeke Miller, "Rand Paul's New Mission: Take Down Trump," *Time*, August 10, 2015, http://time.com/3991699/donald-trump-rand-paul/.

21. Neetzan Zimmerman, "Trump Mocks Fiorina's Physical Appearance: Look at that Face," *The Hill*, September 9, 2015, http://thehill.com/blogs/blog-briefing-room/253178-trump-insults-fiorinas-physical-appearance-look-at-that-face.

22. Lauren Gambino, "Carly Fiorina Defuses Trump on 'Beautiful Face' Retort and Foreign Policy," *Guardian*, September 17, 2015, http://www.theguardian.com/us-news/2015/sep/17/carly-fiorina-republican-debate-donald-trump-sexism-foreign-policy-women.

23. "Constitution and Second Amendment: Donald J. Trump's Vision," https://www.donaldjtrump.com/positions/second-amendment-rights.

24. "Tax Plan: Donald J. Trump's Vision," https://www.donaldjtrump.com/positions/tax-reform.

25. Elenea Schneider, "Trump on his White House bid: 'I'm not a Masochist,'" *Politico*, October 4, 2015, http://www.politico.com/story/2015/10/donald-trump-masochist-214411.

26. Maggie Haberman, "From Donald Trump, Hints of a Campaign Exit Strategy," *New York Times*, October 9, 2015, http://www. nytimes.com/2015/10/10/us/politics/donald-trump-presidential-race.html?_r=0.

27. Nick Gass, "Trump: I'm Never Dropping Out," *Politico*, October 9, 2015, http://www.politico.com/story/2015/10/donald-trump-not-dropping-out-2016-214602.

28. Maya Rhodan, "Donald Trump Won Twitter During the Democratic Debate," *Time*, October 14, 2015, http://time.com/4072688/democratic-debate-twitter-donald-trump/.

29. Philip Bump, "Is it Time to Concede that Donald Trump is Likely to Win the GOP Nomination?" *Washington Post*, October 21, 2015, https://www.washingtonpost.com/news/the-fix/wp/2015/10/21/is-it-finally-time-to-concede-that-donald-trump-is-likely-to-win-the-gop-nomination/.

30. Eliana Johnson, "The Establishment Thinks the Unthinkable: Trump Could Win the Nomination," *National Review Online*, October 19, 2015, http://www.nationalreview.com/article/425750/gop-establishment-thinks-trump-could-win.

31. Johnson, "Establishment Thinks the Unthinkable."

32. Tim Marcin, "Donald Trump Will Win General Election, Republican Voters Tell Pollsters," *International Business Times*, October 21, 2015, http://www.ibtimes.com/donald-trump-will-win-general-election-republican-voters-tell-pollster-2150195.

33. Dylan Stableford, "Donald Trump Triples Down on 9/11 Comments," Yahoo Politics, October 20, 2015, https://www.yahoo.com/politics/donald-trump-triples-down-on-911-comments-160233313.html.

34. Rebecca Burg, "Trump Pounces on Bush's Payroll Troubles," RealClearPolitics, October 24, 2015, http://www.realclearpolitics.com/articles/2015/10/24/trump_pounces_on_bushs_payroll_troubles_128544.html.

35. Brett LoGiurato and Colin Campbell, "The GOP Debate Audience Booed CNBC for Confronting Ben Carson about a Controversial Association," *Business Insider*, October 29, 2015, http://www.businessinsider.com/ben-carson-debate-question-booed-cnbc-2015-.10. Even the headline, however is misleading, in that he did *not* have an "association," rather, had given paid speeches.

36. " 'Not a Cage Match': Cruz, Others Scold GOP Debate Moderators," Fox News, October 29, 2015, http://www.foxnews.com/politics/2015/10/29/gop candidates-face-off-for-3rd-debate/?intcmp=hpbt1#.

37. "The Simple Flat Tax," https://www.tedcruz.org/tax_plan/.

38. "What Trump's Bizarre Iowa Tirade Looked Like Up Close," *Politico*, November 13, 2015, http://www.politico.com/story/2015/11/donald-trump-des-moines-rant-215825.

39. Claire Phipps and Kevin Rawlinson, "Paris Attacks Kill More than 120 People—As it Happened," *The Guardian*, November 14, 2015, http://www.theguardian.com/world/live/2015/nov/13/shootings-reported-in-eastern-paris-live.

40. Anil Dawar, "New Immigrant Crisis on the way: 185,000 Migrants Flood into Europe in Just Three Months," *Express*, June 19, 2015, http://www.express.co.uk/news/uk/585501/3-months-migrants-flood-Europe.

41. David Crouch, "Sweden Slams Shut its Open-Door Policy Towards Refugees," *Guardian*, November 24, 2015, https://www.theguardian.com/world/2015/nov/24/sweden-asylum-seekers-refugees-policy-reversal.

42. Serge F. Kovaleski and Frederick Kunkle, "Northern New Jersey Draws Probers' Eyes," *Washington Post*, September 18, 2001, https://www.washingtonpost.com/archive/politics/2001/09/18/northern-new-jersey-draws-probers-eyes/40f82ea4-e015-4d6e-a87e93aa433fafdc/?postshare=7281448290025183&tid=ss_fb.

43. Salena Zito, "Taking Trump Seriously, Not Literally," *Atlantic*, September 23, 2016, http://www.theatlantic.com/politics/archive/2016/09/trump-makes-his-case-in-pittsburgh/501335/.

44. "FL GOP Presidential Primary," Opinion Savvy, http://opinionsavvy.com/wp-content/uploads/2015/12/FL-GOP-PP-12.17.15.pdf.

45. Jennifer Jacobs, "Iowa Poll: The Inside Skinny on Each GOP Candidate," *Des Moines Register*, December 12, 2015, http://www.desmoinesregister.com/story/news/elections/presidential/candidates/2015/12/12/iowa-poll-inside-skinny-each-gop-candidate/77168608/.

46. Benjy Sarlin, "Of Course Ted Cruz Could Win," *National Review*, March 24, 2015, http://www.msnbc.com/msnbc/how-ted-cruz-could-win-the-gop-nomination; Benjy Sarlin, "How Ted Cruz Could Win," RealClearPolitics, November 22, 2015, http://www.realclearpolitics.com/2015/11/21/how_ted_cruz_could_win_370427.html; Shane Goldmacher, "Ted Cruz's Plan to Pick off the Competition," *Politico*, October 27, 2015, http://www.politico.com/story/2015/10/inside-ted-cruzs-plan-to-pick-off-the-competition-215173; David M. Drucker, "Cruz Makes a Play for GOP Conservative Wing," *Washington Examiner*, October 31, 2015, http://www.washingtonexaminer.com/ted-cruz-a-consistent-conservative-can-win/article/2575391; Chris Cillizza, "Here's Why Ted Cruz Could Win the GOP Nomination," *Washington Post*, December 13, 2015, http://www.thefiscaltimes.com/2015/12/13/Here-s-Why-Ted-Cruz-Could-Win-GOP-Nomination; Fred Barnes, "Can Ted Cruz Actually Win?" *Weekly Standard*, December 19, 2015, http://www.weeklystandard.com/can-ted-cruz-actually-win/article/2000282.

47. Benjy Sarlin, "How Ted Cruz Could Win the GOP Nomination," MSNBC, November 21, 2015, http://www.msnbc.com/msnbc/how-ted-cruz-could-win-the-gop-nomination.

48. Neil W. McCabe, "Panic Mode: *LA Times* Poll Shows Donald Trump Skyrocketing As Hillary Clinton Falters in Black Community," Breitbart, September 18, 2016, http://www. breitbart.com/2016-presidential-race/2016/09/18/panic-mode-la-times-poll-shows-donald-trump-skyrocketing-as-hillary-clinton-falters-in-black-community/.

Chapter Six: On the Campaign Trail: Michigan, Pennsylvania, Wisconsin, and Florida

1 Vaughn Hillyard, *Rachel Maddow Show*, MSNBC, October 27, 2016, https://www.youtube.com/watch?v=NuTTq0UwTTo.

Chapter Seven: "When Did You Become a Republican?" From the Birth of the Parties to Trump's Primary Victories

1. Observers were astounded at the seventy-year-old Trump's stamina and energy. One secret was that he flew home after every event; see Emily Flitter, "Trump Likes to Sleep in His Own Bed and It May Cost Him Votes," *Yahoo News*, January 8, 2016, http://news.yahoo. com/trump-likes-sleep-own-bed-may-cost-him-112155624.htm—at least until the frenetic end of the general election campaign, when, as Joel Pollak was able to observe firsthand, he seems to draw new energy from the exuberant crowds and the late-breaking news from the James Comey/FBI investigation and WikiLeaks.

2. Scott Bland, "Donald Trump's Big Tent," *Politico*, January 8, 2016, http://www.freerepublic.com/focus/news/3381178/posts?page=2.

3. James Warren, "Trump Could Win it All," *U.S. News & World Report*, January 8, 2016, http://www.usnews.com/opinion/articles/2016-01-08/new-poll-shows-donald-trump-is-a-real-threat-to-hillary-clinton.

4. As of this date, with more to be learned, it is unclear if Hillary Clinton was foolish in failing to campaign at all in Wisconsin, and to campaign only minimally in Michigan and Pennsylvania, or if in fact her health was so poor she could not.

5. Some later claimed that Trump was insincere in his suggestion of Sykes, whose brother was radio talk show host and virulent anti-Trumper Charles Sykes. Even after Trump's election, Charles Sykes remained rabid in his negativity about Trump.

6. Sharyl Attkisson, "8 Trump Enemies Helping Him Succeed," sharylattkisson.com, March 15, 2016, https://sharylattkisson.com/8-trump-enemies-helping-him-succeed/.

7. Caleb Howe, "Just Got Real: Ted Cruz Blasts Trump in Presser About Unrest in Chicago," *RedState*, March 12, 2016, https://www.youtube.com/watch?v=ags62-VvwEY.

8. Jim Hoft, "Horror! Conservative Website RedState Calls on Far Left Protesters to Bring Guns to Trump Rallies," Gateway Pundit, March 11, 2016, http://www.thegatewaypundit.com/2016/03/gop-unhinged/.

9. Harry Enten, "It's Still Not Clear that Donald Trump Will Get a Majority of Delegates," *FiveThirtyEight*, March 16, 2016, http://fivethirtyeight.com/features/its-still-not-clear-that-donald-trump-will-get-a-majority-of-delegates/; Enten, "Wisconsin Could Be Trouble for Trump," *FiveThirtyEight*, March 31, 2016, http://fivethirtyeight.com/features/wisconsin-could-be-trouble-for-trump/.

10. J. R. Taylor, "Shocking Claims: Pervy Ted Cruz Caught Cheating—With 5 Secret Mistresses!" *National Enquirer*, March 23, 2016, http://www.nationalenquirer.com/celebrity/ted-cruz-sex-scandal-mistresses-cheating-claims/.

11. Donald J. Trump, @realDonaldTrump, Twitter, March 22, 2016.

12. Gabriel Sherman, "Operation Trump, Inside the Most Unorthodox Campaign in Political History," *New York Magazine*, April 4, 2016, http://nymag.com/daily/intelligencer/2016/04/inside-the-donald-trump-presidential-campaign.html.

13. Sherman, "Operation Trump."

14. Maureen Groppe, "7 Things We Learned From Indiana's Primary," *Indianapolis Star*, May 7, 2016, http://www.indystar.com/story/news/politics/behind-closed-doors/2016/05/06/seven-things-we-learned-indianas-primary/84021796/.

15. Maeve Reston, "Ted Cruz Drops Presidential Bid," CNN Politics, May 4, 2016, http://www.cnn.com/2016/05/03/politics/ted-cruz-drops-out/.

16. Sundance, "Attn: Stuart Stevens and the Never Trump Coalition—the Monster Vote Is Very Real," The Last Refuge, May 9, 2016, https://theconservativetreehouse.com/2016/05/09/attn-stuart-stevens-and-the-never-trump-coalition-the-monster-vote-is-very-real/.

17. "Election 2016: Presidential Primaries, Caucuses, and Conventions: January 2016 through September 2016," TheGreenPapers.com, http://www.thegreenpapers.com/P16/R.

18. Interview of Richard Barris by Larry Schweikart, November 26, 2016.

19. James Rosen, "Trump's Secret Supports Come Clean Now That the Election is Over," *News Chief*, November 26, 2016, http://www.newschief.com/news/20161126/trumps-secret-supports-come-clean-now-that-election-is-over. Later, Trafalgar pollsters would reveal that they reached the same shy Trump voters Davis did but did through a different method, asking not who *they* would vote for but who they thought *their neighbor* would vote for. Trafalgar learned that people would project their own Trump vote onto their neighbor, making its Michigan poll particularly accurate.

Chapter Eight: On the Campaign Trail: From Florida to North Carolina and New Hampshire (Again)

1. Scott Adams, "Why Does This Happen on My Vacation? (The Trump Tapes)," dilbert.com, October 8, 2016, http://blog.dilbert.com/post/151504993671/why-does-this-happen-on-my-vacation-the-trump.

2. Scott Adams, "The Persuasion Scorecard Update—One Week Out," dilbert.com, November 2, 2016, http://blog.dilbert.com/post/152644376081/the-persuasion-scorecard-update-one-week-out.

3. Olivia Nuzzi, Tweet, November 5, 2016, https://twitter.com/Olivianuzzi/status/795076412931764224.

Chapter Nine: The Trump Revolution

1. Philip Rucker,"Trump Promises 'Showbiz' at Convention, but Stars on Stage Will Be Relatively Dim," July 13, 2016, *Washington Post*, https://www.washingtonpost.com/politics/trump-promises-showbiz-at-convention-but-stars-on-stage-will-be-relatively-dim/2016/07/13/2e28d14e-4453-11e6-bc99-7d269f8719b1_story.html?utm_term=.3cc0d4776e35.

2. "Under the Bus: Ted Cruz's Biggest Donors Cut Ties," Breitbart, July 24, 2016, http://www.breitbart.com/2016-presidential-race/2016/07/24/bus-cruzs-biggest-donors-cut-ties/.

3. "Trump: Comments about Judge 'Misconstrued,'" CNN Politics, June 7, 2016, http://www.cnn.com/2016/06/07/politics/donald-trump-mexican-judge-trump-university-racist/index.html.

4. Neil W. McCabe, "Shock Poll: Reuters/IPSOS Radically Changes Methodology to Favor Clinton," Breitbart, July 29, 2016, http://www.breitbart.com/big-journalism/2016/07/29/reuters-ipsos-poll-change-methodology/.

5. "Surveying National Issues: National Poll with *USA Today*," Suffolk University, Boston, October 26, 2016, http://www.suffolk.edu/academics/10741.php.

6. "CNN Oversampled Democrats to Claim Hillary Clinton Won the Debate," Zero Censorship, October 10, 2016, https://www.zerocensorship.com/uncensored/cnn/oversampled-democrats-claim-hillary-clinton-won-debate-336593.

7. Gary Langer, Gregory Holy, and Chad Kiewiet de Jonge, "Clinton Vaults to a Double-Digit Lead Boosted by Broad Disapproval of Trump," ABC News, October 23, 2016, http://abcnews.go.com/Politics/clinton-vaults-double-digit-lead-boosted-broad-disapproval/story?id=42993821. See G. Petronius, "Reuters Poll Giving Hillary National Lead Oversampled Democrats +12%, Women +22%, That Still Only Gave Her a 6-Point Lead," Reddit, October 2016, quoting Bill Mitchell on Twitter, https://www.reddit.com/r/The_Donald/comments/583y64/reuters_poll_giving_hillary_national_lead/. Also see a Morning Call Pennsylvania poll taken in November that had a seven-point Democrat lead when all indicators were that Democrats had lost several points' worth of voters from previous years and Republicans had gained; Muhlenberg College/Morning Call, 2016 Pennsylvania Election Survey, November Version, http://www.mcall.com/news/local/elections/mc-read-november-muhlenberg-college-morning-call-election-survey-20161105-htmlstory.html. Trump won the state by 1 percent.

8. This was true of virtually every poll that reported methodology during this time. See for example, Gravis, a poll considered *favorable* to Trump and Republicans, taken in North Carolina on November 5, interviewed 6 percent more women than men which national averages showed the difference to be only about 4 percent Naturally, Clinton emerged with a two-point lead. See "Current North Carolina Polling," Gravis, November 5, 2016, https://www.scribd.com/document/330329777/North-Carolina-November-5-2016-v3#from_embed.

9. Interview with Richard Baris by Larry Schweikart, November 26, 2016.

10. Richard Baris, "No, the PPD Poll Was the Most Accurate in 2016. It Wasn't Even Close," People's Pundit Daily, November 13, 2016, https://www.peoplespunditdaily.com/news/elections/2016/11/13/no-ppd-poll-accurate-2016-heres-not-even-close/.

11. Richard Baris, "In Defense of the LA Times Poll," People's Pundit Daily, on October 2, 2016, https://www. peoplespunditdaily.com/news/elections/2016/10/02/defense-la-times-poll/.

12. See the RealClearPolitics "General Election" final polls, http:// www.realclearpolitics.com/epolls/2016/president/us/general_ election_trump_vs_clinton-5491.htmlhttp://www. realclearpolitics.com/epolls/2016/president/us/general_election_ trump_vs_clinton-5491.html

13. "No Toss Up States," RealClearPolitics, http://www. realclearpolitics.com/epolls/2016/president/2016_elections_ electoral_college_map_no_toss_ups.html.

14. PPD had the final Pennsylvania margin as Trump at 48.8 and Clinton at 47.6, and had Trump winning Florida by 2 (the margin in the election was about 1.5).

15. SurveyUSA had Clinton winning Minnesota by 10, the *Minneapolis Star Tribune* by 8. Yet the final result was Clinton at +1.5.

16. Interview of Richard Baris by Larry Schweikart November 26, 2016.

17. John Wagner, "Clinton's Data-Driven Campaign Relied Heavily on an Algorithm Named Ada. What Didn't She See?" *Washington Post*, November 9, 2016, https://www.washingtonpost.com/news/ post-politics/wp/2016/11/09/clintons-data-driven-campaign-relied-heavily-on-an-algorithm-named-ada-what-didnt-she-see/?utm_ term=.fa2a77bcc28a.

18. Kate Reilly, "Read Hillary Clinton's 'Basket of Deplorables' Remarks about Donald Trump's Supporters," *Time*, September 10, 2016, http://time.com/4486502/hillary-clinton-basket-of-deplorables-transcript/.

19. Betsy Woodruff and Michael Daly, "Unnamed senior law enforcement official quoted in "Hillary Clinton Appears to Faint at 9/11 Ceremony," *The Daily Beast*, September 11, 2016, http:// www.thedailybeast.com/articles/2016/09/11/reports-hillary-leaves-ground-zero-ceremony.html.

20. Edward-Isaac Dovere, "How Clinton Lost Michigan—and Blew the Election," *Politico*, December 14, 2016, http://www.politico.com/story/2016/12/michigan-hillary-clinton-trump-232547.

21. Dovere, "How Clinton Lost Michigan."

22. Glenn Thrush, "One Man in Hillary's Campaign Warned She Could Lose, and Everyone Ignored Him," *Daily Caller*, December 12, 2016, http://dailycaller.com/2016/12/09/one-man-in-hillarys-campaign-warned-she-could-lose-and-everybody-ignored-him/; Glenn Thrush, "10 Crucial Decisions that Reshaped America," *Politico Magazine*, December 9, 2016, http://www.politico.com/magazine/story/2016/12/2016-presidential-election-10-moments-trump-clinton-214508.

23. Thrush, "10 Crucial Decisions that Reshaped America."

24. Ibid.

25. Ibid.

26. Stephen Collinson, "Can Donald Trump Recover From This?" CNN Politics, October 8, 2016, //www.cnn.com/2016/10/07/politics/donald-trump-campaign-crisis/index.html?iid=EL.

27. "NBC Planned to Use Trump Audio to Influence Debate, Election," TMZ, October 12, 2016, http://www.tmz.com/2016/10/12/nbc-trump-tape-billy-bush-plan-election-debate.

28. Scott Adams, "Clown Genius," Scott Adams' Blog, August 13, 2015, http://blog.dilbert.com/post/126589300371/clown-genius.

29. "2016 November General Election Early Voting," http://www.electproject.org/early_2016.

30. See McDonald's Comments on North Carolina in "Early Voting Stability Despite News Volatility," Huffington Post, October 31, 2016, http://www.huffingtonpost.com/michael-p-mcdonald/early-voting-stability-de_b_12723188.html; and Richard Baris, "Clinton Lost Florida and the Election Because She Lost the Argument," People's Pundit Daily, December 7, 2016, https://www.peoplespunditdaily.com/news/elections/2016/12/07/hillary-clinton-lost-florida-before-election-day/.

31. Richard Baris, "In Florida, Trump in Far Better Shape Than Romney before Election Day; Clinton Lags Obama," People's Pundit Daily, November 6, 2016, https://www.peoplespunditdaily. com/news/elections/2016/11/06/florida-trump-far-better-shape-romney-election-day-clinton-lags-obama/.

32. Baris, "Hillary Clinton Lost Florida before Election Day."

33. Michael P. McDonald, "Early Voting Stability Despite News Volatility," Huffington Post, October 31, 2016, http://www. huffingtonpost.com/michael-p-mcdonald/early-voting-stability-de_b_12723188.html; Baris, "Clinton Lost Florida and the Election."

34. Michael P. McDonald, "Early Vote: Election Eve Predictions," Huffington Post, November 8, 2016, http://www.huffingtonpost. com/michael-p-mcdonald/early-vote-election-eve-p_b_12853864. html.

35. McDonald, "Early Vote: Election Eve Predictions." McDonald called Florida a "tossup" on election eve and said, "There is not enough information about the early vote in Michigan, Pennsylvania or Wisconsin to make a prediction." But he wrongly gave Maine's Congressional District 2 to Clinton, said Ohio "leans Trump"—Trump won it by more than nine points— and agreed only reluctantly that North Carolina "leans Trump." See Richard Baris, "Hillary Clinton Lost Florida Before Election Day" for statistics showing that no one, including McDonald, should have come to that conclusion.

36. Ibid.

37. Alex Leary, "Hispanics Voting in Record Numbers in Florida, Other States, Boosting Hillary Clinton," *Miami-Herald*, November 6, 2016, http://www.miamiherald.com/news/politics-government/election/article112958953.html.

38. "General Election: Trump vs. Clinton," RealClearPolitics final polling, November 8, 2016, http://www.realclearpolitics.com/ epolls/2016/president/us/general_election_trump_vs_clinton-5491.html.

39. Jesse T. Richman, Gulshan A. Chattha, and David C. Ernext, "Do Non-Citizens Vote in U.S. Elections," *Electoral Studies* (December 2014): 149–57. They found that non-citizens likely gave Senate Democrats the pivotal sixtieth vote needed to overcome filibusters in order to pass health care reform and other Obama administration priorities in the 111th Congress.

40. Interview of Richard Baris by Larry Schweikart, November 26, 2016.

41. Bill Sammon, *At Any Cost: How Al Gore Tried to Steal the Election* (Washington, D.C.: Regnery, 2002).

42. Quoted in Ann Coulter, "A Night to Remember," anncoulter. com, November 23, 2016, http://www.anncoulter.com/columns/2016-11-23.html#read_more.

43. Coulter, "A Night to Remember."

44. Gromer Jeffers Jr., "Trump Wraps Up Campaign with Promise to Take Apart Corrupt Political System," *Dallas Morning News*, November 7, 2016, http://www.dallasnews.com/news/2016-presidential-election/2016/11/07/trump-closes-campaign-promise-take-apart-corrupt-political-system.

45. Coulter, "A Night to Remember."

46. Myra Adams, "How the Clinton Victory Party Went from Coronation to Despair," *Washington Examiner*, November 12, 2016.

47. Adams, "How the Clinton Victory Party Went from Coronation to Despair."

48. Ibid.

49. Dave Jamieson, "It Looks Like Donald Trump Did Really Well With Union Households. That's a Bad Sign for Unions," Huffington Post, November 14, 2016, http://www.huffingtonpost.com/entry/donald-trump-did-really-well-with-union-households_us_582367d0e4b0aac62488cc32.

50. Dr. Eowyn, "Hillary Clinton Was in a Drunken Rage on Election Night," *Fellowship of the Minds*, November 16, 2016, https://fellowshipoftheminds.com/2016/11/16/hillary-clinton-was-in-a-drunken-rage-on-election-night/.

51. Tweet from J. Deplorable Valette, https://twitter.com/Jean_de_Valette/status/798357468040441856.

52. Ed Klein on Steve Maltzberg show, http://www.northcrane.com/2016/11/15/cnn-reporter-states-hillary-became-physically-violent-towards-john-podesta-at-midnight-had-to-be-restrained/.

53. "CONFIRMED: Video confirms Hillary Clinton drunkenly attacks Podesta and Mook on Election Night," NC (Northcrane), November 15, 2016, http://www.northcrane.com/2016/11/15/cnn-reporter-states-hillary-became-physically-violent-towards-john-podesta-at-midnight-had-to-be-restrained/.

54. "Hillary Clinton Was in a Drunken Rage."

55. Amie Parnes, "Obama Urged Clinton to Concede on Election Night," *The Hill*, November 25, 2016, http://thehill.com/homenews/campaign/307536-obama-urged-clinton-to-concede-on-election-night.

56. Larry Rosin, "The Hidden Group That Won the Election for Trump: Exit Poll Analysis from Edison Research," November 15, 2016, http://www.edisonresearch.com/hidden-group-won-election-trump-exit-poll-analysis-edison-research/.

Chapter Ten: On the Campaign Trail: From Seven-State Sunday to Election Day

1. Scott Adams, *How to Fail at Almost Everything and Still Win Big: Kind of the Story of My Life* (Portfolio, 2014).

2. Joseph Telushkin, *Rebbe: The Life and Teachings of Menachem Mendel Schneerson* (Harper Wave, 2016).

3. Donald Trump, quoted by CNN Staff, "Here's the full text of Donald Trump's victory speech," CNN, November 9, 2016, http://www.cnn.com/2016/11/09/politics/donald-trump-victory-speech/.

4. Hillary Clinton, quoted by National Public Radio Staff, "Transcript: Hillary Clinton Concedes To Donald Trump," National Public Radio, November 9, 2016, http://www.npr.org/2016/11/09/500715219/transcript-clinton-gives-concession-speech.

Epilogue

1. Ian Hanchett, "Michael Moore: 'Millions' of Obama Voters Changed Their Minds, 'They're Not Racists," Breitbart News, November 11, 2016, http://www.breitbart.com/video/2016/11/11/michael-moore-millions-of-obama-voters-changed-their-minds-theyre-not-racists/.

2. Thomas Frank, "Donald Trump Is Moving to the White House, and Liberals Put Him There," *Guardian* (UK), November 9, 2016, https://www.theguardian.com/commentisfree/2016/nov/09/donald-trump-white-house-hillary-clinton-liberals.

3. Laura Sydell, "NPR Reporter Tracked Down a Fake-News Creator; Here's What She Learned," National Public Radio, November 23, 2016, https://ww2.kqed.org/news/2016/11/23/npr-tracked-down-a-fake-news-creator-in-the-suburbs-heres-what-they-learned/.

4. Frank Luntz, tweet, December 10, 2016, https://twitter.com/FrankLuntz/status/807623515918700544.

5. Alex Egoshin, "TrumpLand and Clinton Archipelago, VividMaps, December 2016, http://www.vividmaps.com/2016/12/trumpland-and-clinton-archipelago.html.

6. All numbers from Wikipedia, by election year and state.

7. Jennifer G. Hickey, "Republicans Build on Their Dominance in State Legislatures," Fox News, November 18, 2016, http://www.foxnews.com/politics/2016/11/18/republicans-build-on-their-dominance-in-state-legislatures.html.

8. Liz Spayd, "Preaching the Gospel of Diversity, but Not Following It," *New York Times*, December 17, 2016, http://www.nytimes.com/2016/12/17/public-editor/new-york-times-diversity-liz-spayd-public-editor.html?_r=0.

9. George Orwell, "Extracts from a Manuscript Note-book," *The Collected Essays, Journalism and Letters of George Orwell: Volume Four: In Front of Your Nose, 1945–1950* (Boston: Nonpareil, 1968), 515.

Index